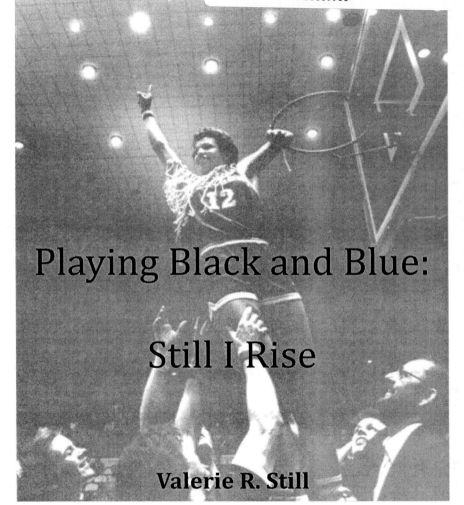

Playing Black and Blue:

Still I Rise

Valerie R. Still

Cover design & book layout by 101 Business Solutions
Harrodsburg, Kentucky

Title page photo from University of Kentucky Special Collections
* Selected University of Kentucky photos credited to:
2007ua023: Still, Valerie (basketball), University of Kentucky Athletics player files, approximately 1904-2009, University of Kentucky Special Collections.

Photo by Adrian R. Rowan/ A. Rowan Photography
Makeup by Kayla Motyka Bittle/ Level Up Makeup
Manufactured in the United States of America

All book order correspondence should be addressed to:
STILL Publications
P.O. Box 606
Palmyra, NJ 08065
valeriestill1@gmail.com

Basketball great Valerie Still's family's illustrious lineage begins during slavery through the secretive and dangerous network of the Underground Railroad. She is a pioneer in women's basketball at the collegiate and professional levels both nationally and internationally. Still survived racism and sexism to become a recognized Hall of Famer. Her magnificent career begins in the streets of Camden, New Jersey where she competed with her brothers. Still's memoir is an inspiration for all.

Charles L. Blockson, *Curator Emeritus*
Charles L. Blockson Afro-American Collection,
Temple University Libraries

"The author is my Goddaughter. It sometimes can be problematical to comment upon anyone's Memoirs; Valerie Still is an exception. Her mother and I were high school classmates and graduated together in 1949."

Valerie's Memoirs describe a "Hero's Journey." They provide us with a rich and compelling description of her life experiences, reminding us, paraphrasing the author Barbara De Angelis, that "the journey" between what she once was and who she has now become is where the dance of her life has really taken place.

Her Memoirs are a "MUST READ!"

Dr. Clarence B. Jones
Political advisor, legal counsel and draft speechwriter for
Dr. Martin Luther King, Jr.

A quest is a journey....
From the ashes the Phoenix arises

Table of Contents

Dedication

**Dedicated to my Mom and ancestors who laid the bridge
I would eventually cross...**

Of Wind and Wings
By Bob Todd

The phoenix, 'twas said of old
burns itself out eventually
then arises anew
from its own ashes.
Those same ashes
have a way of blowing, sometimes
on winds of pain
and alighting upon the soul
of one anguished by weight of loss.

Might not it be wise
to remember, tho through tears
that scattered bitter ashes
may also be carried distant
on winds of hope
thus leaving a clean perch
from which that joyous rejuvenated bird
may fly off into blue cloudless skies
and return, when summoned
to the heart which lent it flight.

Foreword

Playing Black and Blue: Still I Rise is a remarkable book about the life of a remarkable Lady (capital "L" intended). I need not belabor the point that this book tells the story also of a remarkable family, the Stills of New Jersey. That family, once enslaved on the Eastern Shore of Maryland, produced Valerie's great-great grandfather, Dr. James Still, not only a successful but prominent physician with only three months of formal schooling (same as Thomas Edison); her great-great granduncle William Still known historically as the "father of the Underground Railroad"; Caroline Still, one of the first Black woman physicians in this country and great-great granduncles Levin Jr. and Peter, sold as children into Lexington to become playmates of Henry Clay's children who lived across the street where they were enslaved.

Kentucky football fans will of course remember Arthur Barry Still (Art), her brother, who along with his close friend Derrick Ramsey, led UK to its best season since the days of Bear Bryant; no team since has matched the Ramsey-Still-led team.

Valerie Still has long been known as a fighter for women's rights (see for example, her New York Times op-ed piece of June 1999). She has argued for three decades that the great façade put up by those who would deny women athletes their selfhood has not protected the large percentage of players and coaches who are gay, relegating them instead to careers played from the closet when they should have been enjoying the freedoms the rest of us take for granted, those freedoms that allow us simply to be who we are and to be respected and treated accordingly. She is a social advocate for equal rights, equal opportunity, equal work, equal pay and equal play.

Perhaps the cat has nine lives, but this Lady Wildcat had at least four; she was at the point of death over a period of hours or days twice; and barely survived an automobile crash while playing professionally in Italy. She has played on every level and on three continents and has coached both high school and professional basketball. And yes, she, along with her ABL Columbus Quest team, was the first professional women's team to be honored at the White House with the invitation of President and Mrs. Bill Clinton.

Please read a most enjoyable book and get to know my friend and good friend of many years, the unvarnished, not-always-politically-correct (thankfully) but always honest Valerie Still.

Bob Todd

Introduction

Each living soul has the capability to tap into a force that allows us to live a life that is limitless – an existence beyond a fragile, time-restricted reality dependent on a beginning and an end, an existence in which two plus two no longer equals four, but eight or nine or even one hundred; an existence in which a thought becomes reality and mountains can actually be moved. For years I searched for this force, and at times I believed I had harvested its powers. But just as soon as I could grasp that feeling, my demons would resurface to tell me how inadequate and inferior I was, and I would lose my grip on those illusions of limitlessness. The facade of success I maintained was, all the while, being undermined by deep-seated insecurity. I know what it's like to hate myself.

I was born into the poverty-stricken ghettos of Camden, New Jersey where my mother and father raised me and my nine siblings in cramped, low-income public housing. After leaving Camden, which remains one of the poorest and most dangerous cities in the U.S. to this day, I experienced athletic excellence at the University of Kentucky, becoming UK's basketball all-time leading scorer and rebounder (male or female) during a period of social transformation involving gender equality and identification, eventually becoming a pioneer for American women's professional basketball, both overseas and in the USA. I lived as a young naïve American female, right out of college, in a foreign country where I was allowed to break the bondage of America's racially-charged society and its limitations, only to return to the USA having to confront the internal struggles of an interracial marriage of two former professional athletes whose gender roles defied tradition.

I made history as a member of the first women's professional team to be recognized at the White House. I can say that I was the first female player to see my bank account rise to $1 million. But that chapter of my life is just that: a chapter. The rest of my story, often pushed aside in favor of the more appealing sound bites, includes losing my home to foreclosure after a difficult divorce and good old-fashion American racism. Through it all, I have risen beyond not only the social expectations assigned to me at birth, but my own self-outlook.

Many would consider my life and accomplishments as "success-ful." Recognized as an *overachiever*, a *trailblazer*, a *risk-taker* and a *winner,* it seems I lived the quintessential American dream. Instead, I've been on an onerous journey. A quest for acceptance. A quest for security. A quest for normalcy. A quest to understand --- who is Valerie Still?

It wasn't until the unexpected and problematic death of my moth-er in 2010 that I came face to face with an adversary, one that had the greatest potential to destroy me. I was all alone. In all of my years of beating the odds, I had the ultimate teammate, ever-present and ever-ready to go to battle with me. The force that sustained me for nearly fifty years was gone and I was in a free fall heading for a crash landing. Ironically, the year after her death, when I thought I had lost all hope, I began a journey that would lead me directly to the Ultimate Source of unlimited possibility and wisdom my years of graduate studies could never impart.

There is no life without death. No joy without pain. No triumph without struggle. No love without hope. My mother's death forced me to not just reclaim my own life, but investigate its true purpose. A new sense of urgency arose within me — I would have to keep my mother alive for the sake of my own survival. But how would I do that? How could I erase the image of my mother's body being taken out of a thick plastic bag and placed on that cool, stainless steel table at the funeral home? How could I make that cold lifeless body become my lifeline?

On my journey to reconnect with my late mother, I uncovered family secrets, some dating back more than 200 years, that would reconstruct my identity and provide me with an empowered, authentic sense of who I am.

Playing Black and Blue is a narrative of tragedy, struggle, survival, growth, triumph, self-awareness, self-discovery and empowerment. Hopefully, in between the lines and words of each page of this book, the reader will connect with me in an organic, ethereal way. I invite you to experience enlightenment and awakening while appreciating the uniqueness, sacredness of each human's earth journey. After years of searching for who I am, years of working through my complex and arduous childhood, I am at a minimalistic stage in my life. Having shed many convoluted layers of ego to expose the core, the bare essentials, I am finally able to be vulnerable. I now know vulnerability, a skill I once believed was a sign of weakness, provides the opportunity to embrace all of life in freedom. I don't claim to be an expert, scholar, or authority on anything that I present in my writings. I am merely a traveler on my own unique passage.

As time passes, my mother's voice echoes in my inner being with one of her favorite Bible verses:" […] but they who wait on the Lord shall renew their strength; they shall mount up with wings like eagles; they shall run and not be weary; they shall walk and not faint." (Isaiah 40:31). It is my hope that my story will inspire readers of all ages with its message of survival, perseverance, and triumph.

PART ONE: Still Life

"All persons are born with certain gifts, which sooner or later develop in them, and I think those gifts should be cultivated, let them be of what sort they may, so that they lead to honorable pursuits."

Dr. James Still

Chapter 1

A Tribe Called Still

My mother, Gwendolyn Alice Ricketts, was the fourth of eight children. She and her twin sister Geraldine were born on October 3, 1931, just a couple of years after the beginning of the Great Depression. Firstborn "Gerry" was outgoing and daring. "Gwennie," on the other hand, was soft-spoken and reserved. In high school, Gerry always looked for extracurricular activities and adventures, while Gwennie struggled with learning disabilities. It was surprising they graduated.

One night during their senior year, she encountered a handsome, entrancing piano player, James, at a speakeasy after sneaking out. The Dew Drop Inn in Morrisville, New Jersey was a popular nightclub in the 1940s and 50s. It was a short ride over the bridge from Philadelphia. Famous Negro singers and entertainers who performed in nearby Philadelphia would travel to the small smoke filled club to unwind and relax in the wee hours of the night. James Still, known as "Doc," greeted everyone in the club as "cuz". His bad-boy, fun-loving, explosive personality and gifted piano skills made him a club favorite. After a few drinks, he often ended up playing and singing with noted musicians, singers, and entertainers. As he told it and retold it, one night he even outshone one of his jazz favorites, Dizzy Gillespie.

It was love at first sight for the naive Gwennie.

She was stunning and refreshing, a pretty, olive-complexion petite with big dark eyes and long black hair fixed high on her head in her signature beehive hairstyle. He was tall, slightly muscular and lean with high cheekbones, long Grecian nose, black wavy hair and mystifying eyes. As Gerry danced and partied, Gwennie sipped on a glass of ginger ale while tapping her feet to the lively music from across the room, enchanted by the tall, good-looking man tickling the ivories and singing. Even though a crowd gathered around the piano, his improvised love song sung in falsetto was directed at her. Once finished, he picked up his drink, grabbed his lit Pall Mall cigarette from the ashtray and stumbled over to Gwennie.

"Come on, Doc," yelled Sally, his younger gregarious sister and party partner who had had a few drinks already. "Play another song!!'"

"Can't do sis," Doc replied, "I've got some business to take care of."

That would be the beginning of Gwennie's incarceration into Doc's dysfunctional world and would last until his last breaths.

Doc's biggest obstacle in his conquest of Gwennie was Al Ricketts. Gwennie's father was a hard working man and the owner of the most successful minority-owned construction company in East Riverton, New Jersey. Doc planned clandestine visits to Gwennie's house during the day while her father worked. One day as he enjoyed a piece of Gwennie's fried chicken, Al unexpectedly walked in the front door; that chicken leg ended up jammed down into the couch and Doc was kicked out.

Despite the scene that unfolded that afternoon, Gwennie kept seeing Doc and shortly after her eighteenth birthday, she became pregnant. No longer daddy's little girl, she left home and moved in with her mother's sister, Camilla. James Fleming Still Jr. was born July 4, 1950. Nine months later she was pregnant again and gave birth to Bonnie Jean. A year later in 1953 twins Francine Carrie and Francina Gladys were born. Francine was a plump, chubby brown-skinned baby. Small, light-skinned, blue-eyed twin Francina was tiny compared to Francine, giving rise to the nicknames "Porky" and "Peanut." It wasn't until an ultimatum was given that Doc agreed to marry Gwennie. On February 8, 1954, Doc and Gwennie were married and went to live at his parents' home.

With only an eighth-grade education and a growing family to support, life was not easy, but Doc was a hard worker looking for any type of job to make money. Shortly after the birth of the twins, Aunt Camilla suggested the family find a place to live in newly-built Roosevelt Manor, a public housing project in Camden, New Jersey where she was a teacher.

At the time, with its proximity to Philadelphia, Camden was a prominent city; however as blacks moved into cities, whites began their migration out to the suburbs. Doc and Gwennie, were one of the first families to move into a small public housing unit at 809. It wasn't long before 809 Ferry Avenue was too small for the ever-growing Still clan. Soon after their wedding Gwennie, was pregnant again. They moved a few units away to 813 Ferry Avenue, a tiny four-bedroom, one-bathroom public housing unit, which was slightly larger. It wasn't long before the ever-increasing family, responsibility and stress drove the fun-loving Doc to falter. Doc spent hours across the street at Vic's Tavern trying to escape the reality of being a husband and father of five children. The more he drank, the less he worked, which led to violence.

Ferry Avenue became Doc's domain. For Gwennie and her continuously growing family, the initial innocent infatuation with Doc became a dangerously vicious pattern of physical, sexual, psychological, and verbal abuse.

One day Doc stumbled home inebriated from Vic's.

"Gwennie!" he yelled as he busted in the front door. "Where the hell are you?"

She was overly familiar with his rants, yelling, and physicality.

"You've been cheating on me, goddammit. I know it," he said as he grabbed the butcher knife she had laid on the table after cutting potatoes in the tiny kitchen.

She began backing up. "No Doc, No. I'm just fixing dinner...I'd never..."

He lunged toward her with the knife before she could finish her sentence. Terrified, she dashed out the back door. The hairpins in her normally well-kept beehive loosened and her long black hair flowed freely with Doc closing in. Navigating the fence at the end of the yard proved to be too much for Gwennie. Doc pounced on her, dragged her back into the house by her hair and beat her in front of her small children.

For the next four years Gwennie would be pregnant. Tired from long days of taking care of children and the household, she often fell into bed alone, dead tired, only to be awakened in the middle of the night by a drunken Doc forcing her to have sex. Many times she wouldn't even be aware of doing so because of being so tired until Doc would tell her to "get up and go wash." Shortly after moving into 813 Ferry Ave., Wendell Harold was born with blue eyes. Doc did not understand how he could be the father of a child with blue eyes, which sparked his suspicion of Gwennie's infidelity. A year later, Arthur Barry was born. He looked more like Doc. In 1956, Gary Albert was born and was followed by Dennis George in 1959. With each child, Doc's behavior worsened. Raising eight children, including five overactive boys, was definitely a challenge for Gwennie along with meeting Doc's demands.

Searching for relief and refuge from her extremely hostile domestic situation, Gwennie turned to religion. She was desperate for an outlet from 813 Ferry Avenue and in search of truth. She visited at least four or five local churches.

One day Charles Dawson, a young, athletic, baritone-voiced milkman with a million-dollar captivating smile invited Gwennie and her family to attend a new non-denominational, Bible-teaching church that he was starting in downtown Camden.

Pastor Dawson quickly saw Gwennie's need for help with her growing family and in particular with her tribe of boys. He also recognized Doc's need for a mentor and friend. Each day he delivered the milk, he extended the invitation to Gwennie and Doc to attend his church, Broadway Bible Tabernacle. Initially, only the children were allowed to go to church because of Doc's jealousy but eventually he allowed Gwennie to attend as well.

Sunday became the "day of rest" on which no activities would occur other than religious ones. Every Sunday she started early, getting each child dressed and ready to be at Sunday school by 8:00 a.m. With her hair standing high in her signature beehive and shoulders back, Gwennie walked over a mile at a record-setting pace with the youngest in her arms and the other seven children struggling to stay close behind. Morning church service began shortly after Sunday school and could last until late in the afternoon. While Gwennie prepared dinner, the older children attended the Camden Rescue Mission's programs. All returned for dinner, and then headed back for the Youth Service at church from 6-7 p.m.

Though she was exhausted, those walks allowed Gwennie to release, refill, and renew for the following week. For her children it was bonding time and prepared them for life's fast pace. She never looked back and they always kept her in sight.

At 27 years old, she was poor with eight children, a high school education, a dysfunctional marriage, and a troubled husband. It is not clear if she had a vision for herself but she had a strong faith, determination and will, and she no doubt had a vision for a bright future for each of her children.

Her children were her future. Her spiritual foundation and fortitude would be the key to her survival and her legacy. I wonder at what point she let go of her personal dreams and vision for her future?

*****

The Sixties was a decade of volatile cultural and social changes in American society. By the spring of 1961, twenty-nine-year-old Gwennie, with eight children, all under the age of 11, was in the middle of her own volatile social existence. Doc's already unstable mental health, increasing responsibility of a growing family, the sense of his dreams slipping away and the isolation of his small low-income domain, made for the right cocktail for extreme domestic violence. Gwennie and her clan of children held onto a code of secrecy --what happened in 813 Ferry Avenue stayed sealed within its walls.

Doc's abuse began to have an impact on Gwennie. She began dishing out physical and emotional abuse similar to what she received, to her beloved children. As Doc instilled fear in Gwennie as a means of control, Gwennie made it clear to her children that they should fear her or suffer the consequences. Her five active boys were energetic, boisterous and adventurous. She reigned down hard, fearing losing control. The youngest, Dennis, lived up to his namesake – Dennis the Menace. He was an extremely ornery toddler.

On Mother's Day, May 14, 1961, Gwennie began the all-too familiar labor contractions. Another innocent mouth to feed. She didn't go to church that Sunday, instead deciding which of the local three hospitals she would sneak into, for the delivery of her newborn was challenging. Being poor and without health insurance, Gwennie rotated around local hospitals for her children's delivery and medical emergencies.

Gwennie ended up at Cooper Hospital in downtown Camden for this birth. At half past one in the afternoon, as a busload of young American freedom fighters, black and white, were set on fire in the South as they sacrificed their safety and lives for civil rights, I was brought into this world.

When I wasn't more than a few weeks old, as my mother breast-fed me, my father had fallen asleep next to her drunk after coming in late with his friends. The house was quiet as he let out a sudden shriek. His body stiffened and he began to convulse vigorously.

"Sparky, Wendell, Barry...get up, get up and get downstairs!" Mom screamed as my father fell to the floor with his eyes half-opened and foaming at the mouth, nearly knocking me out of her arms.

"Mommy, mommy, mommy...is Daddy dying?" Bonnie cried at the sight of her spasmodic father. She had rushed ahead of the boys.

"Girls, watch the baby. Sparky hold his shoulders! Barry grab his feet! Roll him over! Put him back on the bed! Wendell, get a washcloth. Gary, make sure he doesn't hit his head!"

My mother frantically bellowed out commands as her frightened sons obeyed.

"Not my will, Father but Thy will be done...not my will but Thy will Father..." she prayed under her breath.

"He's coming back mommy...he's waking up..." Sparky reassured her.

"What...what the hell is going on, Gwennie? Where the hell am I?" My father sputtered, confused and gazing at his terrified young daughters cuddled together and crying.

"I don't know Doc...I don't know..." Mom whimpered in quiet shock.

"Kids get back to bed now; you have to get up for school in a couple hours."

This was the first of many seizures that would become a normal reoccurring incident in our household. Most of his "attacks" occurred late at night after he had been drinking but they were never forecast and they were always scary. Eventually doctors prescribed medication for his seizures but he was also advised to stop drinking alcohol. After each seizure Mom made sure Dad took his medicine, but he continued to drink heavily.

I was born the year John F. Kennedy took office and Mom's and Dad's last child, Jacqueline Marie, was born two months after his assassination. Jackie and I were born when people fought to break down labels that caused division and disenfranchisement. Within my family and community, finding an identity was confusing for me.

Chapter 2

The Tomboy

My struggle to understand and embrace who I was began at a young age.

My father's father, James Harrison Still, was from a well-established historical Black family in South Jersey. "Jimmie" was a dark-skinned, high-cheek-boned man who was musically gifted. My father's mother, Carrie George House, was from South Carolina. She was of mixed blood, predominantly German-Jew and Native American but also African American. Her phenotype was that of a white person with fine facial features and long straight hair. Whenever they traveled South, Jimmie sat in the back of the bus as she sat in the front.

My mother's father, Albert Ricketts, was born in Pottstown, Pennsylvania. He was Irish and Black. His family was well-respected in Pottstown. They were physically exceptional and a family of athletes who played professional sports when Blacks were just beginning to break the color line. My grandfather's nephews played in the NBA and Major League Baseball. Dick Ricketts, who stood 6'7", was a star basketball player at Duquesne University along with his brother Dave. Dick was selected by the St. Louis Hawks with the first pick of the 1955 NBA Draft and also was a pitcher for the St. Louis Cardinals. He was one of the first two-sport professionals of the post-integration era. Dave was a catcher for the St. Louis Cardinals, who won the World Series in 1967.

My grandfather was fair-complexioned, with light green eyes, and loved smoking a pipe or cigar. He was a quiet but strong family man who owned his own construction company, Ricketts and Sons. My mother's mother, Gladys Robinson, came from a Black family of teachers, educators, and community leaders. Unlike her husband, she was outgoing and dogmatic.

While society categorized my family as "other" and inferior based on our miscegenation, we were also ostracized and mistreated within our community because of the crossbreeding between white and black. My siblings' skin tones ranged from caramel to "high-yellow," with eye colors of rich brown, green and blue. There was also a wide range of hair texture and colors in my family. Color was a major issue within the community and navigating our differences was often difficult.

If navigating racial norms was challenging, navigating gender norms was even more risky. Before Jackie was born, I connected with my four older brothers. I identified with things they did and embraced their interests, especially sports. Although it was unacceptable for girls to play sports, I loved such activities and being outside.

Growing up in Camden was a test in survival on all levels: emotionally, spiritually, physically and mentally. My dysfunctional domestic situation was equally challenging.

My brothers and sisters and I were exposed to, and nurtured, in the complex setting at 813 Ferry Avenue, a perplexing paradox. The small roach-infested, unhealthy red-brick dwelling was built on a dump site, but Mom took great pride in keeping it Godly-clean. It was venomous yet filled with love and cultivated spiritual growth. Mom was the spiritual alpha and Dad the contrasting force that created the exact tension needed for perfect enlightenment. Labeling experiences as "good" versus "bad" is incorrect. This home was the source of a complex domestic milieu that would eventually leave its imprint on everyone who lived within those walls. Mom always said, "What didn't kill us made us stronger."

As a young girl I spent lots of time with Pastor Dawson and his family. I loved him and his wife. They were like foster parents to me – they were a diversion. When I was with them I received the attention I wasn't getting at home with so many siblings vying for Mom's love and Dad's approval. Pastor Dawson was athletic and when I was in fourth grade, he would allow me to join in his morning run in the woods. He never slowed his pace and I did all I could to keep up. One morning as he jumped over a fallen tree, I tried to hurdle the trunk with my little legs but my foot caught a branch and sent me tumbling to the ground. When Pastor Dawson finally realized I wasn't following closely, he turned and ran back to me.

"Are you okay?" he asked, reaching to help me up.

"Oh, I'm okay, I'm okay, " I said as I wiped away leaves, debris and blood on my knee and choked back some tears, determined to finish the run.

During the following Sunday's church service, Pastor Dawson recounted our training mishap from the pulpit.

"Brothers and Sisters, I want to recognize one of God's little warriors this morning. You all know her for her musical talent and nurturing spirit. Valerie, stand up."

Pastor Dawson often had my brothers stand for their athletic accomplishments.

"Our little sister Valerie has been collecting pennies for missionaries for quite some time but this weekend while she was home visiting Sister Dawson and me, she proved to be a pretty tough little athlete." He chuckled and recounted our episode.

"Her big brothers better keep an eye on her," he said amid laughs and amens from the congregation.

"Keep her and the Still family in your prayers."

As sweet as my heart was, on the flip side, everyone knew I was the tough little Still girl who tagged along with her brothers. One of our favorite indoor activities was our makeshift basketball court in the tiny 4 x 10 foot upstairs hallway. We would untwist a wire hanger and shape it into a hoop and loop a cut of a pair of Mom's nylons as the net. The basket would be lodged on top of the bathroom door frame. A pair of athletic socks rolled up was used as our official ball. Games would start quietly. We knew that if Mom discovered us playing we would all be in big trouble, but most games ended with Mom angrily racing up the stairs after hearing the thunderous play. We had an escape plan with the sound of Mom on the first stair. Someone grabbed the basket from the bathroom door and someone else made sure to hide the rolled up socks, then we all adamantly denied playing basketball in the house. We knew the consequences of playing in the house. Mom's punishments were terrifying. She was physically strong and mentally tough. Her forewarning before each punishment was that "this is going to hurt me more than it hurts you."

After an adventure I took with the boys, handing out flyers for a strange man throughout a few neighborhoods for a quarter, I received one of Mom's most dreaded punishments. She locked my head between her knees to stabilize me from squirming. As I nearly suffocating between her strong thighs, my butt was perfectly positioned for a whipping.

"You stop that crying right now or I'll give you something to cry about," she threatened after the whipping as my little body gently jerked, taking in big breaths through my nose with my mouth clenched.

The boys were sent to bed without eating. I would have taken that any day over her heavy-handed or belt whippings. At times I thought her making me practice my piano lessons was the most severe punishment. I was an overly active child and sitting for an hour or two at the piano was agonizing but mom loved hearing me play. It soothed her and I loved hearing her hum along with my playing.

There was always a piano in the house. Dad loved playing and singing. After a few beers and shots of sherry, he often gathered us all around the piano and entertained us with his feet-stomping, falsetto singing, keyboard-rolling performances while Mom cooked dinner. We would dance, laugh and sing along as he had the entire house rocking with his musical renditions until the liquor took control and he started in on Mom. He became violent and abusive with her. Many times the meals she cooked him didn't please him and would end up thrown at the walls or the dog. We would fight to get a scrap of food. Going to bed with hunger pangs was a regular occurrence.

Even though I hated to sit, I was fascinated with music and the piano. I made up tunes, never knowing that anyone was taking notice, but Mom knew I was musically gifted. For my seventh birthday I began piano lessons with an elderly woman who taught from her home. I took piano lessons each week until I turned seventeen; for $2 a session I became a skilled pianist. I performed concerts, played for adult choirs and participated in contests. Playing the piano provided me with an opportunity to make money as well. I loved making money. Eventually, I learned to play the trumpet, saxophone, French horn and guitar. Mom was so proud of my musical accomplishments. Each time someone visited us she insisted I play.

Unfortunately for Mom, I was a tomboy. I was with my brothers whenever possible. In our neighborhood, hanging out with my wild, hyperactive, adventurous, thrill-seeking brothers was advantageous, but detrimental at the same time. I learned to survive and defend myself. Being a tomboy meant that most of the boys in the community were repulsed by me and my masculine ways, so I didn't fall prey to sexual advances. However, I was extremely daring and would always step up to any challenge. Mom knew the dangers of a young girl in this environment and was extremely overprotective of her children, especially her girls.

While I was in third grade, Mom dressed me for school in skirts and frilly little socks with ribbons and bows in my long two-braided hair only to have me come home with all my ribbons and bows missing and my socks filthy with dirt and my skirt twisted and torn. It was common for me to play with the boys during recess. Once I chased a boy up a tree to be eventually rescued by a teacher.

Despite my brothers' adventurous spirits, we were never allowed to walk the streets of Camden individually. Eventually, when Jackie and I became old enough, Mom allowed us to walk to school, church, or piano lessons together. "Do not split up for any reason and don't talk to strangers," she said as we walked out the door together.

One Sunday, as Jackie and I walked to church early in the morning for Sunday School, because we had been fighting, I forged ahead of her, making turns and cuts so she could not keep up with me until she was out of sight. Once I was sure I had lost her, I noticed a car following slowly and close behind me. I looked back at it and kept walking. It then pulled along side of me, and the driver rolled down the passenger's window.

"Where are you going?" asked a white man with seedy eyes.

Suddenly, I thought of Mom; she would be upset if I left Jackie.

"I'm heading to church," I said as I continued to walk.

"You wanna ride?" he asked as he leaned over and opened the passenger door.

"I'm heading the same way and it won't be a problem at all."

Scaring Jackie was my plan, so I jumped into the car in my little plaid skirt with the big pin in the front slit. As I shut the door and the man pulled away from the curb, I felt a lump grow in my throat. I didn't know this hairy man with the button-downed shirt and khaki shorts. My heart began to pound in my chest. The man made small talk as we slowly drove through green traffic lights. When he asked for directions, I could barely speak. Then he reached over, reassuring me that everything would be okay as he touched my bare inner knee. I felt like I might vomit. His hand moved up toward my thigh. I tried to pull my skirt down past my knees, praying the car would stop but we didn't stop once as the car crept slowly down the street. We were getting closer to the church, but I knew I had to get out of the car. Finally, a yellow light. When the car began to stop, I jumped out and ran in the opposite direction, hoping to find Jackie or someone else from my church. I found Jackie walking slowly toward church with tears in her eyes. I grabbed her and hugged her and told her that we shouldn't tell anyone that I had left her. I could have been another Camden statistic.

I often thought Mom would become a statistic. Watching Dad beat her was frightening. One night as Mom was overpowered and getting bludgeoned by Dad, Dennis jumped in.

"Don't hit mommy, you son-of-a-bitch!" Dennis snapped, grabbing him around the waist, wrestling my drunk, unstable father to the ground.

Without thinking, I sank my teeth into his calf muscle.

"You leave my mommy alone!" I shouted, emboldened by Dennis.

"You little bastards..." Dad snorted, scuffling to his room, shocked that we had joined the brawl.

After that fight, whenever Dennis and I were around and Dad began beating on Mom, we jumped in. As Dennis and I got older and bigger, Dad stopped beating on her as much. We felt like her protectors. Dennis and I had similar personalities. We were born two years and two days apart in May. We were loyal, hard-nosed and stubborn as two bulls. Although Dennis was always hot-tempered, I was normally mild-mannered and reserved, but depending on the circumstances and situation, I could become as enraged as a bull in a Spanish bullfight. Seeing my beloved mother being beaten by my father certainly sparked that rage in me.

Physically getting involved in my parents' fights changed me. I loved my mother and I loved my father, but something changed within me that day. I couldn't understand why he would hurt her. He loved his family and always told us we were his ten little Indians. That was one of his favorite songs to sing to us. We were taught to defend each other when we were outside of the home; now getting involved in my parent's conflict within the home created an internal battle for me.

I sought my father's love, protection and approval. He was proud of his family history and placed importance on family unity. Periodically, he would gather all of us around him and bring out an old dusty, worn brown book. It was an original copy of the autobiography written by his great-grandfather, Dr. James Still, published in 1877. We didn't understand what the book was but knew Dad valued it. He cherished his great grandfather's autobiography, *Early Recollections and Life of Dr. James Still*. Whenever we had an opportunity to touch the little brown book or look at the portrait of Dr. James Still, we felt inspired just by being in its presence. Dad, named after his great-grandfather, understood the priceless treasure. It held Dr. James Still's teachings, philosophy and life lessons. Such a legacy could either inspire one to excellence or overwhelm with unrealistic expectations. Passing on the legacy to the next generation without overpowering his children was Dad's goal. At times he hit the mark and the legacy pushed us to excellence; however, most times during my childhood we were unable to utilize the wealth of knowledge and wisdom from the pages of that little brown book.

A feeling of great pride comes over me when I share the fact that Dr. Still was my great-great-grandfather. Born on April 9, 1812, he lived through and past the Civil War and past the Emancipation Proclamation, being born free to a self-liberator, Sidney, and an enslaved father, Levin, who had bought his own freedom.

My own personal strength, my often-fragile courage in facing an always-uncertain future in such a changing world has been significantly uplifted, enhanced, by reading and re-reading Dr. James Still's book. Just having the original book in my hands and with the very thought – the knowledge – that an African American man born to enslaved parents who escaped from the American South over half-a-century before the Emancipation Proclamation, could and would one day write and have published the story of his life gives me more fortitude than I can express. The fact that my great-great grandfather became one of the most respected and successful doctors in South Jersey with only three months of formal education continues to inspire me. I believe his spirit and Providence protected and guided me as a child.

*****

One morning in third grade I became extremely ill and couldn't get out of bed; I couldn't walk. I was hospitalized in isolation. Although Mom never showed any signs of fear, I can only imagine her terror. She was our provider, protector and defender. On the hospital bed lay her listless once-hyperactive daughter and none of the tests were able to determine why I was unable to walk.

Eventually, I was diagnosed as having the sickle cell anemia trait and periodically I would have these types of incidents. Doctors warned Mom that I should not play sports or be too active. Instead of chasing boys up trees at school, now I was chasing them around the children's ward at the hospital. Once back to my normal self, I was released.

By the time I was eleven years old, Dad was unemployed and Mom was forced to get a job. Joining the workforce at forty years old with only a high school education, and after being a stay-at-home mom for so many years, this wasn't easy. Mom didn't have a driver's license and she was dyslexic but didn't know it. She did finally pass her driving exam after a few attempts, obtained her license and began working at a pre-school; Dennis, Jackie and I celebrated. We were her three youngest children, her three musketeers, and we shared a special bond with her.

Mom never asked for help from her father. She held onto the belief that she had dishonored and disrespected him when she got pregnant as a teenager and vowed she would never return home once she left. She had made the decision to be with Dad and, wrong or right, she would make it work. Her father loved her and would support her regardless of her decision but she fought the demon of disappointing him. Family was important to her and because of the dysfunctional situation she was in, she would make sure that her daughters would not make the same mistakes.

One way of making sure we would not fall into the same pitfalls as she had and to maintain control was our indoctrination of rigid Christian beliefs and tenets. Even when there wasn't much to eat, we always gathered for family devotions before each evening meal. These devotions included reading from the Bible, praying and moral teachings. She mixed in her life philosophy as well which included the importance of education and that we should always stick together, protect and defend each other. The only music that was allowed in the house beside Dad's playing and our classical music from lessons, was religious music. With ten children, maintaining control was a must but not easy as we became teenagers.

I was faster, taller, stronger and more athletic than most of the boys in my neighborhood when I became a teenager. Because of Mom I was also one of the best musicians in school and an honor roll student. Regardless of my grades, Mom's standard comment on my report card was "there is always room for improvement." She continued nudging me toward "lady-like" activities and discouraging me from playing sports. Girls participating in sports was unacceptable and doctors had warned Mom that physical exertion would cause health problems for me. None of this mattered to me; I loved basketball.

Chapter 3

Fighting to Survive

Our house was built on a dumpsite, many believed a toxic waste site. During the hot summers, the stench of decay filled the air for days at a time. Roaches and mice were a constant reminder of our unhealthy living environment. There were twelve people living in that small row-house with a small kitchen, small living room, four little bedrooms and a small bathroom without a shower. My nine siblings and I used the three bedrooms upstairs and my parents' bedroom was on the first level. I can't remember the exact arrangements but I always shared a bed and at least one roommate.

Initially I roomed with my older sister Peanut, and later with my younger sister Jackie. Sharing those last moments of the day with someone, reflecting and reliving what had been experienced that day and planning for the next created strong, intimate relationships. Peanut was eight years older than I. She was a very angry, solitary person who went to bed early. There was not much interaction and conversation with her at bedtime. Sneaking into bed as quietly as possible so as not to wake her was my main objective. She was extremely hostile and aggressive when awakened. Often she would punch me as hard as she could, knocking the wind out of me, or practice her martial arts skills on me. Regardless of her abuse, I was in awe of her.

Jackie and I lived a whole different life once the sun went down and we were in bed snuggled together. No longer were we living in a dreaded nightmare but we soared the universe. Those hours were filled with laughter and tears, songs and crying, happiness and despair. We talked of imaginary places and of traveling the world. We shared our dreams and a life so wonderful, we giggled for hours. Inevitably, we began to sing and eventually grew tired and fell asleep.

Many things happened in the quiet hours of the night; our reality never left us. Often Jackie was jarred awake from a nightmare, shaking and crying; we would hold on to each other, comfort each other...we understood, without saying a word. Many times we woke up to the feel of cold urine, a problem I frequently experienced. It seemed that all of the light-skinned children in our family were bedwetters. Other nights we could be unexpectedly awakened by Dad's seizures or domestic terrorism.

Once back in bed from any of the nocturnal interruptions, Jackie and I collapsed; throughout the night we clinched each other tightly. Hugs were not a common occurrence in our household. The sun rose and I knew, as I rolled over, there Jackie would be; my comforter, my dreamer, my support, my laughter, my security, my music maker and my best friend. A shout from mom to start the day, a glimpse at Jackie and we were back...to the real world, another chaotic day, filled with challenges too great for an adult to face, let alone two young girls.

When one grows up in an environment such as I did, many fears develop. I was an adult before realizing I had a fear of waking up alone. The fear of hunger, abuse, loneliness, illness and rejection, the fear of not being worthy, of not fitting in, the fear of anger and jealousy are just a few fears that I have experienced. With time I have experienced new fears but more importantly I am discovering the sources of those fears. Although it may seem important to recognize and discover the source of one's fear, the most important factor in dealing with it is recognizing that I could overcome and get rid of it by being aware of my thoughts. For me it was empowerment.

The fear of not having money or enough of anything as a young impoverished girl caused me to be practical and to develop an entrepreneurial mentality. One of my earliest aspirations was to work as a cashier at the local supermarket. Practical Valerie decided that

that would solve two of her biggest problems - food and money. I couldn't think of a better job. With my musical talents I could also make money. I played the piano for a few local church choirs and also performed concerts. Not only did I generate income, I saved and protected what I had.

I hated housework. There was no money to be made in housework. I was insulted that I was made to do it. All of my brothers were exempt from housework. Housework was designated for girls. My brothers played sports. It was the girls' job to do housework and clean up after everyone. I was an athlete and regardless of gender, I felt I should be exempt from housework. This became a major conflict between Mom and me.

My real passions were animals, being outside, and sports. I loved animals and would often bring stray wounded animals and birds home to nurse back to health, only to be heartbroken having to let them go. I wanted to be a veterinarian and loved James Herriot's series of books about his experience as a rural veterinarian in England. Although we didn't have many books in our house, I loved reading because I was able to escape my limited, constricting world. Herriot's books placed me in rural Britain with green pastures, smelly farm animals and lively characters. That's where I longed to be.

Mom's fears in regard to my participation in sports during my childhood were perpetuated by sexist attitudes; I would get cancer if I got hit in my breast (which I didn't even have at that time); I would become a lesbian; I wouldn't know how to be a lady; I would be denigrated because girls were not supposed to play sports. The pinnacle of the fight for women's equality in the workplace and in sports was reached in 1971 while I was still in elementary school. Title IX of the Education Amendment of 1972 tackled the issue of gender discrimination and inequality. I was a Title IX girl in every sense, free-spirited, strong and willing to fight for my passion, playing sports. Fear and ignorance was the driving force behind sexist attitudes and gender discrimination. I was Mom's contrasting force.

It is said that fear is "false evidence appearing real." All the things Mom feared about my playing sports were neither real nor true. Although she would never admit to fearing anything, my passion for sports and my willingness to do whatever it took to participate helped dismantle her fears in regard to sports and girls and more importantly her view of the importance of women in society. My determination and drive to stand up for what I loved helped change her antiquated ideology about women and women's role in society. My rebellion in playing sports may have given Mom solidarity in her fight for empowerment in her home situation. Although she was a battered woman, her daughter would be strong, empowered, determined and able to protect and defend herself.

The origins of Title IX were in the souls of women who tapped into their authentic power and needed to see that manifestation in American society. Although Title IX was a necessary law, women's collective vibrational signals caused the social change, not the legislation alone. Women needed to be given the same opportunities as men whether being selected as department chairs in universities or given athletic scholarships to those same schools. Being rejected systematically based on gender dismantled fear for women who had felt the sting of discrimination. I was one of those females. I hadn't petitioned for the legislation as had Bernice Sandler, but I had persevered and played sports despite the humiliation and ridicule of those around me.

Fear can drive people to do incredible things, but when fear is part of your make up and you cannot control it, you live in a constant state of confusion. At 813 Ferry Avenue, fear could have easily overtaken all of us but each one was born with a passion and reason. I recognized that at an early age.

*****

By high school my brothers had made names for themselves as athletes. My oldest brother Sparky was a 6'7" musician in the band, towering in the hallways of Camden High when the basketball coach discovered him his junior year. By his senior year he was highly recruited and accepted a basketball scholarship to the University of Maryland. Wendell, Barry, Gary and Dennis were inseparable. I tagged along as much as I could. Wendell was light-skinned with light green eyes and light brown hair. Barry (whose first name was Art but who we always called by his middle name) was Wendell's walking companion to and from school. Wendell was hot-headed and Barry mild-mannered. Wendell was chased home nearly every day from school by bullies, which meant Barry was running from them as well.

One day after school a pursuit ended with a thunderous backdoor slamming. Wendell and Barry dropped their books outside the door and jumped inside the house just in time not to get snatched by the swarm of assailants. The mob chasing them banged and kicked on the door, taunting them as Mom hurried from the bathroom upstairs. The streets of Camden were filled with violence but she had raised gentle giants.

Enraged at the sight of the group kicking the back door and yelling obscenities; she snatched Wendell and Barry, who had found safe hiding places in the house, and dragged them out the backdoor into the raging mob. There were at least ten boys, older teenagers, some bullies and other followers wanting to catch the action. Mom stood between the mob and Wendell and Barry.

"Okay, you want a fight?" she shouted as she grabbed colossal but frightened Barry from behind her to in front of her and the mob.

Barry was huge and towered over the little runts who had chased him home. When he started crying it seemed he garnered the strength of Hercules. Whether happy, sad or mad, everyone in our family knew that once Barry produced tears something out-of-the-ordinary was going to happen. As Mom continued while holding Barry, tears began to well up in his eyes.

"One at a time, just one at a time...who wants to be first?" Mom challenged the mob as trembling Barry clenched his hands into fists and held back tears.

By this time the crowd had grown and a circle was formed as if this was a nineteenth-century bare-knuckle fight in the backlands of the deep South. One of the bullies stepped up, egged on by his groupies, and stood face to chest with Barry. Mom called for all of her children to come out to make sure there would be no group attack as the two combatants stood in the middle of the circle.

The diminutive challenger rushed Barry and threw a couple of sucker punches, which seemed to go unnoticed with Barry clenching his fists tighter and tighter. This went against Barry's non-aggressive nature.

"Fight, I said fight!" Mom yelled at Barry as she pushed him towards the bully. Dennis and I could hardly contain ourselves. We were like two Pit Bulls trained for fighting and accustomed to jumping into any confrontation.

After Barry inflicted a few excruciating hits, he easily wrestled the much smaller kid into the dirt and began an all-out trouncing, as the teenagers in the crowd began shouting at their little buddy to be tough and get up. Mom stepped in and pulled Barry off the bully.

"Okay, who's next?" she asked as the demoralized, beaten and exhausted bully scuffled to escape.

Barry stood in the middle of the circle like a Roman gladiator with fire coming from his nostrils – finished with one opponent, ready to take on the next beast. There were some murmuring heard among the group of bullies as to who would be next but not one of them stepped up to face Barry who stood bigger than life. Barry was done crying. His chest seemed to grow in size with each breath he took and everyone there was in awe of this gentle but powerful superhero. In that moment, Barry became a hero. I was totally in awe and had the utmost respect for him.

I had also been consistently bullied as well, in particular by two dark-skinned sisters who were spiteful and mean-spirited, and who teased us as being the White family or "half-breeds." Anyone who was White or looked White was considered the enemy. Those two Black girls would attack me for no reason whenever I walked past their house and I had to do so to go to school and back home. I wondered why Black girls were so mean and was frightened by them.

Jackie and I were walking companions and without Dennis I didn't have much of a chance, but now with Barry in the middle of the circle, mom officiating and Dennis in eyesight, I felt safe.

Although Mom may not have done the right thing, she knew it was what needed to be done. She didn't believe in violence but in this environment she understood that if her boys would not defend and protect themselves they would be prey to any and all. After that day, my brothers didn't have much trouble from the boys in the neighborhood. It was a rite of passage; they established themselves as men. From that point on I was no longer included in their group.

Chapter 4

Playing to Escape

I had a one-block boundary. Going farther meant getting into big trouble with Mom. Thankfully everything I needed was across the street on the corner of Ferry Avenue and Phillips Street: a basketball court, a baseball diamond (which served as our football field) and the public swimming pool. I spent every moment possible on those outdoor basketball courts. I believed that one day I would play with Dr. J and the 76ers. When things were crazy at home, or there wasn't food to eat, or I was teased and bullied at school, or Dad was acting crazy, I escaped to the basketball court. There I was told time and again, "go home" or "go down to the other end...you're a girl...you don't belong here." In those moments, I learned to overcome my fears.

When I wasn't selected for pickup games, I continued to play by myself and each time another game started I would get in line for picking teams, only to be rejected, until one day there were only nine guys on the court to play. I had slipped on a hat to cover my hair to look like one of the guys. It wasn't long before I was asked to play. I was ecstatic. I finally had my chance. I played like a mad-woman, using all the skills I had practiced by myself and with the passion that burned inside of me. When the game was over, my team had won. I was so excited and sweaty with the big wool hat on my head that I pulled it off. When my long braids cascaded past my shoulders the boys were shocked and embarrassed; they had just been "schooled" by a girl.

"Hey, that's Still's little sister…girl you can ball!"

Although I still had to prove myself to get picked to play, I played with the boys. My biggest obstacle was Mom. She didn't want her young daughter playing with boys and men on the court where there were drugs, alcohol and fighting. But that didn't deter me.

"Valerie! Valerie! Mom screamed busting through the front door one night after Wednesday night prayer meeting.

"Yes, Mommy," I replied, barely making it through the back door, trying to catch my breath and wiping a few beads of sweat from my forehead.

I usually timed her returns from Wednesday night prayer meeting at the church but the last pickup game on the court had run longer since a team had to be up by two buckets to win. I had spotted her car at the red traffic light at the intersection of the basketball court and hoped she hadn't seen me. It was dark but those big floodlights on the court made me an easy target as Mom glanced at the court where a couple players were disputing a call. It was a close game and no one wanted to lose. I usually made it back in the house by the time she parked the car and entered the house without her noticing I had been out. I hoped she hadn't seen me but by the tone of that yell, I knew she had spotted me.

"If I catch you on that court one more time at night when I'm not home, you'll wish you were never born," she yelled while grabbing my arm and getting face-to-face. "That court isn't a place for girls. You could get hurt and you're wasting time! Did you get your homework done?" She continued, totally exhausted from a conversation she had had with me quite a few times.

"But Mommy…I wasn't…" I tried to diffuse the tension.

"But Mommy, nothing! Go to bed!" She ended the conversation perplexed, aggravated and disheartened.

That outdoor basketball court was a savior for me. I had a dream and I believed in my dream.

Establishing myself on that court before starting high school facilitated my transition from middle school to high school. Mom had other plans for me – music. Playing in the band was mandatory. I played saxophone in marching band, trumpet in stage band and French horn in concert band. I was also selected to be the pianist for the school choir and began taking private piano lessons from the band director. I did all of this to appease Mom, so I could play basketball. Try-outs for the team were in October.

Mom knew the dangers and pitfalls of living in a place like Camden, New Jersey. Our neighborhood was also home to pimps, prostitutes, pedophiles, drug addicts and high school dropouts. She did whatever needed to keep her precious children safe and protected. One of her mantras was "an idle mind is the devil's workshop." Although petite in stature, she controlled us, including her oversized boys, like a small bridle controls a wild mustang. We feared her in every way. Yet even in her domestic pandemonium, she created an environment that could nurture most physical needs and enlighten any spiritual one.

By the fall of 1975, Barry, who had earned a scholarship, was heading back for his second year at the University of Kentucky. He and his high school buddy, Derrick Ramsey, had signed to play football with Kentucky for the 1974 season. They were exceptional athletes and had led Camden High to state championships in football as well as basketball. At Camden High the football and basketball coaches were authoritarian figures with lots of control over players. They were influential people in the community who made deals with college coaches for young players and then placed those players with colleges.

Barry was highly recruited. His main objective was getting out of Camden; not going to the NFL. Most of the NCAA Big 10 conference schools were interested in him; his favorite was Michigan State but Coach Hinson convinced him Kentucky was his best choice.

"You can go to a program like Michigan, Michigan State, Penn State, Ohio State or Minnesota which already have great teams or you can go to Kentucky, which has an upcoming program and start your freshman year," Hinson promised Barry. Plus, UK would also give Derrick a football scholarship. Eventually, Derrick became UK's first black quarterback. I'm not sure if Hinson was aware of UK's history with Black athletes or the environment his young athletes would be placed in. Mom nor Barry was aware it had only been seven years earlier that UK had begun to recruit and offer scholarships to Black athletes. Nor were they aware of what had happened to UK's first black football player.

The Southeastern Conference was the last major conference in America to be integrated. In the mid-1960s UK president John Oswald promised football coach Charlie Bradshaw as enticement, employment for life at the school if he recruited black players. At the height of the civil-rights era, UK had signed two Black football players, Greg Page and Nate Northington, making it the first school in the SEC to sign Black players. They arrived on campus after the game that changed American cultural and sporting ideology on Black athletes and Blacks in general, the 1966 NCAA basketball championship game – University of Kentucky versus Texas Western, now the University of Texas at El Paso. Losing the national championship to a team that only played its black players was humiliating and forced legendary basketball coach Adolph Rupp to recruit black players as well. It was not an easy transition for Page and Northington with the UK football program. Playing in the deep South was the least of their concerns; they would have to navigate UK's campus.

Greg Page, one of the best players on the football team, died tragically. He was projected to be the first Black to play in an SEC football game once the season started but a month before the start of the season, during a non-contact practice in which the team was not in full pads but only shoulder pads and helmets, Page was fatally injured in the "pursuit drill." When the drill was over, ironically, the intimidating defensive end lay on the ground lifeless. He died 38 days later without leaving UK Medical Center.

Wilbur Hackett and Houston Hogg, two black freshman football players, were on the practice field when Page was injured and experienced the racially hostile, unwelcoming, uncomfortable environment at UK. Many in Kentucky's Black communities were suspicious of Page's death. Hackett's friends questioned his return to UK, "you gonna stay where they killed Greg Page?" Hackett and Hogg were so upset during their first year they discouraged any black athletes from signing with Kentucky.

Black players suffered Jim Crow discrimination, death threats and hate incidents. Many of UK's white football players didn't want black players on the team; most had never played with black players. After Page's death, Northington, who was never given a new roommate, believed this to be a form of Jim Crow segregation. He eventually became the first Black to play in SEC game the day after Page died, but left UK after playing only three varsity games.

Jim Green, a black track star and the first black athlete to graduate from UK in 1971, was accustomed to racial slurs, often being called "nigger" but once retaliated by spitting at a group of white males on campus who verbally attacked his girlfriend and her friend, with racist comments.

In 2014, Northington's autobiography recognized Page's sacrifice of being one of the first black football players in the SEC, noting, "Greg and I had successfully accomplished our mission of desegregating football in the Southeastern Conference, although at a terrible price."

Mom was unaware of Page's tragic death or the environment at UK when Kentucky's handsome coach, Fran Curci, sat in our tiny public-housing living room to meet her. This was only a formality; Hinson had already had Barry commit to UK before Mom knew.

Camden High School had been known for its boys' sports programs. By the time I arrived at Camden High, I was known as "Still's little sister." I had five exceptionally athletic brothers; four had already received athletic scholarship offers to Division I colleges. With my brothers I was aggressive and tough; I had to be in order to survive. With no formal basketball training, my aggressiveness made up for my lack of skills. Apart from when I was actually playing with my brothers or participating in some sport, I was quiet and shy.

Jackie and I were dreamers breaking down the illusion of what seemed to be our reality, the ghetto of Camden. Dreaming came easy to us. As a minority child living in poverty, all I had of value was my passion, my vision, my dream —what I envisioned as fulfilling. I was submerged in an authentic reality of limitless possibility and the law of attraction.

As I headed to high school, Jackie began middle school and our relationship began to change. Dennis and I spent more time together, but Dennis had had lots of behavior problems. At one point he was expelled from all Camden public schools until he was seen by a psychiatrist. Mom walked over 2 miles to his therapy sessions and back home a few times a week until he was allowed back in school.

With Dennis and me in high school, Mom began working full-time, leaving the house before we were up. Dad was at home but still had no involvement in our lives. Some mornings my oldest sister Bonnie, who at this time had finished college and was an elementary school teacher, stopped by the house with donuts and took us to school.

Sometimes Dad admonished his boys and told them he would not allow any dark-skinned girls in his house. I wasn't sure if he was joking or serious as the boys laughed hysterically as he joked about this. He had no advice for his daughters in terms of relationships and dating.

My passion was basketball. I knew in order to play basketball though, I would have to appease Mom, which meant I would have to get good grades, practice piano, and do housework. If I didn't, there were repercussions. I was not allowed to go outside and play. Mom continued to warn me that if I didn't do my housework, I would not play for the high school basketball team. She was strong-willed and always stuck to her word, but I was stubborn and detested washing dishes.

Tryouts were tough but my young gym teacher and coach of the girls' basketball team, diminutive Ms. Williams with a close-cropped afro, loved the energy and passion I had for the game. I had an organic talent that was enhanced by my experience playing unorganized street ball. Fundamentally, I was raw. I had never attended a camp or clinic or had any organized skill development, but I was aggressive and had a gift for anticipating where the ball would be and grabbing any loose ball or rebound. After the three-day tryouts, I was selected to play varsity as a freshman. Ms. Williams and my friends were excited for me as well. I could barely get home fast enough to tell Mom the good news.

"Valerie, I don't care what your coach thinks or your teammates or if you never speak to me again. You're 14 years old and not a little girl anymore. Since you can't wash dishes then you won't be playing basketball."

I pleaded with a lump in my throat. "But Mommy--"

"Go practice your piano lessons; that's the gift God gave you."

"Yes, Mommy."

It didn't matter to her that this was probably the most important thing that had happened to me; she wanted to make sure I understood that in life I would have to follow rules and in her house the rule was: no washing dishes, no basketball. I cried and cried but to no avail; she had made up her mind and she was not going to change it for anybody. My hurt turned into anger, bullheadedness and a battle of wills. I despised Mom and her crazy rules.

After the initial shock of not playing basketball my freshman year, I recuperated. I excelled academically, becoming a member of the National Honor Society and staying active in band and choir. Camden High had an excellent music program and our marching band was one of the best in the country. Mom loved the band and watching her sons play sports. She was Camden High's number one supporter and supplier of athletes. She was animated at the games and by the time her last three began high school, she was a sports' appassionato and expert.

My sophomore year, Mom and I came to a non-verbal agreement. As long as I kept my grades up and participated in band and choir, she would allow me to play basketball and not wash dishes.

I was so excited, but ill-prepared for the season. I was accustomed to playing aggressively and physically with the guys on the playground. I fouled out of every game. Mom and Jackie sat in the stands embarrassed, and later criticized me about being a "butcher," but they attended all my home games. Even through my unorthodox and crude manner of playing, I was honored with post-season awards. I now was on the radar of the girls' basketball world in South Jersey and the Philadelphia area.

Over the summer I progressed tremendously, training with a police officer, and by my junior year of high school I was slated to be a star in South Jersey. Camden High hired a new girls' basketball head coach for my junior year, Ms. Stanfill, and made Ms. Williams assistant coach. Ms. Stanfill was a sweet young white blond-haired newlywed Christian who loved us as if we were her own children. She baked cookies and had the team over to her house for pizza, shared her religious beliefs and took some team members to a Christian summer camp in upstate New York. We were having a fantastic year. I was averaging over 20 points and 16 rebounds per game, when I suffered an ankle injury that sidelined me for the last ten games of the season.

In the state tournament, with my ankle healed, I scored 17 points and had 17 rebounds in our first-round win and had 20 points in our second-round overtime loss to Millville. While post-season honors and all-star selections poured in, Dennis won both football and basketball state titles at Camden. He was receiving offers from Division 1 schools across the country and Barry had finished up a record-breaking career at Kentucky and was heading to the NFL draft.

In May 1978, Barry was selected by the Kansas City Chiefs as the second overall pick of the NFL draft. With his signing bonus, he bought a house in Cherry Hill, an affluent suburb. Going from the ghettos of Camden to the gated communities of Cherry Hill was a cultural shock.

We had endured the turbulent years of racial tension and being poor in the USA. Fitting into the black community was complex and conflicting. We were targeted as different because of our miscegenation. Within our neighborhood, the fact that not only did the blood of the "enemy" run through our bodies but that blood resulted in us having a lighter skin tone; we were sometimes the surrogate enemy. Barry's national recognition filled Centerville with pride. There were only four of us living at home, Mom, Dad, Jackie, and me. Dennis had had a physical altercation with Dad the previous year and moved out. Dad had come home drunk while Dennis was preparing for his sports banquet after winning state championships in basketball and football and had begun hurling Dennis' trophies to the floor and cussing at Mom. Once Dad stepped toward Dennis, Dennis tackled and punched him, breaking his nose. Blood squirted out like a water spout as Dad stumbled to get back up off the floor while mom screamed for Dennis to leave the house. After the incident Dennis lived with his high school coach. I missed him. When we moved to Cherry Hill, Dad decided he would not move. He remained in Camden.

Mom was now unofficially a "single mom." Barry bought her a car and furnished her new spacious home in the suburbs. She was hired by a reputable home healthcare provider in Cherry Hill as a nurse's aide. I found a job working in the mall's pet shop and opened a bank account.

We moved into the beautiful two-story house with a basement, four nice-sized bedrooms, tons of space and an attached garage. The Downs Farm subdivision had its own country club with a swimming pool, but we heard that Blacks were not allowed to join. Cherry Hill was predominantly white, with a large population of Jewish and Italian residents. Mom enrolled Jackie and me in Cherry Hill High School East shortly after moving. I was one of only twelve black students in a class of over 800. My first semester, along with required courses that included British Literature, I chose vertebrate anatomy and a photography class as electives. The massive school had manicured football, baseball, field hockey and soccer fields. They offered swimming, bowling and gymnastics, sports that Camden High didn't have.

"Life is what we make it," Mom insisted.

If something needed to get done, we just had to get it done. No excuses, no backing down. She had learned to stand up for herself and did not allow others to treat us as inferior. She had had her confrontations in terms of discrimination and we had watched her handle situations boldly. Now she only had Jackie and me left.

Grandpa Ricketts died the first month we were in school; Mom continued on as if nothing happened. I'm sure it broke her heart but she had to be strong for us just like he had been for his family. Mom had made amends with her father and he was proud of her and our family. He was an avid sports fan. Mom was glad that her father had the opportunity to see the NFL draft and watch some of Barry's professional games on television. They buried Grandpa Ricketts and Mom carried on without showing emotion or expressing any feelings about her loss. I don't remember, as a child, ever seeing her cry. Life continued.

In Downs Farms, we didn't make friends but we had eliminated the element of physical harm. At Cherry Hill East, as social teenagers who needed acceptance and inclusion, our pain was inflicted by exclusion. Socially, we weren't invited to many events outside of school with other students. Jackie and I had each other. We were tall, athletic, smart and pretty. Jackie was a towering six-foot beauty who led the freshman team and I led the varsity team. The basketball teams embraced us, knowing that I would instantly get varsity to the state tournament and Jackie represented the future of the program. The local newspapers heralded East as the team to beat in our conference and I was the reason.

I learned new fundamental basketball skills but brought my own set of life survival skills, which enhanced my game. My aggressiveness, determination, speed and instinct for always knowing where the ball was gave me a big advantage.

We started the season with seven non-conference games. Our first game against Audubon was a fairly easy one; we beat them by eleven points. After losing our second game to Gloucester Catholic by sixteen points we regrouped and went undefeated in the conference, becoming conference champions. Cherry Hill East went from an 11-11 record the previous year to a 21-1 record, and headed to the state tournament.

The University of Kentucky offered me a basketball scholarship, which I accepted immediately. Since Barry's experience at UK, I had dreamed of attending as well. I averaged nearly 18 points and 21 rebounds a game as we headed into the South Jersey Conference playoff game. My season ended during an aggressive dive for a loose ball. I fell and broke my left wrist. I would not be able to play in the state tournament.

Cherry Hill East was eliminated in the second round of the state tournament but I was selected for awards across the country and also for the New Jersey All-Star Game. I was anxious about the game. Anne Donovan, a 6'8" center for Paramus Catholic High School, was considered by most to be the best player in the country. Anne was selected for the North and I was selected for the South. I would finally get to play against this giant.

The South Jersey All-Stars lost the game 70-78. "Still Stands Out For South Stars," was the headliner in our South Jersey newspaper. The Philadelphia Inquirer wrote, "The major reason the heavily-

favored North trailed at all was Still's inside moves on Donovan."
I was heading into college and the matchup with Anne was a gauge
for me. After that game I believed I would be able to compete at the
collegiate level.

Mom watched proudly as I graduated from Cherry Hill East as a
member of the National Honor Society, East Academic Society, and
Cum Laude. The poor little girl from the projects of Camden had
not only survived in Camden but had survived and thrived in Cherry
Hill and was ready for her next adventure. My journey would continue in Lexington, Kentucky, a place that was unfamiliar and unknown to me.

Chapter 5

My Ol' Kentucky Home Far Away

On my official visit to UK for a women's basketball game, a local reporter questioned me as to what I saw in the underdeveloped program. The team was coming off a 13-16 season and was playing poorly when I was approached during the second half of the game. His article the following day noted that another observer of the game was not impressed with the Lady Kats, but I was. I thought they looked good and had good freshmen even though only one of those freshmen would make the team the following year. I made it clear that UK was my number 1 choice. I was only seventeen years old, and yet I knew I had to be in Lexington, Kentucky.

Having spent all of my life North, I had no idea how my own history and heritage would unfold when I set foot in Kentucky. Time and again, I was questioned as to why I would want to attend UK: not only why I wanted to play basketball for such a program but how a person of color from Camden, NJ could fit into a place like Lexington, Kentucky with its history. The Bluegrass State was one of the border states that remained "neutral" during the Civil War. Kentucky had been a center of interstate slave-trading. When I set foot on the UK campus, I didn't know that Lexington was the largest and wealthiest town west of the Allegheny Mountains at the turn of the nineteenth century. It was the capital of the slave trade. The city's location in the heart of the Bluegrass region was ideal for trading slaves; it had the highest number of enslaved African Americans and it was difficult for enslaved individuals to escape. If I had known, I would have said, "But that was history. I went to UK to play basketball, to walk in the shadows of my big brother, maybe even step out of those shadows to stand on my own, not to relive a past that had little to do with me."

There was much I didn't know about Kentucky's history. When I accepted my athletic scholarship I was not aware that the University of Kentucky, a land-grant university, founded in 1865 did not become racially integrated until nearly 85 years later. In 1904, Kentucky Day Law prohibited Blacks and Whites from attending the same schools. In 1948, Lyman T. Johnson, a Black man, won a lawsuit challenging the Day Law to be admitted to UK's graduate program.

My enchantment with Lexington, Kentucky was palpable and mysterious. Whenever we visited Barry, I felt more and more like I had already walked Lexington's roads and experienced it – it was familiar to me in a way I could not possibly understand. Barry had enjoyed much success and made many friendships during his four years at the University of Kentucky but our gravitation to Lexington was more than hospitality or accomplishments.

Located in downtown Lexington was Cheapside Auction Block. During the antebellum period enslaved African Americans were sold, traded and bought there. By the time I arrived at UK, Cheapside Bar & Grill was a local hangout for UK students. Along with my classmates, it would be one of our favorite college-town bars. Many UK fans and athletes gathered there to celebrate victories. Then, and even now, most Kentuckians, and certainly UK fans, and athletes who continue the tradition of celebrating UK's sporting events, do not know the dark history and significance of the Cheapside Auction Block between 1833 and 1865. I didn't know.

I wasn't familiar with UK's decorated men's basketball program and the women's basketball program barely existed. Women's athletics at UK was treated as an inferior product that the school was forced to offer because of Title IX. Women's basketball was an oxymoron, almost sacrilegious at the great University of Kentucky.

Many years after the fact, I was told that Pat Head, a young, vibrant and upcoming coach for the University of Tennessee, who was transforming their women's basketball program, was interested in becoming UK's coach before I arrived. UK administrators would not agree to pay her moving costs...so she remained at Tennessee. Kentuckian Cliff Hagan, a beloved and revered former UK basketball player and Naismith Hall of Famer, was the athletic director at UK during this period. One can only imagine where the UK women's basketball program would have gone under the leadership and coaching of Pat Head (later Pat Head Summitt). What a loss. And all because of moving costs from Knoxville to Lexington?

When I accepted my athletic scholarship I was not aware of this history and couldn't explain my deep infatuation for the foreign quaint southern city of Lexington.

*****

As a student, I didn't know that at the turn of the nineteenth century, my enslaved great-great-great grandparents made one of the toughest decisions of their lives – to risk everything to gain their freedom. After my great-great-great grandfather bought his freedom and headed north, his wife later successfully escaped with their two young daughters, leaving behind their two sons, six-year-old Levin Jr. and four-year-old Peter. It was her second attempt at escaping; the first escape with all four children resulted in their being recaptured by slave hunters.

After the second successful escape, their enraged owner sold their two boys to a slave-trader known as Kincaid, who took them to Kentucky. Their journey from the Eastern Shore of Maryland to the Bluegrass State was the beginning of an oppressed life filled with suffering, torture, dehumanization and pain, something I could not imagine, nor was focused on as I walked through the UK campus and around the streets of Lexington.

Kincaid sold the two little brothers to John Fisher, a brickyard operator in Lexington, Kentucky who lived across the road from the "Great Compromiser," Henry Clay, who himself enslaved people. As I enjoyed an Ale-8 soft drink at the Cheapside Bar and Grill, I had no idea that in all likelihood, my great-great granduncles were sold at Cheapside Auction Block. Those two terrified boys stood among men in shackles, sold to the highest bidder on the same spot where I played and dreamed about basketball.

Although I was not aware of the history of abuse, torture and dehumanization of my ancestors in the Bluegrass State, Levin Jr. and Peter, two sweet innocent boys whose childhood and lives were snatched away by the peculiar institution called slavery, they would be my guardian angels as I navigated the culture of Lexington.

Although slavery had been abolished for over a century, I would have to fight against other forms of enslavement, entrapment, and oppression as a female and as a person of color that would last longer than the years my ancestors had been in bondage in Lexington. I was a daydreaming naive female teenager in my wonderland. I was a conduit. In now knowing, in order for me to achieve total authentic power and enlightenment and step into my destiny, the Universe would have to expose all the despicable sins and atrocities my ancestors had suffered in Lexington, Kentucky. Mom often said, "Be sure your sins will find you out." It would take me nearly 35 years to understand what she meant.

Levin Sr., Charity, Levin Jr. and Peter had paid the ultimate price for my opportunity to attend the University of Kentucky and their sacrifices had gone unrecognized.

"The sun shines bright on my old Kentucky home, Tis summer the darkies are gay..."

*****

The summer of 1979 was a very eventful and restless one for me. I was sent the UK basketball summer training program. Reality hit. I showed Mom the long schedule of activities. She told me I would have to figure it out and that's exactly what I did. Each day, I did all the track and conditioning exercises listed with required time allowances. I competed against myself, pushing past my limits, most days without a stopwatch. It was me against myself and I knew if I could compete against myself I would be able to compete against anyone.

Often my brothers and I drove around South Jersey trying to

find outdoor courts for pick-up games. There was always trash talking about having a girl play, so my brothers usually asked the guys to "put their money where their mouths were," and a friendly wager was put on the game.

"How about letting my 'lil sis play, pussies," Dennis taunted the opposing team he had just beat. "She's better than you punk asses."

Opposing players usually had the same responses.

"Nah, man...I ain't playing against some little girl. She'll get hurt!"

"Are you fucking crazy? Hell no! This ain't recess...have her go get us water..."

"What? Are you babysitting!? Take your sister back home man."

Gary or Wendell or Barry sealed the deal after winning the first game without me.

"Okay, pick your team, we've got ours...how much you got? Winners take all."

After the first win with me playing, racking up money became easier as the male egos couldn't stop the double-or-nothing bets and leaving the court with a loss to a girl. With the extra cash, we'd stop to pick up a few soft drinks and snacks (sometimes beer and cigarettes for my brothers) courtesy of the losers. Our car rides home were filled with laughter, bantering and sharing our favorite moments from the games. I missed these moments together with my brothers once I left for UK.

Before reporting for school in the fall, all incoming-freshman players had to attend Lady Kat's Girls Basketball Camp as counselors for two weeks at UK. This is where I met my teammates. The upperclassmen were welcoming but I bonded right away with the other incoming freshmen. Lea Wise, Patty Jo Hedges, Sharon Garland and Lori Edgington were all from Kentucky. Lea and PJ had strong Kentucky accents and they teased me about my East Coast enunciation. Lea was a gorgeous blond who looked like Farrah Fawcett. She was one of the best shooters I had ever seen. I was stunned by PJ's quickness and ball handling skills. Although Lea and PJ were competitive, Lori was the edgiest competitor. Outgoing, funny, hard-nosed, she was the leader of the group. Regardless of who she was defending, she played physical and aggressive. Sharon, a quiet redhead, led her high school team to three state championships. Her shot was deadly. I couldn't believe the talent of these players. We bonded immediately. These girls loved the game as much as I did and could flat out play. When we weren't working camp, we spent every moment playing basketball. Sometimes we arrived early at Memorial Coliseum without lights on and played in the dark. After camp was over each day, we played inter-squad games for the campers.

Head coach Debbie Yow was an attractive, mild-mannered blonde with shoulder-length hair and a heavy southern accent. I connected immediately with her and would always be loyal to her because of the opportunity to play at UK. She was a former star basketball player in North Carolina. At Elon College, Debbie and her sisters, Kay and Susan, won a North Carolina State Championship. Older sister Kay was the head coach, Debbie, the captain of the team and younger sister Susan, the All-American. Two years after graduating from college Debbie became head coach for the University of Kentucky women's basketball team. Her assistant, Coach Beauchamp, was a soft-spoken, petite blonde in her second year with UK. She was from Macon, Georgia but graduated from UK in 1978. Both were young and inexperienced, but during that first week of camp, they understood that they had a special group of incoming players.

I made it through the first week of camp a little homesick, but excited. On Friday, the other freshmen players headed home for the weekend. Lea, who was from Lexington, invited me to stay with her at her home. Lea's family was different than mine; her dad owned his own business and Mrs. Wise was the nurturing mother of three children. They were incredibly nice, showing me around Lexington. I gained a respect and love for Lea after my visit with her family.

Even though I enjoyed my 2 weeks of Lady Kat Camp, I was ready to get back home to Mom.

"Mommy, you got to meet all my new teammates...they're so nice and I went to a horse farm, it was beautiful...and UK's campus is so big and you gotta see our home basketball court...and there were a few of the UK 1978 championship players I met and a few new freshmen coming in that I met too..."

I rambled on and on in the car ride back from the Philadelphia airport as Mom and Jackie listened.

"Well, Valerie...this is only the beginning for you...the Bible says better the end of a thing than the beginning thereof." It seemed Mom always spoke with Bible verses, from the King James old English version, making it difficult for me to understand the meaning of most of her biblically-laced advice.

*****

Before I set off for UK in the fall, Mom gave me her last bits of advice and assured me that I would be ok if I kept my faith in God. No matter what happened or came up, I would never be alone because God would always be with me.

"Keep God in your heart...Wait on the Lord: be of good courage, and he shall strengthen your heart. Don't forget that God will be with you always, even unto the end of the world. And when life gets rough be strong and of a good courage; be not afraid, neither be dismayed: for the Lord your God is with thee whithersoever thou goest."

While Mom rattled off her string of Bible verses in a Shakespearean mode, I recited them in my mind word for word. We all believed she knew every word of the Bible from beginning to end.

*****

Freshman orientation was scary. Unlike summer camp, there were thousands of students on UK's campus as I tried to schedule classes and get my dorm assignment. As I hopelessly roamed around Memorial Coliseum, now set up with dozens of tables for processing incoming freshmen, someone from the women's basketball office spotted me. It wasn't difficult to spot me -- a tall, skinny, light-brown-pimple-skinned girl with a big Afro. Although the Afro had been out of style for quite some time, I sported mine proudly. Mom had never let me wear my hair in an Afro it had been a symbol of rebellion. She was extremely upset when Porky had cut my long braids without Mom's consent. Now that Mom didn't have a say in how I wore my hair, I made my statement of independence.

All the Lady Kat basketball players lived in Blazer Hall directly across from Memorial Coliseum. We were all assigned another basketball player as a roommate.

"Hey Val, good to see ya again," Debra greeted me after I fumbled to get my dorm room unlocked after a long day of scheduling classes, getting my ID card and meal ticket.

"How's orientation going?"

"It's okay..." I said feeling scared, lonely, and homesick already.

"Don't worry, it gets better. Let's get a bite to eat."

Debra was awkwardly quiet and I was conspicuously frightened. We were roommates. Not much was said as we walked down the stairs to the cafeteria in Blazer Hall. Debra Oden was UK's first black female basketball player. Tanya Fogle bustled through the front doors causing a scene as we crossed the lobby of Blazer Hall uneasily.

"Hey ladies!! How's our lil' east coast Lady Kat doing?" Tanya hollered, sprinting towards us and throwing her arms around my neck.

"I got you lil' sis. I own this town, it's my town...we're gonna have lots of fun," she continued, answering her own question with a hearty laugh.

I had met Debra and Tanya during summer camp and felt some comfort in their presence.

Tanya, a sophomore, was UK's second female black player, and I was its third. Debra and Tanya were from Kentucky but complete opposites. Debra was from a tiny town of less than a thousand people, located in Eastern Kentucky's Appalachian Mountain Coal Fields. She was an attractive 5'8" browned-skinned sinewy forward who played aggressively on the court but off the court was extremely quiet and reserved. She was the most athletic and respected player on the team. Debra dated Lavon Williams, who won the NCAA 1978 men's championship with UK. Tanya was about the same height as Debra but weighed at least forty pounds more. She was deep chocolate-colored with the most contagious smile with a striking set of white teeth. Tanya didn't know a stranger and could make anyone laugh. She was big but fast, agile, aggressive and a gifted athlete. Along with her physical aggressiveness, Tanya was the most sociable and enthusiastic player on the team. She was a hometown favorite from Lexington. Her first cousin was Jack "Goose" Givens, who was the star of the UK 1978 championship team.

Blazer Hall was home for the next nine months. It was a dorm for female students, both athletes and non-athletes. Unlike all the other dorms on campus – one stood out, the newly-built "Wildcat Lodge"—home of the men's basketball team. I could see The Lodge and Memorial Coliseum from my dorm room window. Wildcat Lodge was built the previous year after Kentucky won the 1978 NCAA championship. Although it was supposed to be a dorm, it was more like a luxury resort, hence the name "Wildcat Lodge." The male players were treated like gods; even I was in awe of seeing players who I had watched win the championship in 1978 on TV.

Classes began. Most of the other incoming-freshmen were undecided in their major. Mom wanted me to major in music, but I majored in Pre-Vet/Animal Science even though not many athletes were a part of the College of Agriculture, which was located on the other side of campus. I had to take a bus to get to my classes and getting back in time for practices was often a challenge. Afternoon labs would be a problem once the season began. Almost any other major would have been easier and less complicated for me and basketball, but I had my sights on going to Vet School in four years.

Within a couple of weeks, I missed home. Mom. My siblings. Dad. To keep my mind off my sadness, I kept as busy as possible. During the first month we could not practice, so often my freshmen teammates and I would sneak into Memorial Coliseum and play pick-up games with the lights out. One day we arrived around lunchtime and discovered a small group of old men playing. One was short and balding with a long piece of hair combed over the top of his bare head. Each time he came into contact with opposing players his long comb-over hair fell down, exposing his shiny bald head. My teammates and I could barely keep from giggling out loud as we watched him constantly replacing his hair flap. Another one was skinny and wore an elastic knee brace and glasses. Although he had a limp, he was pretty agile for an old man. The one that really stood out though was a tall, handsome, distinguished man with a head-full of perfectly-styled silvering thick black hair with each strain gelled neatly in place. This Hollywood-actor-looking middle-aged man had a signature smooth right-handed hook shot -- automatic two points each time he took the shot.

A Black muscular player was assigned to play against him and challenged him physically under the basket. He looked like he was young enough and athletic enough to play for UK's football team. I later learned he was the wrestling coach. He used some of his wrestling techniques to tie up the hook-shot guy. The guys were really mixing it up, pushing each other, elbowing and fussing about calls, and each one seemed to believe he was playing in the 1978 NCAA championship game.

Lea, PJ, Lori, and I watched quietly from a distance until the game was over. As we headed toward the group, Mr. Hollywood looked at us oddly as one of us asked, "Can we play?" We were newcomers to town and didn't know this was the daily lunchtime games session open to faculty and staff. These were UK male professors and coaches and the good-looking guy with the right-handed hook was Cliff Hagan, our athletic director.

Basketball in Lexington was a man's thing. That had not changed. We knew we could easily take on these guys. I wanted a chance to shut down that right-handed hook. I didn't know Cliff Hagan but everyone else in Kentucky did.

"Hey guys, we got next." Lori insisted. "Us girls against you guys?"

Hagan looked at Lori begrudgingly and shouted out to the big Black players from the losing team heading off the floor.

"Fletcher, c'mon you're playing with us!"

Fletcher was the first African American head coach at a major college. He was hired at UK in 1973 as an assistant football coach but became the head wrestling coach. It seemed he was good friends with Hagan. Girls against guys? They would beat us once and then have us get off the court.

"Okay, boss. Real quick. I have to get to the other side of campus." Fletcher responded.

Instead, that group of guys would be the first to experience the birth of the Kentucky women's basketball program. They didn't know what hit them as teenage girls proceeded to man-handle them at the sacred male game of basketball. It wasn't long before frustration set in.

Lea hit bombs from the outside effortlessly while stealing the ball from opposing players.

"C'mon put a hand in her face and protect the ball!" Hagan scolded the comb-over guy.

PJ dribbled circles around her defender and dished out pin point, no-look passes, making her defender look pathetic.

"I know your knee is bothering you but you have to put more pressure on the ball. For God sake, she's not Kyle Macy!"

Lori played her aggressive defense and didn't back down from anyone, not even the wrestling coach.

"Fletcher don't take it easy on her...post her up!"

And I finally felt like I was back in South Jersey with my brothers, surprisingly showing some clueless guys that girls could play basketball while snatching all the rebounds from Cliff Hagan's missed hook shots.

"Hey boss, I guess the banks not open today," Fletcher chimed back after Hagan missed a couple shots.

We beat the lunchtime crew, much to their amazement and frustration, in what would become our venue for female empowerment, Memorial Coliseum. More importantly, we planted the first seeds of enlightenment in regard to women's ability in the minds of UK's educators, leaders and policy-makers. Although this wasn't a public display and was only witnessed by a handful of individuals, it was the start of a transformational shift in how these men viewed us.

We played often with the lunchtime group in Memorial Coliseum. It was one of the places I found comfort. I had been at UK for less than a month but was extremely homesick. All of my teammates were from Kentucky except senior Linda Edelman. The freshmen players returned home on the weekends or had family come visit.

My telephone calls home were stressful because I wanted to come home, "....but Mom was always willing to listen. She knew what if I could get past this initial period, I would be fine. She had gone through eight other children who had been through similar experiences in college. I usually called Barry after calling home. Although he was busy preparing for the Kansas City Chiefs' upcoming season, he always made time to talk to his little sis. He had had a great rookie year with the Chiefs during my senior year of high school, becoming an immediate starter and making the NFL All-Rookie Team in 1978. Watching him play professionally on TV was thrilling for me. I always adored Barry and loved his goofiness. Hearing his voice soothed me as we talked about what I was doing in Lexington. Before getting off the phone, he told me that he would have Bonnie, one of his best friends from Lexington, call me and that I should arrange to spend time with her.

Bonnie Hutton was an avid UK fanatic. She met Barry accidentally outside a class, in 1976, her first year at UK. The pretty, petite blonde with a bubbly personality noticed the gentle giant and struck up a conversation. He invited her to the next football game, and she never missed a game after that.

Bonnie called me and arranged to pick me up. She had never met me or seen me so we arranged to meet in front of Blazer Hall. As Bonnie pulled up she was shocked to find standing on the corner a tall, skinny, pimpled-face, homely girl with a big afro. We hit it off immediately. I was shy and reserved and she was outspoken and bold. She was a senior and only a few years older than I but she took me in like a mother duck with a little ugly duckling. Bonnie lived in a townhouse (close to the football stadium) that would become my second home for the next year.

Any time I was free, I was with Bonnie. Her mother and stepfather lived in Lexington. Her stepfather was Dean of The College of Agriculture, Dr. Charles Barnhart. During the summers she worked in the Vet Science building. That was where autopsies were done on famous racehorses and unusual animals. It was a small garage-like building that not many on campus knew about, but Bonnie knew all the doctors and people who worked there. Since I was in Pre-Vet, Bonnie asked if I would be interested in visiting; of course I was.

As we entered the parking lot, a man was hoisting a dead horse out of a truck. As we entered the building, a pungent smell of formaldehyde and old blood immediately hit me. I thought I was going to faint but didn't want to seem weak. I looked around the small room with an array of stainless steel tables and noticed a saw-table with an enormous blade. A disheveled elderly man with stubbly facial hair stood hosing down the blood-stained cement floor with a drain in the middle. On a shelf behind him sat large clear jars with animal organs and heads and a baby pig. There were also a few stalls with live animals.

"Hey Dr. Tobin, this is Valerie. Art Still's little sister. She's a freshman," Bonnie shouted out to someone entering the building.

"Y'all just in time. We just got a horse in. Wanna watch?" he asked Bonnie.

I was curious. Bonnie and I stayed as an autopsy was performed on the horse. The first task was sawing the head off. My first horse autopsy was gruesome. I had never seen anything like it. I didn't vomit; in fact, I was hooked. The autopsy lab became a second home to me. Bonnie and I became best friends quickly. She accepted me for who I was and gave me suggestions and advice that would help me fit into this new world of college. We never saw each other in terms of race or class. We were two college students, inquisitive, adventurous, young, wild and carefree. Nothing was off limits for us. One of the first bits of advice from Bonnie was after one of our first home games in which we had surprisingly beat a ranked team. I had dominated the game and Bonnie busted through the crowd to reach me right before I headed into the locker room. I extended my hand for a high five, excited to see her.

"Valski, you gotta whack off all that nappy, nasty armpit hair...I could see it from where I was sitting!"

Armpit hair? What was she talking about? I had just dominated in a college game against a ranked team and she was talking about hair?!

"You don't shave? She continued as I stood sheepishly. "If you have all that hair under your arms your legs must be a forest! Hurry up, I'll wait for you, we're going shopping after you're done in the locker room."

Once in her car Bonnie ranted on and on.

"If you want Sam to notice you, or any other guy... you gotta shave that hair!" Bonnie warned me.

Mom had already chastised me for allowing Porky to cut my hair; there was no way I was cutting any hair.

"I'm not shaving my legs, I barely have any hair on them..." I rebutted, "Feel 'em!"

"Wow, that hair is fine," she said, rubbing my legs. "But I've seen that nasty hair under your arms...no compromise there...it's gone. Don't worry, I'll show you how it's done." She said after pulling in the parking lot of Kroger Supermarket.

We badgered each other up and down the aisles as Bonnie put shaving cream, razors, acne cream and personal hygiene items in our shopping basket.

"Yeah, you're a Lady Kat but that doesn't mean you're some hairy wild funky beast... you're a college girl," She joked. "And none of the Wildcats will come close to you with all that hair!"

"Hey Bon, but what about us Lady Kats tonight?" I asked once back in the car.

"You all rocked. And Val...wow! All jokes aside, you were awesome!" Bonnie said like a proud mamma bear.

Every free moment I had I spent with Bonnie; she was an older sister/mom to me. When I wasn't with Bonnie I filled my time by joining Christian clubs at UK. Mom wanted me to read my Bible every day and stay strong in my faith. Along with classes and studying, these activities helped keep my mind off being home.

The end of September is a beautiful time in Lexington. The leaves begin to change colors and the weather has a pleasant chill. On the first day of conditioning, the veterans shared all their horror stories. Some of them questioned Coach Yow's ability to coach, but her ability to motivate and inspire and her conditioning preparation were exceptional. After stretching and warm-ups, we were tested on the three-mile run. Guards had a different time limit than post players. On Coach Beauchamps' command, we took off. Lea, PJ, and Lori sped out quickly and I trailed behind them. Some of the other veterans seemed shocked as we took off. I was the first big player to finish behind the guards. Next were the 100, 200 and 400-meter sprints, all done within certain time limits; two 400-meter sprints, followed by six 200-meter sprints, followed by ten 100-meter sprints. I thought I had pushed myself during summer workouts, but they were nothing compared to the pain of these sprints.

The coaches were pleasantly surprised by the freshmen; not only had we pushed to make our times; we pushed the veterans by competing in each conditioning skill. Walking back to Blazer Hall, we joked about the torture we had just endured. My legs felt like wet noodles. I could barely make it back across campus. This would be the first day of preseason training without a basketball for the next two to three weeks. I thought once preseason started I wouldn't think as much about home, but it made me long for Mom and home even more.

We eventually began basketball workouts. Practices were intense and competitive, and ended with a series of "suicides," conditioning sprints usually run in under twenty-five seconds. Our workouts and practices were brutal. Coach Yow was merciless. All players were required to wear big blue knee pads. We thought they looked horrendous but she wanted us to have an aggressive mentality; that meant we would be diving on the floor for every loose ball. We did drills to practice diving on the floor and taking offensive charges with one player barreling over another. The harder the collision, the louder and more spirited the praise from teammates and coaches.

Four of the returning veterans were starters from the previous season: Liz Lukschu, Debra Oden, Linda Edelman, and Geri Grisby. Debra, Liz, and Maria Donhoff were former All-Kentucky Women's Intercollegiate Conference players. Liz was a 6'4" post player who wasn't very fast or aggressive, but she had a soft, precision touch and seldom missed shots. Her hanging partner was Maria, an antagonistic, physical 5'11" forward but who, like Liz, didn't have great speed and agility. Debra was smaller than Liz and Maria but more athletic. Debra could outrun, out-jump, and out-hustle Liz and Maria. The front court veterans included 5'9" forward Tanya Fogle. She was a powerful, strong, big player who had great agility and speed for her size. Tanya was the team's comedian, keeping everyone laughing with her antics. We only had two returning guards. Linda Edelman was a tall guard at 5'9" and in the past had played small forward as well. She was a smart, solid player who didn't commit many turnovers. As a guard she was a tenacious rebounder with a height advantage but she was also a scorer. She was UK's third all-time leading scorer and only needed 266 to move into second place. Along with me she was the only other out-of-state scholarship player on the team. Geri was the smallest player on the team at 5'5" but one of the hardest working. She was a former Kentucky Miss Basketball and had once scored 81 points in a high school game. Coach Yow picked up a 5'7" freshman walk-on, Cathy Barber from Maryland, who had a full track scholarship. Cathy was lightning-quick and an aggressive player. Everyone could see the direction the team was moving, from a methodical, non-aggressive, but efficient team to an athletic, competitive, shorter, fast-breaking team. The team consisted of six veterans and six freshmen.

It wasn't long before media day arrived in late October. We were all excited because at summer camp there had been a buzz in the air about the new generation of Lady Kats. The overlying theme of our media day was the expectation of the freshman class, but also how the veterans would accept the new talented group of freshmen who would be going after their positions. Just from practices the media knew that something special was about to happen with the Lady Kats and the new group of freshmen.

Most UK fans knew the other Kentucky freshmen players; they had had stellar high school careers in Kentucky but not many people knew who I was. I was "Art Still's little sister." Barry was loved at UK and closely followed with the KC Chiefs. I would have his legacy to uphold. Media day ended and November was scheduled with scrimmages and intrasquad Blue/White games across Kentucky.

Despite our excitement, the men's basketball team overshadowed the Lady Kats. As a UK student, I was excited about the men's team and its run at a national championship. I couldn't help but notice this was a group of good-looking guys. The 1979 class of freshmen, Sam Bowie, Dirk Minniefield, Derrick Hord, Charles Hurt and Tom Heitz was much anticipated after a 19-12 record and a 6th place finish in the SEC the year following the national championship. UK fans were ecstatic about McDonald's All-American and national high school 7'1" basketball sensation, Sam Bowie. At the time, it was arguably UK's best recruiting class ever. Coach Hall had landed four All-Americans. I had a crush on Sam until Bonnie informed me he had a high school sweetheart.

Sam and the men's team had media day before the women's team. I sat and watched in awe as TV news stations from across the state and nation set up cameras and lights for interviews and stories.

I had never seen so much hoopla.

We had three Blue/White scrimmages and I led in scoring with 21, 29 and 36 points. Our final Blue/White game was held in Memorial Coliseum in front of fewer than 300 fans. With butterflies in my stomach and heart racing, I sprinted from the locker room down the hallway that led to the middle of the court in Memorial Coliseum. Neil Diamond's "Kentucky Woman" blasted over the loudspeakers as we stepped onto the court.

"Kentucky woman, she shines with her own light...she gets to know you, she gets to own you."

One of my dreams was becoming a reality. Coach Yow pitted the freshmen against the veterans for our last scrimmage.

The game was a battle and although the freshmen lost 81-76, it was clear that UK women's basketball was at the beginning of a new era. The freshmen, in Kentucky blue uniforms, played an exciting, aggressive, fast-paced, in-your-face style of basketball. We played scrappy, persistent defense, causing lots of turnovers, which ended in transition fast break points. Lea and Lori sank long-range bombs from the outside. PJ dazzled with her between-the-legs, behind-the-back dribbling, escaping traps to find a teammate streaking to the basket for an assist and I challenged every shot in the paint, stole passes, snagged rebounds, passed out to the guards and sped down the sidelines to finish at the opposite end of the court with lay-ups. I was 6'1," less than 150 pounds and assigned to play post against a bigger and more experienced Liz but I blocked shots, rebounded and scored at will. I finished with 36 points, 23 rebounds, four blocked shots, five steals and only two turnovers.

Coach Yow, who usually didn't show much emotion, could hardly conceal her excitement as she spoke with a reporter from the newspaper after the game. The team had gotten stronger in every area of the game. Two weeks earlier Coach Yow had said she would go with experience at the start of the season. After this game she decided she would go with the strongest lineup. Our first game of the season was in less than a week and Coach Yow decided to start three freshmen: Lea, PJ, and me. Liz would play in the post and Maria and I would be forwards.

I was not the most skilled athlete, but what I lacked in skill I made up in determination. When I missed an easy shot under the basket, I got the rebound on the other side, threw it back up, sometimes missed again, got the rebound on the other side and finally put the ball in for a score. I was an unpolished player with lots of potential. Coach Yow allowed me to learn while playing at the top level.

The University of Kentucky women's athletic program was a member of the Association for Intercollegiate Athletics for Women (AIAW) while UK men's athletic program was a member of the National Collegiate Athletic Association (NCAA). The two organizations had contrasting philosophies in regard to collegiate athletics. The NCAA raised money to help fight Title IX while the AIAW consistently fought against sex discrimination and for gender equality in collegiate sports. The AIAW, founded in 1971, was the governing organization for women's sports and national championships. The NCAA, a 73-year-old, multi-million dollar organization was the governing body for men's collegiate athletics and tournament. The AIAW did not want women's sports to suffer the commercialization and corruption that had infiltrated men's collegiate sports but the fight against an NCAA takeover of women's collegiate sports was overwhelming for the AIAW. UK women's basketball team played in the Kentucky Women's Intercollegiate Conference (KWIC), which included seven Kentucky teams; Eastern Kentucky, Western Kentucky, Louisville, Murray State, Morehead State and Northern Kentucky. The first KWIC championship began in 1972 shortly after Title IX was passed. We would also participate in the NCAA Southeastern Conference (SEC) tournament held at the University of Tennessee. This would be the first year the SEC offered a women's basketball tournament.

A couple weeks before the start of the season Rena Koier, a sportswriter for the Lexington Herald-Leader, pulled me over for an interview.

"Hey Val, have you seen this?

She handed me a booklet with Coach Yow centered on the cover between our two seniors Debra and Linda. It was the UK women's basketball 1979-80 media guide. It may have been the first women's media guide. I hurriedly flipped through the pages.

"Check out page 35."

Wow. I had to contain my emotions. An action shot of me in a UK uniform and tons of information about me. My personal profile listed my brother Art as the athlete I admired and my mother as the non-athlete that I admired. Wait until Mom sees this! My quote was "A winner never quits and a quitter never wins" and my thrilling moment..." being able to play for Lady Kats basketball team." I flipped to the back of the book, where all the records were kept. Most Points. Highest Scoring Average. Most Rebounds. Most Field Goal Attempts. Most Field Goals Made. Most Free Throws Attempted. Most Free Throws made. Best Rebounding Average. Career Point Leader. Pam Browning. Pam Browning. Pam Browning. The only name in the 1,000 Point Club - Pam Browning.

"Who's Pam Browning?" I asked Rena.

"She was a beast, Val. The best player to ever play here. Now she's playing pro ball in your neck of the woods with the New Jersey Gems."

Pam had been UK's first female to receive an athletic scholarship in 1974 when the program became a varsity sport. She now held most of UK's records. As I read and re-read her name over and over again, I had an overwhelming sensation.

I have to get my name on these pages where it will last forever.

The season started with an explosive game against the University of Cincinnati, December 1, 1979 at Cincinnati. We ripped them 81-45 with next-day headlines reading, "Freshmen Star in Debut." I had 18 points and 14 rebounds and Lea had 14 points to lead UK. The newspaper article noted that Lea and I, even though we were freshmen, "looked wise beyond their years in their first college game." Whether I was playing on the playgrounds of Camden or on the most historical college basketball court, a force guided me. Our next game was a double-header with the men's team at legendary Rupp Arena, home of the legendary Kentucky Wildcats - University of Kentucky Men's Basketball.

Rupp Arena was a male domain, a sport's sacred sanctuary. With an official capacity of 23,500, it was the largest arena designed specifically for basketball, as well as the largest indoor arena by capacity, in the United States. In Kentucky, men's basketball was king and anything done with the men's program must be larger than life. Purchasing a ticket to a UK men's game was nearly impossible.

Season tickets were traditionally passed down to family members through wills and contracts. The men's games were typically sold out in Rupp Arena while the Lady Kats could barely get 300 people into the stands when I arrived.

On December 8, 1979, I stepped under the bright lights of Rupp Arena. Not only was this the first home game of my college career; the thought of playing in the biggest and most prestigious venue in the USA was exciting, but as we ran out onto the court, our 300 loyal fans looked like a few ants among the numerous empty seats. I made eye contact with Bonnie, who snuck down to the lower section behind the UK bench. "Kentucky Woman" sounded angelic yet ominous and sacrilegious in this men's basketball Mecca. On press row sat our two local newspaper reporters who followed the team, while the local TV stations began arriving to set up for the men's game. That didn't matter – we just played. I was at center court ready to jump for the tipoff of the game. As the ball left the ref's hands I leaped high, looking for Lea or PJ to tip the ball to. I knew if they had the ball we would get a good start.

As the half was ending and UK men's basketball fans began to pour in for the men's game, we held a 47-32 lead, but in the locker room it felt as if we were losing by 20 points. Even though we had outshot our opponents 56.3% to 40%, and we had outrebounded them 24-11, we knew we were not playing to our full potential. The UK men's fans were now in the building along with TV and newspaper reporters, as well as the many grumblers who didn't believe in women's sports.

The first seven minutes of the second half we put on a basketball clinic. We clicked up the intensity level and speed control and had the crowd off its seats. Liz picked up her fourth foul less than five minutes into the second half. She was replaced by Lori, and I was pushed to the post position. Lori was only 5'8" and more competitive than anyone I knew; this meant we started our run-and-gun game of aggressively defending, causing turnovers and then converting them into easy transition layups or jumpers. Coach Yow unleashed her spirited, young, win-crazed, basketball-loving team, and some of the men's fans started cheering for us.

At one point, Lori scored eight straight points from 20-foot jumpers. The cheers grew louder and stronger. When the buzzer sounded, we had destroyed our opponent 96-56, holding them to just 24 points in the second half. I had my second double-double with 19 points and 11 rebounds. The crowd was astonished. The cheers filled the stadium. They didn't know that girls could have such skill and that a girls' game could be so entertaining. As I looked up into the crowd of thousands of screaming UK fans I wondered how a poor little girl from Camden, NJ could garner such applause and approval from this sea of Blue and White enthusiasts? We had planted thousands of seeds tonight but we would have to wait to see if they would grow.

Our next game was a KWIC conference game, our first conference game and against our cross-state rival, the Louisville Cardinals. Coach Yow had them favored to win the conference this year. They were big and experienced. Our practices were extremely physical and challenging as Coach Yow tried to do something unconventional –give her young freshmen players college experience. What she didn't realize was that although we had only played two college games we were on a mission and open to all possibilities. We took the hour-long bus ride to Louisville and stunned Louisville by nearly 20 points. A few days later we were back in Rupp Arena where three of our first four games were scheduled. Against Indiana, the fourth game of the season, and in front of over 10,000 fans, I broke the single-game scoring record with 38 points, and grabbed 19 rebounds in 31 minutes (my fourth consecutive double-double).

With each basket, each steal, each well-executed fast break the crowd grew louder and louder. We beat Indiana 102 - 52. Coach Yow had played all of her players in all of the games thus far, even our walk-on, Cathy Barber. When I left the game with 38 points, Indiana's team had only scored 41. Coach Yow told reporters she had never experienced such a lively crowd in her four years at UK. A quote from the newspaper the following day: "I don't believe it," said one UK fan who accidentally caught some of the Lady Kats' game by coming early for the men's game that followed. "Those girls can solid play. And Art Still's sister (Valerie) is unbelievable." The seed had broken ground and sprouted.

Whenever possible I watched the men's team practice. They

practiced after we did in Memorial Coliseum and we would interact between practices. I loved watching them practice. Bonnie said that was mainly due to my crush on Sam Bowie. Coach Joe B. Hall was like an army drill sergeant during boot camp, hurling out insults and punishment to indoctrinate his players into his system. He had been an assistant coach with legendary Adolph Rupp. Watching them run timed suicides at the end of practice until some players vomited or dived over the baseline finish to make the allotted time showed me what I thought it took to become a champion. I was surprised when Debra told me that junior Freddie Cowan liked me; he was her boy-friend Lavon's roommate.

The first time I visited Wildcat Lodge was with Freddie.

"C'mon Val," Freddie whispered one evening as we entered the backdoor of The Lodge after a late practice.

"But Freddie, I thought girls couldn't be in The Lodge," I re-plied, scared that I would be caught.

"It's fine, Lavon's out and I want to show you my room."

I was excited and nervous walking through the sacred edifice that commoners were not privy to. I tried not to make eye contact with the two Wildcats playing billiards on the oversized pool table covered in Kentucky Blue felt, while others lounged on the big luxu-rious leather sectional couches watching the theater-screen TV.

"Hey Sam," Freddie shouted to the Wildcat cueing up a shot.

Wow...that's Sam Bowie. I nearly died. I had heard he loved bil-liards. I nearly tripped heading up the stairs.

"Here's my room!" Freddie announced turning the key and opening the door. "Make yourself comfortable."

I sat on one of the specially-made oversized beds as the door shut. My heart raced. Wow... this is how the Wildcats live?

"You want something to drink?," Freddie offered, opening his personal refrigerator.

"No...no...I'm okay," I stuttered, still in shock as Freddie plopped down close to me on the bed.

"I think you're really cute," he said bringing his face close to mine as he rolled on top of me.

His slobbery kiss was a little repulsive and awkward to me.

It was unbelievable that an upperclassmen who had won a national championship was interested in me. The male players were high-profile personalities on campus. We spent a few minutes making out before he walked me across the street to Blazer Hall.

Freddie and I began seeing each other regularly after that first kissing encounter in his room but my first love was basketball.

Our last game of 1979, but first game in Memorial Coliseum, was a conference game against Eastern Kentucky. It was right before the Christmas break and everyone was looking forward to getting home for the holidays.

We beat Eastern Kentucky, 100-77 in front of 600 screaming fans. We had doubled our attendance in Memorial Coliseum in less than four games without a marketing budget or much support from the athletic department. I had my fifth consecutive double-double, 25 points and 15 rebounds. Lea, PJ, Lori and I were beginning to become familiar names in Lexington as I anxiously flew home for Christmas break.

Since the season started, I was a little less homesick but still ready to get back to Mom. She was excited that I was doing so well and adjusting. The fact that I was going to church and attending Bible study each week made her happy. Bonnie teased me about the suitcase full of bags of chips and snacks for everyone at home I had saved from my meal ticket allowance.

While I was at home, the UK men's basketball team fell from its #2 national ranking; the UK women's basketball team climbed into the top 20 at 18. It was the first time the Lady Kats were nationally ranked and recognized for their aggressive, up-tempo, fundamentally-sound, entertaining, dominating playing style.

Chapter 6

A Seed is Planted

Christmas break was short but sweet. I didn't want to miss one moment with Mom. I snuck in her bed at night, sharing all my UK experiences until falling asleep. Mom and I reminisced about my funny high school episodes as well. Some of the funniest stories centered around menstruation. I started much later than most girls and suffered with severe debilitating effects.

"Why did God make girls have periods? "I hate being a girl! This isn't fair!"

"Honey, this has nothing to do with God...just try and relax. You're not the only girl going thru this." Mom assured.

"I don't want kids! I can't take this pain...Mommy, mommy hold my hand...Jackie, please hold my hand...I'm dying!"

"Okay, Valerie..." Jackie soothed me while grabbing my hand.

Often Mom and Jackie had to hold back laughter during the painful cramps and dramatic vomiting episodes.

Now Mom was shocked to find out that I wasn't having those issues at UK. I hadn't had a period since being at UK. I had dropped my body fat dramatically. I was nearly 6'2" and barely weighed one hundred and forty pounds. Mom always told me I had the upper body of a giraffe and the lower body of an elephant.

"Thank goodness you have big legs."

I didn't like the idea of having "big legs."

Mom had always been my number one supporter. We were more like girlfriends than mother and daughter. Returning to UK was difficult. I missed being with Mom and Jackie. I wished they were able to see me play in front of thousands of screaming fans. Strangely, my success as a Lady Kat didn't lessen the pain of not being with them. My pleas to stay home fell on deaf ears though.

Over Christmas break, Coach Yow married Lynn Nance, he had been an assistant coach at UK but was now head men's basketball coach at Iowa State. She had warned us when we left for Christmas break to keep our focus and return ready to play. Hopefully she hadn't lost hers.

I received my grades once back at UK. In high school I had been an honor roll student, graduated cum laude; at the end of my first semester at UK I had straight Cs and one B. Bonnie told me not to be so concerned; the first year of college was always the most difficult to adjust to.

The New Year started with three away games. This road trip would be a big test for Coach Yow-Nance's young team and she prepared us as if we were heading into a war zone. With her heightened intensity in practice, we joked amongst ourselves that married life must not be so enjoyable. We ended 1979 undefeated, 5-0, but more importantly we were beginning to build a special aura around the UK women's basketball team.

On January 3rd we travelled to South Carolina to play our first nationally ranked team. UK's heralded fabulous four freshman finally played like freshman against the strong veteran Gamecocks. South Carolina had four returning starters from their 1978 NWIT Championship team. They were big and strong in the middle, led by Sheila Foster, who overpowered anyone who came near her. I thought Sheila Foster was crazy as she swung her elbows to clear opposing players each time she rebounded the ball.

One of their best newcomers, Evelyn "Sweet E" Johnson, was a big 5'10" guard who had incredible ball handling and passing skills along with a deadly jumper. We all knew Sweet E's older brother Ervin, the number one pick in the 1979 NBA draft for the LA Lakers. Playing against Sweet E would be the closest I would get to Magic.

Although I scored my sixth consecutive double-double with 14 points and 10 rebounds, I got into foul trouble early. We suffered our first loss against the 12th-ranked Gamecocks, 61-84. Two days later we recuperated and beat South Carolina State and headed back to Lexington before going to Northern Kentucky and chalking up another KWIC victory.

While the UK's men's basketball team continued to slip, the Lady Kats continued to impress. We were ranked 18th nationally with a 9-1 record heading into the biggest game of the year and on the biggest stage in college basketball. January 12, 1980, we played Theresa Grentz's 7th-ranked Rutgers team at Rupp Arena in a double-header with the men's team.

The Big Blue Nation was now aware of the Lady Kats and over 10,000 fans roared as we took the court at Rupp Arena. They loved our fast-pace, high-octane style of play and expected to see an engaging game of basketball regardless of the outcome or that we were girls. With my adrenalin overflowing, Coach Yow watched as I would miss a shot, get my own rebound, throw it to the other side, miss, get my rebound and finally make a basket time and time again. She called a timeout in an effort to calm our nerves. Before sprinting back on the court she grabbed my jersey and pulled me face to face.

"Gather yourself, focus, and concentrate on your shooting form Val...take your time," she spoke quietly while looking into my eyes hoping to calm me. "If you take your time, you'll be fine."

"Coach, don't worry," I replied with an uncanny sense of confidence mixed with nervous energy." If I don't make the shot I'll just get my rebound and if I don't make it, I'll get my rebound again and eventually I'll make the bucket!" With a slap on my back, she turned to sit on the bench with a smile knowing that her young star would do whatever was needed to get a win. In only a short time she understood my unassuming spirit of determination. I would not be denied.

We established credibility both in Lexington and nationally, annihilating Rutgers by nearly 20 points, 97-78. I poured in 32 points and pulled down 26 rebounds, breaking my previous record for most rebounds in a game. UK's men's team lost to Alabama in the second game of the double-header.

For the next seven games we crushed opposing teams by an average margin of over 30 points per game, averaging 90 points while holding our opponents under 60. After Rutgers we played a conference game against Western Kentucky, winning by 56 points. We won our own Lady Kat Invitational Tournament, destroying Georgia, led by its star junior guard, Bernadette Locke in the first round. Mississippi State was our victim in the finals, 86-68 victory. We finished January on a victorious note, stomping in-state Murray 95-59.

UK athletic and sports information departments began experiencing a new phenomenon — media interest in, and coverage of, the women's basketball team. People wanted to know more about this group of young, strong, bold, and beautiful women who could play basketball. I was featured in a few articles in the two local newspapers. UK's Kentucky Kernal loved covering their Lady Kats and "The Cats Pause," a weekly tabloid devoted to UK sports, began giving us more space in their publication as well. Around town we were beginning to be recognized.

At a local Burger King someone had stolen pictures of Lea, PJ, Linda, and me off the wall. Coach Yow-Nance warned us to stay focused and not get caught up in the public's new interest in the Lady Kats. February was demanding. Coach continued to push us to our limits in practice. We were the most conditioned team, could run effortlessly 40 minutes a game and loved our run-and-gun style. Some thought that Coach Yow-Nance didn't have great strategic coaching skills because we played so effortlessly. I really didn't care what type of coaching skills she had; I loved her and I would do whatever was needed to make coach happy. And I despised losing. I was the consummate underdog from my days in Camden, always willing to pick up a few stones and slay Goliath.

Regardless of my production or achievements, I always expressed my need for improvement. My secrets to success? My family, God, my passion for the game and my teammates, especially Lea and PJ. We had played most games with composure and maturity considering we were freshmen. February would start off with a bang, playing our archrival, the Tennessee Volunteers.

The Tennessee and Kentucky rivalry was one of college's longest and fiercest rivalries, dating back to their first college football game in 1893. The University of Tennessee is less than 200 miles from Lexington. I was told the bus ride back after a loss was unbearable. The Lady Vols had become a national powerhouse in the last few years since the arrival of a young graduate student, Pat Head. She was a pre-Title IX athlete. While coaching Tennessee, in 1976, she co-captained the first US women's national basketball team as a player, participating in the first women's tournament at the Summer Olympics, and winning a silver medal.

Pat brought her competitive and determined mentality to Knoxville. By the time I arrived at UK, she had quickly established one of the most respected women's basketball programs in the country. Rumors were that Pat wanted to coach at UK but the athletic administrators were not willing to pay her moving expenses of less than $200.

The Tennessee game attracted the largest crowd ever for a Lady Kats' game in Memorial Coliseum with 6,000. Thirty minutes before the game more than 2,000 fans were already seated in Memorial Coliseum and a long line had formed at the ticket window. Kentucky was ranked 17th nationally. The 6th-ranked Lady Vols were led by junior 6'5"center Cindy Noble, senior 6'3" All-American forward Jill Rankins, and senior All-American guard Holly Warlick. The up-tempo first half ended with the Lady Vols holding a two-point advantage. Warlick picked up her fourth foul with two minutes remaining in the first half. Heading into the locker room, we believed we could pull off the upset. The Memorial Coliseum crowd was crazed.

We jumped out on a 10-4 run to start the second half with Liz and me leading the way. I had never heard such a deafening sound or felt my heart beating harder as a group of crazy male students led the boisterous crowd chanting.

"Go Big Blue! Go Big Blue! Go Big Blue!"

Tennessee regrouped and took the lead when Liz and Maria fouled out. Coach Yow-Nance decided she would make a bold move: Lea, PJ, Lori, Linda, and me. A small lineup of four guards and me and I was playing with four fouls. We kicked and clawed our way back into the game, with the adrenaline from a boisterous crowd. Warlick fouled out with less than four minutes to go in the game. With 33 seconds we had tied the score, 76-76, and had possession of the ball. Coach Yow-Nance called a timeout. We would hold the ball for a last-second shot. With time winding down, Lea took a 15-foot shot that hit off the rim with 3 seconds on the clock as Lori and I crashed the boards. Lori snatched the offensive rebound over top of the towering Lady Vols and threw up a desperation shot with less than one second as fans held their breath. The ball rolled around the edge of the rim and fell out as the buzzer sounded.

Coach Yow-Nance stuck with her small lineup for overtime. I cut Tennessee's lead to one, 84-83, but fouled out with a minute and a half left, trying to block Rankin's shot. We lost in overtime 83-91. Three freshmen finished in double-figure scoring. PJ had 14 points, Lori had 10 and I had 28 and 14 rebounds. Lea finished with 8 points and I was the only player for both teams with a double-double.

The crowd of 6,000 stood and cheered us on as we walked dejectedly to our locker room. Not one person had left the building. This had never happened at a UK women's basketball game.

We were now averaging more than 3,000 spectators at home games. Although that paled in comparison to attendance at UK men's basketball games, nationally we were among the top in game attendance for women behind Tennessee and defending national champion Old Dominion. The UK's women's basketball program had gained varsity status only six years earlier and only one year prior began awarding full scholarships.

The group of male students dressed in white t-shirts with blue lettering with "Love Those Lady Kats" sat in the seats directly behind our basket, holding signs and noisemakers. They had passionately cheered us on during the game, harassed Tennessee players and coaches, and moved onto the court after the buzzer, forming a human tunnel for us to walk through. The high fives and pats on our backs took away some of the sting of losing to our archrivals. They were the "Rowdy Bunch" and became a fixture in Memorial Coliseum. To think that at our first games we were barely getting a few hundred people and here stood a group of that many, in the midst of thousands, who were loyal to the team and willing to celebrate and support women playing sports, was overwhelming. The game was a tremendous boost for women's collegiate basketball and it showed us we could compete with the best in the country.

After the game Pat Head told a UK newspaper reporter, "This is the best team UK has had. When you see all freshmen on the floor and the veterans on the bench, you know they've got talent." We had talent but more importantly we had support and validation now from a fan base that traditionally only valued male athletics. One male sportswriter claimed he'd rather watch UK's women play than the men because the women weren't afraid to shoot the ball.

A week later we were in Knoxville for the first SEC women's basketball tournament. The Lady Vols and Lady Kats had the two best records going into the tournament and were seeded 1 and 2, which meant we would possibly have a chance to avenge our home loss against Tennessee. Tennessee was ranked 5th and we were ranked 15th in the nation.

Arriving in Knoxville, our main objective was to beat Tennessee. I was mesmerized as I walked into Stokely Athletic Center for practice. Stokely's bright-orange, hard-rubber, Tartan flooring was like none I had ever seen before. I had only played on wooden floors indoors or asphalt courts outside.

We earned a bye in the first round and would play the winner of the Alabama/Vanderbilt game. Tennessee totally devoured Florida 118-44 in front of their overexcited mob, sending a psychological statement of domination to everyone at the tournament. In the following game, we beat Alabama 77-69 with Tennessee fans still packed in the stands and celebrating their victory. Saturday we watched Tennessee's win against Auburn in the semi-finals by only 11 points before we played Ole Miss.

Unlike teams in the KWIC with predominantly in-state players, SEC teams consisted of players from across the country. Some teams had foreign players as well. Although our young team could compete with any team, our inexperience would make us vulnerable to teams with more diverse and experienced players.

Mississippi and Auburn had both seasoned, talented players and male coaches. Joe Ciampi was new to Auburn, and the previous year, Ole Miss hired a young male coach, Van Chancellor. With his heavy southern accent, Chancellor bellowed out commands to his group of veteran players, led by Peggie Gillom and Carol Ross. Ranked 15th in the nation, we were no longer a surprise in women's basketball and our success was no longer considered lucky. Ole Miss watched us play the night before and was well-prepared for us. I began to face more double-team and triple-team defenses.

Ole Miss and the SEC atmosphere proved to be too much for us. We lost to Ole Miss, 62-79. We wouldn't be playing against Tennessee for the first SEC Tournament Championship. We were devastated but had to recover quickly and make necessary adjustments for the consolation game the following day against Auburn.

We crushed Auburn 88-59 to take third place in the first SEC women's basketball tournament and Tennessee beat Ole Miss, becoming the first SEC Tournament champion. I was selected to the first SEC All-Tournament team along with Peggie Gillom and Carol Ross from Ole Miss, Lori Monroe from Auburn and Cindy Noble, Holly Warlick and MVP Jill Rankin from Tennessee. We piled onto our bus along with coaches and cheerleaders after watching Tennessee hoist up the SEC trophy, and took the long dreaded unending ride back to Lexington.

We finished the KWIC regular season undefeated and won the KWIC Division 1 Tournament in Memorial Coliseum. We were KWIC champions with a 24-3 record heading to the AIAW Region II tournament. The Regional tournaments were qualifying tournaments for the national tournament. Region II was traditionally the best in the country. Six of the eight schools in Region II were ranked in the nation's top 20: four of those schools were in the top 10. On March 6, not only did we play one of those top 10 teams, Coach Yow-Nance would be competing against her older sister, Kay, and the North Carolina State Wolfpack. We lost to NC State 63-71 at NC State in the first round of the regional tournament but received one of the eight at-large bids to the national championship.

After an incredibly successful year, the defeat to NC State was heartbreaking for Lea, PJ, Lori and me. But we still had a chance to redeem ourselves. We were ranked 11th in the country and heading to the national tournament. As an inexperienced team, playing away from home was always a disadvantage. With our aggressive pressure defense we were more prone to get into foul trouble. Our first round opponent was Region 9 Champions, the University of

Oregon, which meant a cross-country trip to Eugene, Oregon. I had never been to the West coast.

Like the Lady Kats, the Oregon Ducks, led by six-foot sophomore Canadian Bev Smith, had only lost four games and was a high-scoring team. Unlike us, the Lady Ducks had a team of veterans with four starters averaging double figures. Oregon's experience and home court advantage proved to be key in their 85-81 win.

The national championship game was broadcast on NBC. Old Dominion University defeated Tennessee and was crowned national champions for the second straight year. This was just the beginning of Old Dominion's domination of women's collegiate basketball. It was bittersweet for me as I watched our archrival Tennessee go down in defeat but my North Jersey rival, Anne Donovan, cut down the nets.

With the season over, I could focus on school work and being a normal college student again. But before I could, Couch Yow-Nance suggested I try out for the 1980 USA Olympic team. "It will be a great opportunity," she said.

The Olympics were hosted by the USSR and scheduled to be held in Moscow. However, rumor was that the USA would boycott the Olympics in protest of the Soviet Union's invasion of Afghanistan. I packed my bags and headed to Colorado Springs.

The first stage was an "open" trial held March 24 and 25. I was one of over 200 players, mainly from AIAW schools. The second stage from March 26-28 consisted of 18 invited players who were joined by seven players from the "open" trial. I was one of the seven players to be invited to the Final Trials. Most of the players at the final trials were All-Americans or players who had been in AAU for years. Fundamentally, these players were much more polished than was I.

I was in amazement just looking around at who I was competing with, players such as Nancy Lieberman, Carol Blazejowski, Lynette Woodard, Jill Rankin, Holly Warlick, Cindy Noble, Denise Curry and of course my fellow Jerseyan, Anne Donovan. The Amateur Basketball Association of the United States of America (ABAUSA) selected a 12-member team and three alternates; I didn't make the final cut. I called Mom, crying.

"Pick your head up and remember that you're always a winner," she told me.

The return to Lexington was the first time I felt good being back at UK. The Lady Kats had gone from a 13-16 team to being ranked just outside of the top 10 in the nation at 11th. I led the team in scoring and rebounding with 22.1 points per game and 13.9 rebounds and was among the leaders nationally in both categories. I was one of two freshmen named to the first annual SEC All-Tournament team, and was one of three freshmen named 1980 All-KWIC, also receiving other recognitions and awards. I broke four individual SEC tournament records and four Lady Kat records. What many people didn't realize was that my success was a direct result of Lea and Patti Jo. They were two unselfish unsung heroes.

A few days after I returned from the Olympic Trials, the first Lady Kats Basketball Banquet was held. Local businesses sponsored the event and awards. Lieutenant Governor of Kentucky, Martha Layne Collins, was the guest speaker. All the scholarship freshmen received awards besides Sharon Garland. I received awards for Most Valuable Player, Leading Rebounder, and Rookie of the Year. I couldn't help but think I was living a dream. Classes began to get better, and Bonnie and I were starting to have fun like most college students. One of the places we loved to hang out was "The Library," the club were everyone went to dance and party. The Library Lounge was a notorious club with ties to organized crime but it was also the perfect alibi when Mom questioned my Friday or Saturday night activities.

"Mommy, Bonnie, and I are heading to The Library tonight," I bragged, holding back my laughter while Bonnie mocked me, holding up a drink and a textbook.

"Valerie, you've been blessed with a wonderful friend. Tell Bonnie I said hello and thanks for keeping you on the straight and narrow. Make sure you get some fun time in too."

"I will Mommy...we'll be sure not to study too much. I'll survive. Gotta go...love you!" I hurried slamming the phone down.

"As long as I know how to love, I know we will survive, " Bonnie howled as we jumped in her car with Gloria Gaynor blasting on the radio and sipping her 7-and-7 out of a little red plastic cup.

Freddie and I stopped dating. Although I wanted to be in a relationship, I had a difficult time allowing anyone to get close to me. Basketball was my first love and it was a good surrogate for intimacy. I had a few guys whom I would go out with but that was as far as I was willing to commit.

In April, I was selected to be on the National Team that would participate in the William R. Jones Cup Intercontinental Basketball Tournament in Taipei, Taiwan. Being selected to represent the USA and the bonus of travelling outside the country was exciting. As children Jackie and I fantasized about our future world adventures, travelling to exotic places around the globe. After training with the team at the Olympic training facility in Squaw Valley, California for a couple of weeks, on May 21st we set off for my first international adventure.

Stepping off the plane in Taiwan was like stepping into a sauna. The heat was smothering and the humidity ridiculous. I had just turned 19 a week earlier and here I was in another world, with a group of people I barely knew, representing my country. It was suggested we only eat at the hotel and not stray around the city by ourselves. Our hotel was always surrounded by young Taiwanese basketball fans who wanted to see and meet foreign players, especially American players. We were one of the strongest teams and a favorite.

Our assistant coach, Vivian Stringer, was head coach at Cheyney State University. I couldn't understand how Coach Stringer wasn't head coach. She was a better coach than our head coach, but she was also black. She was four months pregnant but that didn't slow her down. She was intense but yet nurturing. She teased me about all the new friends I had made during our stay in Taiwan.

Thousands of fans packed the arena to watch women's basketball and each day there were newspaper articles with game photos and stories. I made friends with the staff from the hotel and the young girls who came and stood outside our hotel regularly with little gifts and trinkets. Some days they brought me food to taste and other days they just wanted to hang out with me and share their stories. I became friends with one of the male Taiwanese waiters at the hotel as well. The handsome Chinese with his beautiful dark eyes and layer-cut thick black hair caught my attention right away. He told me to call him Fulago. He would always wait on our table as my teammates joked about our attraction. Once the games were over, he suggested he show me around the city on his moped.

We won the bronze medal. Mary Ostrowski from Tennessee and I were selected to the All-Tournament Team. There was no curfew the night the tournament was over; we would leave the next day to visit Hong Kong and then return home.

Fulago met me at the hotel after the championship game. I hopped on the back of his moped, wrapped my arms around his waist tightly as we whizzed in and out of traffic-filled streets of Taipei. We stopped at a few interesting landmarks and night markets and then visited the small side streets and eateries. He spoke only a little English.

After a few stops we headed to Snake Alley. He parked his moped in front of a glass store window then walked in and sat on the small wooden stools at the counter of the bar. The bartender took Fulago's order then opened the lid behind the counter. This was a bar that served snake's blood and other snake fluids. These drinks were supposed to be healthy. The man dipped in the box container with a metal hook at the end of a long pole and pulled out a snake to show Fulago as I pushed back from the counter. He poured three shots. Fulago drank each one, leaving just a little of the dark red liquid in the glass. It was my turn for a taste. I quickly chugged the liquid with the guys cheering me on and laughing. I had never backed down from a challenge. The semi-viscous consistency nearly made me vomit instantly but I was accustom to swallowing Mom's daily shots of cod liver oil. Nothing tasted worse than straight cod liver oil but drinking warm blood made me queasy. We got back on his moped and headed back to the hotel. It was late and I had a flight to Hong Kong the next morning with the team. Fulago gave me a little kiss and we exchanged our addresses so we could stay in contact. I promised him I would return next year for the Jones Cup.

Early the following morning, all my new young Chinese friends came to the hotel to say goodbye. I had played a championship game, celebrated with the team, been up all night with Fulago exploring Taipei and returned to the hotel in time to pack my things and hop on the bus. As children, Jackie and I had fantasized about travelling the world and living a life of adventure.

"My son just bought a mansion on the French Riviera and he's sending his private jet for me to visit him," Jackie would boast during a tea party.

"Well, I just returned from an African safari and visiting the Pyramids with my son and we'll be heading to visit Italy and Greece soon," I countered.

"I've already visited the Pyramids, the Great Wall of China and the Taj Mahal...they're all fabulous!" Gloated Jackie, always with a more expansive imagination.

Now, I was living my dream. Just as the bus was pulling off for the airport, I spotted Fulago.

Mom and Jackie picked me up from the airport. I felt like a new person – no longer the girl from Camden. Before I could tell them much about Taipei, Mom blurted out, "Barry bought a house in Kansas City." As she and my sister talked about our move, I realized I was too tired to even think about Taipei and a little sore from the long trip. Talking about my trip would have to wait until tomorrow.

The movers had taken everything but a few blankets. I awoke the following morning in excruciating pain. I cried as Mom and Jackie helped me get to my feet after sleeping on the floor. Mom thought maybe it was because of the long flight from Asia. She told me to try to rest and stay calm but even in a resting position I was in pain. She called our childhood doctor from Camden.

Dr. Brimm knew our family well. He knew I never cried. After examining me he gave me a muscle relaxer shot to relieve the pain and sent me home. I cried in pain the entire car ride home and suffered through Saturday night and Sunday before Mom scheduled another visit with him.

The second visit I was pale and listless and had a very high fever. I was admitted to the hospital immediately and placed in traction until other tests were done. Mom had planned to drive to Kansas City with Jackie, Barry's dogs and me on Saturday. Instead, Jackie flew to Kansas City and Mom stayed with me.

A battery of tests were ordered as my temperature continued to rise and I began to slip out of consciousness. With my temperature alarmingly high, Dr. Brimm and a team of specialists warned Mom that I was seriously ill. They were not sure if I would survive whatever was attacking my body.

I was finally diagnosed with salmonella enteritidis with septic arthritis in my right sacroiliac joint. The bacterial infection combined with my sickle cell anemia trait could be deadly. Dr. Brimm and the specialists had never encountered such a case and didn't have a prescribed cure; they began administering large doses of antibiotics.

Mom sat by my bed and prayed. She had gone through a scare like this during my illness in third grade. She believed God had blessed her with me and she was willing to give me back if I didn't get better. She held my hand as she spoke healing over me. "You're a fighter. You're a survivor."

Although I was unconscious, Mom talked to me. She let me know of honors I was receiving and all the people praying for me. Coach Yow-Nance had sent me a note before I became sick, congratulating me and encouraging me to enjoy the summer with family but to keep working hard. I was also selected as one of the top women college basketball players in the USA for the 1979-80 season by the Women's Pro Basketball League (WBL).

Mom knew my dream was to play professional basketball even though women's professional basketball was very uncertain. Now she didn't know if I would make it through the week. She was proud of me and what I was able to accomplish in one year at the University of Kentucky, but she feared I might not be able to defeat this opponent.

*****

Now, as I lay in the hospital where I was born, fighting for my life, a battle raged within my own source of life, my blood. Mom continued to pray.

Mom had sat quietly in my room for over a week waiting to see if the treatment would be successful. The bacteria had moved through my intestinal tract and bloodstream, settling in a joint in the back of my hip. Flowers filled my room, sent from well-wishers mainly from Kentucky. She shared stories with the nurses about her sweet tomboy with a heart of gold wanting to help the helpless, mistreated and wounded whether stray animals or needy children.

How many times had she punished me for sneaking out of the house to play basketball on the court across from our house? I got a spanking. Other times I tagged along with my brothers canvassing outside our neighborhood, handing out flyers for a stranger for a quarter. That also ended in a spanking for me and no dinner for them.

Dr. Brimm warned Mom that even if the infection was cleared out of my blood, with the sickle-cell trait and salmonella I could suffer permanent damage to my bone structure. That evening as I lay unresponsive and doctors had done all they could and nothing seemed to be working, she held my hand and prayed the Lord's Prayer. Regardless of the outcome Mom never showed any outward signs of emotion. She had come to a peace about my situation and knew that it was out of her control.

"Valerie, you can do all things through Christ who strengthens you," she whispered in my ear as she kissed me and left my hospital room that night. What was impossible with doctors and anyone else was possible with God.

The following morning before she left for the hospital, Mom had a call from Coach Yow-Nance for an update. I wasn't conscious of the ice baths every day to reduce the 104-degree fever in my week-long sleep induced by medications to kill the bacteria. Coach Yow-Nance had tried to keep my situation from the media but after I had been in the hospital a week, newspapers in Kentucky and local TV stations in Lexington began to report that I had become seriously ill and was fighting for my life.

"Mrs. Still, make sure you give Val a big Kentucky hug from me. I'll be praying for her," Coach Yow-Nance assured Mom before she hung up the phone and headed to the hospital.

Stepping into my room, Mom was surprised to find me sitting up as nurses combed my hair. The antibiotics had killed the bacteria and I began to feel better, regaining my strength and the nearly 30 pounds I had lost. Nearly three weeks after entering the Cooper Medical Center, I left with a walker. The following day Mom and I flew to our new home in Kansas City.

I continued treatment with a Kansas City Chiefs' orthopedic surgeon while Dr. Brimm stayed in touch with phone calls.

"Promise me 15 points and 15 rebounds every game," Dr. Brimm joked over the phone as I told him I was feeling better.

Coach Yow-Nance called nearly every day. She insisted that I focus on resting and getting better. I had just beaten the deadliest opponent I had ever faced.

Mom was making the big adjustment moving from the East coast to the Midwest after dealing with the possibility of a dying child for the last month along with all her other children's issues. We were in a new city, a new state, and a new home. Mom, a fifty-year-old woman, had always lived in South Jersey near family and friends, but had agreed to move when Barry asked her. He loved the Kansas City area. She found work as a nurse's aide at a senior retirement community. Jackie was enrolled in the local high school and in the fall, I was on my way back to UK. I wasn't sure what Dad was doing.

*****

I still walked with a slight limp and hadn't regained the pounds I had lost while ill when I returned to Lexington. There were notable changes in the women's basketball team. Unlike the previous years, when incoming freshmen were usually from Kentucky, this year only one freshman was from Kentucky, Lisa Collins. Lisa was a sought-after 5'9" guard who had led her high school team to three consecutive state championships and was named Kentucky's "Miss Basketball." Being a nationally ranked team gave UK the possibility of attracting top out-of-state players. Three of those players were Jody Runge, Kathy Lokie and Beth Kogoy. Jody Runge was a 6'2" post player from Iowa, with big curly blonde hair. She had only played 6-player basketball and was an offensive player in that system. Now she would have to learn how to play 5-player basketball and defense. Like Jody with her signature blonde curly hair, Kathy Lokie's long, thick, bright-red mane that fell below her breast drew attention immediately. Kathy and I quickly became friends. She was 5'11"and from Virginia, with a bubbly, carefree personality.

Patty Jo, Lea, Lori, and I shared our summer stories and team rumors. We could barely wait for the upcoming season. Sharon Garland transferred to Western Kentucky University. We weren't surprised; she was unhappy nearly all season.

One week back Coach Yow-Nance held a team meeting. We all packed into her office, buzzing with giddiness. This would finally signal the start to a new season; for me it was a new chance at life. I still was uncertain as to whether I would fully recuperate, but I was thankful for each second, and right now I was thankful to be with this room full of people I loved and missed during the summer. Coach Yow-Nance was my mom away from home. I would do anything for her and was anxious about the future of the Lady Kats.

Talking with Coach Yow-Nance while we filed into the room was a beautiful, shoulder-length-feathered blonde-haired woman who could have been Coach Yow-Nance's twin.

"I have an important announcement to make," Coach Yow-Nance began in her soft southern-accent voice. She never raised her voice even when she was in the middle of games and shouting out instructions.

"But first let me introduce Coach Berry," she continued. I thought that was going to be her important announcement. My mind wandered trying to figure out what the important announcement was as she told us about Coach Berry and their morning meeting to discuss her decision. Decision? What decision?

Coach Yow-Nance had hired a new 27-year old assistant coach, Dorothy Berry, from Georgia. She was a high school coach with a Masters' degree, who had experience working at basketball camps and clinics, but this was her first collegiate job. She would monitor my progress until I was ready to work out with the team.

"Ladies, I've decided to resign as head coach here and join my husband at Iowa State," she said.

What? There was no way she would leave at this point when we were about to take this program to the next level. She would leave us and for what? A man? Not Coach Yow. She was making the biggest mistake of her life, I thought.

She was always independent and strong and taught us the same. She wasn't going to honor her commitment to her team and in particular, her commitment to me, Patty Jo, Lea and Lori. Everyone was in shock.

Kentucky wouldn't begin a national search for a replacement until September. Coach Berry filled in as interim coach. During the transition, Coach Berry stepped up and reassured everyone that we would continue to move forward in a positive way. By the middle of September she had already begun our preseason training and was doing a little of everything in preparing the team. One of Cliff Hagan's requirements for the head coaching position was that it had to be someone with at least two years of college coaching. That disqualified Coach Berry. What was that all about? College coaching experience? Why would college coaching experience really matter in women's basketball during this period?

Cliff Hagan hired Terry Hall, the head coach of the Louisville Cardinals. Disappointment was one of many things we felt. Louisville was our in-state archrival. Coach Hall was never able to win a state tournament or advance to national tournament action. How was she going to be able to help us achieve our goals?

Lea, Patti Jo, Lori, and I had a special bond with Coach Yow-Nance and felt blindsided by her resignation. How could we do it without her? Why did she leave us?

*****

September meant mandatory breakfast and study halls. I had survived my first year of college classes, taking the minimum number of credits. Our academic advisor suggested I continue taking the minimum number of credits and classes so that I could stay eligible for basketball. I agreed not knowing I would be short. The first week of September was also testing for strength and conditioning. I had been out of the hospital for nearly two months.

Since returning to UK, at six o'clock every morning, I ran sprints in the parking lot between Memorial Coliseum and Blazer Hall, desperately trying to regain all I had lost with the illness. In the weight room, I was weaker than all of my teammates. On the track, I couldn't run one sprint with the team. As I limped back to Blazer Hall from the track the first day of conditioning, dejected with tears streaming down my face, Coach Berry caught up to me and put her arms around me.

"Val, you're gonna be okay," she said in a strong Georgian accent. "It's a process and you have to give it time. You're a great athlete but this is gonna show you who you really are. I know you're gonna be better than before; just hang in there, girl. I believe in you and I'll be right here with you."

The first week of testing was demoralizing for me. As the team conditioned with sprints, running, weights and track work all together, Coach Berry trained me individually in hopes of being ready for our first official practice October 6.

My calls to Mom were filled with tears, panic, anxiety, and uncertainty. Mom loved Coach Yow-Nance but I would have to focus on whoever was with the team. I told her about Coach Berry. I didn't even know this woman but she had taken an interest in me and motivated me to push myself. Mom said she was sent from God and that no matter what happens, God always provides everything we need; there was a reason I was still alive and I had to have faith that God would always be with me and for me.

"Valerie, once you're determined to do something or not do something, no one can change your mind," Mom said. "Even if it's to your detriment, you stick to what you believe. Stick to believing what's in your heart and regardless of what other people think or feel, do what you know to be right."

I loved Mom; she always supported me and would defend me to the end.

*****

Coach Berry created the Lady Kat Booster Club, soliciting sponsors and supporters in the community. She began by searching for former players who might have a loyalty to the team. One of those players was Maryanne Daughaday. Maryanne played basketball between 1968 and 1971 as an undergraduate. She had entered UK as women's sports were re-instated on the club level for the first time since the 1920s. Maryanne married Steve Simmons from Paducah, Kentucky, they bought a house in Lexington, and started a family with the birth of their daughter in 1978. They loved UK sports. Coach Berry thought Maryanne would be perfect as the president of the Lady Kat Booster Club. Along with increasing and developing interest in the team in the community, one of the objectives of the club was to be a support system for players, especially out-of-state players, which UK was beginning to attract.

Maryanne was among the first female players on UK women's teams that began playing intercollegiate competition. She was excited how things were changing positively for women's sports at UK.

Coach Berry proposed a sponsor program, matching up local families and individuals who would nurture and assist a player. If Maryanne agreed to be president, Coach Berry promised her she would give her a "special player." Maryanne agreed and I became the Simmons' sponsored player.

Maryanne was a beautiful, athletic, thirty-year-old blonde with an out-going personality and was a pharmacist until she had Kelly Beth, then became a stay-at-home mom. Steve, an insurance agent a couple of years older than Maryanne, was a tall, good-looking, former basketball player with a dry sense of humor. He had been a basketball coach for a junior high school in Lexington.

Steve, Maryanne and Kelly Beth were the ideal American family. They offered me stability and love and became my family. Bonnie was my surrogate sister and Maryanne, Steve and Kelly Beth were my surrogate family. At their home, I had the comfort, security and support of a healthy family setting – something needed during the first few months of my sophomore year when I wasn't sure if I would be able to play again. I loved spending the weekends in front of a cozy fire in their den, sitting around the table enjoying one of Maryanne's tasty meals and attending church on Sunday with them. Maryanne's mother visited sometimes and she treated me as if I were her granddaughter.

Maryanne loved telling me about her experiences as a UK female athlete before Title IX.

"Val, you wouldn't believe how bad we were treated when I played," Maryanne shared with a bit of melancholy but pride.

" Adolph Rupp was the coach for the men's team and he wouldn't allow the school's newspaper to cover women's sports or interview female players. We weren't allowed in Memorial Coliseum period, not even for practices. They gave us a tiny isolated space in the

ROTC building for practices and games. Do you know where that is? The space was so small that every time one of us went up for a layup, we were scared we would run into the wall. That claustrophobic court was surrounded by walls less than three feet away from the perimeter. Often we'd smash into a small pad on the wall. Now look at the Lady Kats! Ya'll are getting record crowds in Memorial Coliseum!"

I didn't understand and appreciate the significance of Maryanne's pre-Title IX collegiate experience; playing before women's basketball received varsity status at UK in 1974. She had sacrificed like many female athletes, allowing us to break down more barriers for the next generation of women athletes.

Media day arrived and drew more attention than the previous year. Unlike the days of Coach Rupp, now Memorial Coliseum was the women's home and we attracted media from across the country wanting to talk to us. I still wasn't 100% recuperated physically but I had begun practices with the team. Unlike the year before when the men completely overshadowed us, there was a heightened interest in us, partly because of our success, partly because of the coaching change, and mainly because people wondered if I had totally recuperated and would be able to repeat what I did my freshman year.

The coaching transition had not gone as smoothly as everyone within the program hoped. Lea, Patti Jo, Lori, and I couldn't make the emotional detachment from Coach Yow-Nance because she continued to contact us. Coach Hall had an unemotional personality compared to Coach Yow-Nance and we picked Hall apart for the smallest things, whether it was her socks that didn't match her outfit or the fact that she always wore pants. Rumor had it that Coach Hall was a lesbian.

However, I had been given another chance at life and I would not bring in any negativity. My personal basketball goal was to improve my game by playing better defense and working on my outside shooting and becoming an All-American. My goal for the team was to win a national championship.

Sportswriters, broadcasters, TV stations, and newspapers from across Kentucky arrived for our Media Day. The overall sentiment was a desire for national honors. I thought I was at about 95 percent but expected to be full-strength by our season opener at Memorial Coliseum the first day of December.

Once the cameras, lights, and reporters were gone and we began preparing for the first game, I realized that this year would bring a set of different and challenging issues. We now had the experience we needed; we understood what we would have to do to get to a national championship and we had all gotten better over the summer; but now we would have to deal with non-basketball issues. Championship teams do not necessarily have the best or most talented players; yes, playing ability is important but the chemistry of a team, the intimacy of a team, the heart of a team dictates its success. We were young and we were working through a coaching transition.

Coach Berry was a people's person and an effective unifier between Coach Hall and players. Coach Hall was a strategic coach, precise, and structured in her procedures and game plan. Coach Yow-Nance had understood she had a talented group with a lion's heart. She prepared us so that we would physically outlast and out-run any team and unleashed us to do what we instinctively did. Coach Hall was an analytic coach who could make clear-cut game-deciding decisions, which took that stress off players. With Coach Yow-Nance, we'd grab a defensive rebound and sprint to the basket for an easy score before our opponent got back on defense. Coach Hall understood that we were a fast, explosive, athletic team, and encouraged us to be a transition team, but she had an organized transition game with options for any situation that might occur. She had certain set rules that would not change regardless of the game situation or the player it affected. One such rule was that as soon as a player committed two fouls in the first half, that player would sit for the remainder of the half. In practice we spent lots of time on end-of-the game situations; we didn't understand why but she was preparing us so that nothing would be a surprise or catch us off-guard.

Little did we know that the two distinctive coaching styles and personalities would be our biggest obstacle to overcome. Liz and Maria, who were less athletic and instinctive, loved Coach Hall's methodical approach. They thought Coach Yow-Nance had sometimes gotten disoriented in certain game situations in the past and this had factored into last year's losses. Liz, PJ, Lori, Tanya and

I loved the more carefree approach and we definitely loved Coach Yow-Nance.

For our first game, the screaming and out-of-control Rowdy Bunch, in their "We love the Lady Kats" T-shirts, stood at the edge of the court to meet us as we turned the hallway curve from the locker room and sprinted to halfcourt. Leading the Rowdy Bunch was Ottie Feedback, an old, puny, white-haired, toothless man whom I had befriended the year before. He hadn't missed one home game last year. We had become good friends after the first Blue/White games and would eat together whenever possible. He didn't have family and I was a long way from my family so we hung out together. Ottie lived by himself in a room at a boarding house close to campus.

As I ran through the Rowdy Bunch-made tunnel, I reached out for Ottie's outstretched hand and gave him a high-five. He slapped my back so hard I nearly fell over the teammate in front of me. I had eaten with Ottie the day before and told him my first basket was for him. He had been so worried over the summer when he had found out that I was sick and couldn't do anything. He had waited patiently and anxiously for news in the newspaper. Once I was back at UK, he pestered me to eat so that I could regain my strength. We spent lots of time at "Tally-Ho's," the favorite greasy spoon on campus. Now after gaining some weight back and losing the last remnants of my illness, I would be tested.

We beat Charleston easily. I had 26 points and 10 rebounds and played 32 of the 40 minutes. That night on the local TV news, the sports segment was headed by a story on me and my comeback. As I ran onto the court, after slapping Ottie high five, "I'm Coming Out," Diana Ross' hit, played in the background for the story. After a near-death summer, I was finally coming out and so were the Lady Kats.

We took up where we had left off in March. December flew by and by Christmas break we were undefeated with a 5-0 record and ranked 15th nationally. I was on my way to setting six individual UK records, including breaking the single-game scoring record I had set last season with a 39-point game against Indiana three games into the season. But still bumping heads with Coach Hall.

I headed to Missouri to spend my first Midwest holiday. Mom was glad Christmas had arrived; she would finally see me fully healthy.

The last time she had seen me I was limping around the house. Also, she was concerned about the issues I was having with Coach Hall. Phone calls home had been tense leading up to Christmas break.

"Mommy, I just can't do this anymore. This coach really doesn't get me, I don't think she likes me."

"You have to give it time Valerie. She's new and I know you loved Coach Yow-Nance but a quitter never wins and a winner never quits."

"I'm not quitting, I would be closer to y'all if I go to the University of Missouri. They have a good basketball program, the coach is nice and they have a veterinarian program I can get into."

"You've worked too hard. Get thru the next few games and we'll discuss this when you get home," Mom insisted.

I returned to Lexington and celebrated New Years with Steve and Maryanne. I talked to them about the situation. I talked to Coach Berry as well.

"I'm miserable and need to leave," I explained to Coach Berry.

"That would probably be the worst mistake of your life at this point Val," she said. "I understand that Coach Hall isn't the most outgoing or personable person. I'm not totally satisfied with my experience as well. Just between us, I was thinking about leaving too, but leaving now just isn't a good solution."

"Val, I promise you, I will stay at UK until you finish and help you with whatever it is to make your experience the best it can be, but you have to promise me you will stay, " she confided in me. "At least until this season is over, put all your energy and thoughts into what you are doing right now."

Coach Berry convinced me to focus on the bigger picture of reaping the benefits of my hard work coming back from a near-death experience. If I could fight back from nearly dying, I should be able to see the positive in everything that was happening in my life, and that included my experiences at UK with Coach Hall.

We got off to a great start in January. The first four games of 1981 we trounced teams on an average of slightly over 20 points per game; we garnered a record of 9-0 and a 14th-rank standing in the nation, setting us up for our biggest game, against third-ranked Rutgers in New Jersey. Rutgers gave us the first loss of the season.

After losing 67-69 in overtime against the #3 team in the country, we moved into the top-ten national ranking at #9. This was the first time UK had been ranked as one of the top ten women's collegiate basketball teams.

Losing by two points in overtime was demoralizing but we bounced back and won our next seven games for a 16-1 record, including winning the Lady Kat Invitational Tournament. I was selected to the All-Tournament team. On January 27, we defeated Eastern Kentucky 74-60 in Richmond. With 15:30 remaining in the game I passed the 1,000-point mark, making me the youngest player in UK history, male or female, to reach that milestone. Although we were the visiting team, at 14:54 the game was stopped and I was presented the game ball. I finished with a 30-point and 19-rebound performance. This was a great accomplishment but I still felt my greatest one was my recovery from illness the past summer.

We finished January playing in the second SEC Women's Basketball Tournament, held at Louisiana State University, losing in the semi-finals to Auburn, 66-70, and started February with a loss in the consolation game against Georgia, 62-73. I was selected to the SEC All-Tournament team. This was the first time we had ever lost two consecutive games. The SEC tournament had replaced the KWIC tournament. We went undefeated in the KWIC with a 12-0 record but no tournament was held in 1981.

It was time for post-season play. The NCAA did not offer a national tournament so we participated in the AIAW Region II National Tournament. We played North Carolina State in Memorial Coliseum for a come-from-behind, overtime 75-74 victory in the first round. Our reward was a semi-final matchup against top seed, 3rd-ranked Tennessee. We had never defeated Tennessee since my arrival at UK and in our last game against them at Knoxville, we had suffered our most humiliating and worst loss of the year. I was held to only nine points. This time we would play the Lady Vols in the Region II semi-finals, held at Old Dominion University in Norfolk, Virginia. In a low scoring game, Tennessee beat us 58-49. Tennessee had knocked us out of the championship game and we would have to settle for winning the consolation game against South Carolina and taking third place.

We were headed to the AIAW National Tournament for the second consecutive year, beating Syracuse in Memorial Coliseum for our final home game of the 1980-81 season and first round of the tournament. Our next game was against 9th ranked Maryland at College Park. We scored the game's last nine points but were eliminated from the tournament by Maryland 82-83.

Another basketball season at UK had come to an end and without knowing it we had closed the gap between the men's and women's basketball program. Although we weren't in competition against the men's program, it was clear that we would always be an inferior and secondary program for UK administrators. A "Kentucky basketball fan" summed up our reality in an editorial published in the Lexington newspaper:

After watching the Wildcats' listless loss to the University of Alabama –Birmingham last week in the NCAA tournament, then listening on radio to the Lady Kats' AIAW tournament one-point loss to Maryland this past weekend, it seems clear that the final games of both teams symbolized their own seasons. While 23,000 fans filled Rupp Arena per game to watch a disappointing Wildcat season of generally uninspired play (except for LSU, Indiana and Ohio State), the Lady Kats played with heart and determination throughout most of their season. It is a shame that only two to four thousand fans per Lady Kat game were present to watch a Kentucky team whose pride and class much better represented the University than this season's Wildcat team in Rupp Arena.

Chapter 7

Season of Awakening

Honors and awards flooded in after my sophomore season; numerous All-American teams for me, selection to the top national team, and UK became a top ten nationally ranked college women's basketball team. I averaged a double-double, 20.9 point-per-game and 10.9 rebounds-per-game. Someone would have to pinch me and awaken me from this wonderful dream. It was a miracle that I was alive. To think only a few months earlier, Dr. Brimm had said I wouldn't be able to walk without a limp but here I was with another great season. The Lady Kats had made it through an internally challenging season with a coaching change and finished with more support and confidence. We were still fighting for equality at UK but it was better than when I had arrived.

Lea, PJ, Lori and I hadn't lost our unbridled passion for basketball. We were always in search of a game. We played on the outdoor courts located adjacent to Blazer Hall and spent hours at night playing under the streetlights against anyone who was on the court. We were frequent visitors to Seaton Center for open gym, playing pickup games against UK male students until word got back to Coach Hall. She prohibited us from playing outside of her organized practices and games. Banning us from playing was like taking crack from a drug addict.

Restricting when I could play basketball was the straw that broke the camel's back. By the end of the school year Coach Hall and I still were in a major control battle. On my way back to Kansas City, I stopped by the University of Missouri to visit with the coach. Mom insisted I stay at UK and finish what I had started. I would have the summer to decide.

Once June arrived, I filled my time coaching at the Lady Kats Summer camp the second week of June and then at a summer basketball camp in the Pocono Mountains in Pennsylvania. A week later I flew to NC State University where the USA Women's Basketball National Team was trained under Coach Kay Yow for a week before heading to Europe for the World University Games in Romania. I was thrilled about being selected for the World University Games. This was the USA's top women's basketball team.

Our first practice, I was in awe. Most of the players on the team had already been in the USA basketball circle and Coach Kay Yow was a well-respected coach in women's basketball. We had played against her but I didn't know what to expect now that we were all on the same team. I felt like an outsider needing to outperform. The team was made up of three players from the 1980 Olympic team, four players from the 1980 Jones Cup team, and five players who had experience with ABAUSA. Coach Yow's former NC State player, Trudi Lacey, who had just graduated, was on the team as well. We stood in a circle at half-court as Coach Yow explained her philosophy; there was a lot of talent on this team; she was open and without bias, and players would earn playing time. She would play the best five at any given time. I was so pumped; I would earn some quality playing time. We ran through conditioning and skill-developing drills and learned Coach Yow's defensive concepts and offensive system. The last thirty minutes of the practice would be intrasquad scrimmaging. Coach Yow called out, "Anne, LaTaunya, Denise, Lea and...Trudi," for one team. They would become the starting lineup from day one. Anne, LaTaunya, and Denise were on the 1980 Olympic team and Lea Henry, from Tennessee, was our best point guard. Trudi was not the most talented forward but she was Coach Yow's player. Once I determined in my mind that there was something other than playing ability that would determine my role on the team, I would enjoy the experience as best I could. It didn't matter that I had reached the top level of women's basketball and was on my way to fulfilling my destiny; after all the years of being treated as inferior, my perception was askew. After that first practice with Kay Yow, I would compete and improve my game, but more importantly, I would see this opportunity as a chance to travel to Europe, meet new people, learn other cultures and live life. I lost respect for Coach Yow's word and proceeded with my immature, inexperienced perspective.

Valerie Walker and I became friends. We were both from New Jersey. She was an All-American and Wade Trophy finalist who played for Vivian Stringer at Cheyney State. Although quiet and reserved she was one of the best players in the country. The team left for Yugoslavia June 29th to scrimmage for two weeks. During an exhibition game near the end of the Yugoslavian tour, I suffered a severe ankle sprain. When we finally arrived in Belgrade to end our scrimmages, I was still rehabbing my ankle and not playing much. We finished the World University Games with a silver medal. Although I had met lots of new international friends, I was looking forward to returning home.

Coach Yow met with each player before we returned to the States.

"Val, you have great potential. This summer must have been challenging for you with your injury and playing at this level," Coach Yow began the meeting. "But now you have to continue working on your game. And more importantly, work on being a team player."

"I really don't think you were fair," I hesitated. "From the first practice, the first five you chose ended up being your starting lineup. I never had a chance."

"Playing for USA Basketball is a whole new level; you have to understand the importance of the concept of team, working within the system, playing with the best players in the world and representing our country."

"I just took you at your word, and don't think you even gave me a chance," I ended the conversation.

"I'm sorry you feel that way about the situation, Val," she said in her strong North Carolina accent. "Stay positive and focused."

Walking out of Coach Yow's room, I had to shift gears and take away the positives; this was my first trip to Europe and I would be going to Japan with UK in less than three weeks.

The beginning of August the Lady Kats headed to Japan for a two-week exhibition tour. We had games scheduled in seven Japanese cities, playing against the Japanese National Team. Arriving in Japan, I felt a strong connection. While some of my other teammates complained about the differences in culture, food, and playing, I loved Japan. We travelled by bus mainly, along with the Japanese National Team. Occasionally we took the Bullet Train. We played in front of packed arenas in each town and were treated like celebrities. In Lexington we were beginning to be recognized but here fans rushed our bus when it entered the arena's parking lot a; they asked for autographs and pictures. After being delegated to a bench player with the USA team, playing in Japan made me feel validated again. Each game an MVP was named and awarded a nice gift from the host city. I received a crystal clock and a glass-encased Japanese Geisha doll.

The Japanese National Team consisted of older and more experienced players. We were beaten five out of seven games against the tough international-style play but it helped prepare us for the upcoming season. Over the course of the two weeks, I became good friends with a few of the players. With our language barrier we didn't communicate much but just loved being around each other. On the last night, we enjoyed Tokyo, even stopping into a few discotheques. I would see them all next summer. When we said our good-byes, I knew I would see them all the following summer.

*****

I was home for less than a week before returning to UK for my junior year. The Japan trip with my teammates made me want to return. We had progressed each year in the national tournament and this year everyone was optimistic that this would be our chance to reach the Final Four and have a legitimate shot at the national championship. The excitement and pressure were strong, but I also had to focus on academics because in addition to agriculture and animal science classes, I had registered for organic chemistry.

In 1982 the NCAA decided to sponsor Women's Basketball, holding national championships for women. The 1981-82 season would be a two-championship season. The AIAW, suffering from a twenty percent drop in membership because the NCAA decided to hold national championships for women, was on life support. Many of the supporters of women's sports thought of this as a "take-over." The NCAA claimed it simply wanted to offer women more options and wasn't trying to monopolize women's sports, and allowed non-member schools to participate in NCAA national tournaments until 1985. To many, it seemed like an attempt to drive the competition out of business. Some saw the NCAA's interest in women's sports based solely in gaining control of increasing revenues, particularly from lucrative TV contracts. Others felt the move was strictly a power move, in the hope of strangling the AIAW with its alternative philosophy for collegiate athletics and its advocacy for federal enforcement of Title IX. Women also had the choice now of playing professionally in the USA. In 1978, the Women's Professional Basketball League (WBL) was formed. The WBL was always considered inferior to men's professional sports leagues in the USA and treated as such.

UK chose to drop the AIAW and join the SEC in hopes for a berth in the first NCAA Division I women's basketball tournament. I was totally focused on my junior year and a national championship.

With Liz and Maria having graduated, we would have to make major adjustments. The biggest one for me, and the team, was that I would have to change positions from forward to post. Jody was still adapting to the 5-player game and would be a backup center. I was an All-American forward, which was ideal for my style and size, but now I had to make the transition quickly. I didn't think about it; it had to be done. We were ranked 9th in the pre-season polls and no longer a surprise or underdog, and in Lexington, we had gained respect and fans. The UK's women's team was given more space in the local and school newspapers and I was recognized now on campus and around town.

Tanya was our only senior. Lea, PJ, Lori and I had to provide guidance and direction for the team. We had made the transition from Coach Yow-Nance to Coach Hall, making the year free from personality conflict and drama – almost. A rumor surfaced about Coach Hall being gay. In UK's homophobic environment, she had to conceal this fact even though she was living with her girlfriend. There was much discussion about this among the players. In some ways, given the atmosphere, we were surprised UK hired her.

The outbreak of AIDS had brought homosexuality to the forefront of American society in a negative way. The stigma for women playing sports and particularly women's basketball was that it was a breeding ground for lesbians. Traits associated with basketball-playing were not considered acceptable feminine ones. Strong, assertive, muscular, aggressive, confident, bold athletic women challenged the status quo of femininity in American culture.

Many in the gay community loved, supported and followed women's basketball and there were many players and coaches who were gay but had to hide their sexuality because of the negative backlash of being homosexual. The thought that young girls would be exposed to and subjected to the possibility of being transformed into social misfits was part of the reason women's basketball was not readily accepted in American society. The Lady Kats had gained respect and acceptance because we were talented basketball players but we were also seen as pretty and feminine. Would having a lesbian coach affect the team's popularity?

We now had a Lady Kat Booster Club, a sponsor program and the "Rowdy Bunch." In our first game of the season at Memorial Coliseum we beat UT - Chattanooga 82-51. Playing the post position, I scored 30 points and grabbed 21 rebounds. It was business as usual for me. We played our first SEC game ten days later against Vanderbilt with an 84-61 win at home.

Six games into the season, we had already lost two games and weren't playing well. Our first big game of the season in Memorial Coliseum came on December 21, before the Christmas break, against UCLA. We were now ranked 13th and they were ranked 12th. UCLA was a national powerhouse and had Jackie Joyner and legendary coach Billie Moore. We won 83-72 in front of nearly 2,500 spectators. PJ had a career-high 23 points and seven assists, and Lea finished with 16 points and I had 30 points and 14 rebounds.

We ended 1981 with an SEC win against Florida and started 1982 with a big win over 7th-ranked Georgia. By mid-January, heading into the Lady Kat Invitational Tournament, we were ranked 10th nationally with a 10-2 record and first in the SEC with a 3-0 record. We beat Cincinnati in the first round of the LKIT, 79-66. With 32 points and 17 rebounds, I tied the University of Kentucky women's scoring record.

After tying the record, I received calls from everyone I knew, offering congratulations and wishing me luck in our championship game on Sunday. Three and a half minutes into the LKIT championship game, I hit a free throw to pass Pam Browning on the UK all-time women's scoring list with 1,599 points. Two minutes later, I hit a layup and the game was stopped to present me with the game ball. Strangely, the thrill of breaking the women's record was overshadowed by my desire to win the LKIT championship. Cutting down those nets always felt exhilarating.

We defeated Southern Illinois 74-56. I had 27 points, 16 rebounds and five assists and sat out the last nine minutes of the game. For the second straight year I was named MVP of the tournament. After the game, Maryanne, Steve and Kelly Beth hugged me and told me how proud they were of me; Steve joked that I should stop being such a ballhog and learn to play defense. Ottie celebrated with the Rowdy Bunch, wearing the USA national team jacket I had given him when I returned from the World University Games. He wore that jacket to every game. Bonnie grabbed me as I headed to the locker room to shower. "Valerie Stillery...you're number one!" she chuckled.

The euphoria from breaking the women's scoring record was short-lived. A few days later, we travelled to Norfolk, Virginia to play Old Dominion and Ann Donovan. We were defeated, 68-91. We lost five of the next ten games, including two losses to Tennessee. February 9th, against National College, I broke the UK single-game rebounding record, pulling down 27 rebounds. Although I was able to set personal records, our losses against Tennessee were demoralizing. We regrouped and won the last two games of the regular season, and I broke another record – the single-game scoring record with 41 points against Florida. Breaking records was an indirect result of my flowing in the energy of my purpose. It was exciting but winning collectively as the Lady Kats and the team's success overshadowed any personal records I set. The relationship between PJ, Lea and me and their unselfishness produced a magical environment where I was able to excel. Their names will always be associated with any record I set at UK.

We headed into the SEC tournament with a 19-7 record. We had to find a way to defeat the Lady Vols to get to the NCAA tournament. Coach Hall was concerned that we would not make the 32-team NCAA field without an impressive showing in the SEC tournament hosted by UK.

While the team prepared, I found myself struggling in my advanced Animal Science classes. I had dropped one meat production class that included slaughtering animals. I loved animals. Now I was learning how to kill them. After a live slaughter demonstration, I dropped the class and became a vegetarian. Coach Hall didn't like that idea; I was already thin, had the sickle-cell trait and needed size to be successful playing the post position. But she hadn't witnessed what I had.

After the Tennessee loss, Lori was suspended from the team. Lori had a strong personality, was extremely competitive and often clashed with Coach Hall. We barely won the last two games of the season. Against Louisville, Coach Hall played her five starters, with Donna Martin and Kathy playing a few minutes. Although the media questioned why Lori was suspended, we were not allowed to comment, and in reality, I really didn't know why. Lea, PJ, Lori, and I had always shared a special bond and a dream. Now we would have to navigate around our quest for a national championship and our commitment to each other. Lori was not allowed to practice with us nor sit on the bench for the last two games.

Without Lori, we pressed on and as a sign we had finally gained respect, Lexington's most popular sportswriter and radio personality, D.G. FitzMaurice, wrote an article about me. It was the first article he had written about the women's team. FitzMaurice asked UK fans to name the youngest Kentucky basketball player to reach the 1,000-point plateau in UK's history; of course most would think of a male player; instead I was the answer to his question. He suggested the only thing that could possibly keep me from topping Dan

Issel's scoring record was "cupid's arrow." I was quoted as saying that "basketball was just a game and I would give it up if I found the right guy," perpetuating the notion that finding a man was more important than any athletic accomplishment for me.

D.G. and I eventually became good friends. He was a tall, stout man who looked like Grizzly Adams with his full beard and mustache. His witty remarks in his high-pitched voice followed by an infectious laugh filled any room. He had a keen sense of humor, was funny and smart, and loved jazz. In his old, dilapidated Oldsmobile, we traveled across the Lexington and Cincinnati area in search of jazz clubs and concerts. Having D.G. as an advocate for the Lady Kats legitimized the women's program. He was revered by sports fans in Lexington, and getting recognized in his article a week before the SEC tournament was significant.

Lori was reinstated with the team but Tanya, who had been gaining weight, wasn't feeling well during practice. The SEC was the toughest conference in the country with five nationally ranked teams, and we had been playing with only five players late in the season. It was good having Lori back but Tanya was fundamental for us. We had to have a great tournament for a chance to go to the NCAA tournament but we had never beaten Tennessee in my three years at UK.

Mom came to Lexington for the SEC tournament. This would be her first time seeing me play in Lexington. She was staying at the Simmons' house for the weekend and I had hoped to stay as well; instead I had to be back at Blazer Hall before curfew. Maryanne cooked a delicious dinner and we sat around a cozy fire in their den afterward. Mom was so proud of me and thankful for Maryanne and Steve. She knew I was a little nervous as Steve prepared to drive me back to the dorm.

"Trust in the Lord with all your heart and lean not into your own ways. Acknowledge Him in all your ways and He will direct your path," Mom told me as she hugged me.

The next night in front of 3,300 screaming fans, Coach Hall played her starters nearly the entire game. After a slow start, playing zone defense in order to rest our limited players, we headed to the locker room with a 43-43 tie at halftime. Less than four minutes into the second half and trailing 52-51, we went on a wild seven-minute, 23-0 massacre to put the game out of reach for Alabama and beat them in the second round SEC tournament. Memorial Coliseum exploded. Four starters finished in double figures. I played 39 minutes scoring 23 points and grabbing 12 rebounds.

Louisiana State beat Ole Miss by four points in our bracket in the other second round game. We would play LSU in the semi-finals. Georgia and Tennessee advanced for the other semi-final game. The NCAA would probably take two or maybe three teams from the SEC tournament. Getting into the finals would solidify our chances of going to the first NCAA women's national championship.

We defeated LSU 85-71, playing only five players. I had 34 points and 14 rebounds and PJ had 15 assists and no turnovers. The NCAA tournament was secured but we had a new target - defeat Tennessee. Tennessee advanced to the SEC finals with a 55-44 win over Georgia. The stage was set. Tennessee had beat us twice in the regular season. We were ready for our revenge. I had spent hours studying Tennessee scout video.

I barely slept the night before the game. I didn't know what made me more excited – playing against Tennessee for the SEC championship or having Mom here to share my passion. She had spent years supporting her boys playing sports and hoping that I would pursue something more "lady-like," but I knew the last two days she had gained a new respect for me. I had matured and become an independent adult who could survive on my own. Her dream for her children was that they would thrive and be happy.

Mom received compliments and congratulations from everyone she met in Lexington. She was personable, fun and outspoken. Maryanne and Steve treated her like a queen. Bonnie Hutton was a daughter to her. Mrs. Singletary, UK's first lady and the Lady Kats #1 fan, who sat with the Rowdy Bunch, squeezed Mom tightly and told her after the LSU game how appreciative she was that the Still children had come to UK.

"The school is a much better place since they've been here, Mrs. Still," she said, "and we're going to beat Tennessee tomorrow!"

Mom's words to me after a game were always the same, win or lose: "You're always a winner, regardless of the score." Although I would always be a winner in Mom's eyes, I wanted to show her that I was a winner and the best way to do that would be to beat Tennessee.

Eighth-ranked Tennessee was predicted to win the tournament. The Lady Vols were on an eleven-game winning streak and was one of only two teams that had beaten us in Memorial Coliseum. They were favorites to win the national championship as well.

From the ball-toss to start the game to the final buzzer, the deafening crowd of well-over 5,000 noisy Kentucky fans along with the Lady Vols' brave, loyal supporters in their Tennessee orange enjoyed an ultra competitive contest. Our desire to beat Tennessee superseded the importance of winning the SEC championship.

Our emotional high and normal jitters with the start of the game subsided immediately with a quick 4-0 run. We knew Tennessee now; successfully beating them would entail beating them down physically and psychologically. We had to hit hard from the start and never look back. At halftime we led, 40-33, while shooting 61 percent. I had 20 points in the first half but knew Tennessee would make necessary adjustments and be ready for the second half. We would not be denied; it was our time. We took the Lady Vols' punches but unlike our last encounter, we remained composed and calm. With 10:24 left in the half we pulled away with a 57-51 lead as Lisa and I scored baskets. Our inside-out game was working to perfection. With each long-range basket, Lisa's confidence skyrocketed as the Lady Vols became frustrated. Normally, they could successfully sag in to stop me but with Lisa and Lea hitting the outside jumpers, destiny was on our side. Lea and I hit crucial bonus foul shots to secure the victory in the last seconds of the game. With the sound of the final buzzer, tears flowed. We had just won the SEC tournament; we were going to the first NCAA national tournament; we were on our home court in front of our home crowd, and we had just beaten Tennessee for the first time. And Mom was in the stands!

Our fans rushed the floor as I was tackled by my teammates. I needed to get up and find Mom. I made it back to my feet and spotted Mom, Maryanne, Ottie and Bonnie heading toward me. As photographers clicked photos for the local newspapers, Mom and I shared an intimate moment that no one recognized in the middle of the chaos. She had always been the one to hold me up and support me. Now I was able to return the favor in a little way, and show her that her sacrifices were not in vain. Regardless of the outcome of the game, I was always a winner to Mom but it felt satisfying to be able to climb up the ladder and cut down those nets at Memorial Coliseum with Mom watching. I had played the best three games of my life. This would be a moment I would never forget.

As a team we had never been as consistent and mature as we had in the SEC tournament. PJ and I were named to the all-tournament team and I was named MVP for the tournament, scoring 90 points and grabbing 34 rebounds in three games.

After the tournament I received national recognition by being named Division I Player-of-the-Week by the American Women's Sports Federation. I led the nation in rebounding with 14.5 per game and was seventh in scoring at 25 points per game. The SEC tournament was our most consistent team performance of the season. It was perfect timing heading into the NCAA tournament.

We waited anxiously to see which region we would be placed in now that we were SEC champions and one of the 32 teams who would participate. Of the four regions, Midwest (Louisiana Tech in Ruston, LA), MidEast (Tennessee in Knoxville, TN), East (North Carolina State in Raleigh, NC) and West (Stanford in Palo Alto, CA), we definitely didn't want to be placed in the Midwest. La Tech was the number one team in the country with a 30-1 record, defending national champion and would be playing at home.

Five teams from the SEC were selected to participate in the NCAA tournament; that was the most from any conference. Although we were the SEC champions, we were put in the most difficult region, the Midwest, as a #2 seed while Tennessee with a 19-9 record was placed in the Mideast as a #2 seed and would enjoy home court advantage throughout regional play.

Two weeks after winning the SEC, we beat Illinois 88-80 in the first round of the first NCAA national tournament for women's basketball. I had 21 points and 13 rebounds. We were in the "sweet sixteen" and heading to Ruston, Louisiana to face South Carolina in the Midwest Regional semi-finals.

The atmosphere was electric as we stepped off the plane in

a small airport in Louisiana. Women's basketball was popular in Ruston, a small town of 25,000, located about six hours north of New Orleans. I was shocked that people could be this excited about women's sports. In 1974 Sonja Hogg, who had never played basketball, started the program with a total budget of around $5,000 and only three home games. Now the program had a first-class recruiting budget, four different sets of uniforms, sellout crowds at every big home game, had won the 1982 AIAW National Championship and could win the first NCAA Division 1 women's basketball championship. I hadn't felt this type of energy at a game anywhere.

Coach Hogg had built the program in Memorial Gymnasium. The NCAA Midwest Regional semi-finals and finals would be the last games played in Memorial Gymnasium before the women's and men's basketball teams would move into the $15 million Thomas Assembly Center next season. Just a week earlier, "Memorial's Marvelous Machine" had disassembled Tennessee Tech 114-53 in the first round of the NCAA playoffs. The emotionally-charged environment engulfed us as we walked into the facility to take on South Carolina. There weren't many South Carolina or UK supporters who had made the trip to Ruston but the gym was filled to capacity with rabid Louisiana Tech fans scouting the Lady Techster's future victim.

South Carolina jumped out to a commanding 10-2 lead in the first four minutes of the game as we struggled to process the chaotic atmosphere. PJ and I stepped up our defense and shifted into our running game and the rest of the team followed. In the final five minutes of the first half we outscored South Carolina 16-4. By halftime we had stormed back to take a 38-34 lead with PJ and Tanya finishing the last thirteen seconds of the first half turning two South Carolina turnovers into two easy layups. Going into the locker room we had calmed down the early game jitters and gained some support from Louisiana Tech's fans, but we knew the game was far from being over.

We continued putting on the pressure, increasing our lead to 10 points seven minutes into the second half but went cold at the foul line, allowing South Carolina to tie the game 65-65 with less than four minutes left. We were too close to being in the regional finals to let it slip from us. I pinned Sheila Foster behind me and PJ pinpointed a pass into me for a quick move and a foul with 2:45 left in the game. I hit both foul shots; Carolina missed a shot and followed with another basket; that would be the end of South Carolina's hope for reaching the finals.

As the final buzzer rang, the arena erupted. We had beaten South Carolina 73-69 but the cheers were not for us but for the Lady Techsters who had run out to the middle of the court to prepare for their semi-final game against Arizona State. Louisiana Tech had blazed the tournament, beating teams by an average of 30 points and after our postgame talk we would finally get a chance to see this Goliath of women's basketball live.

We watched as the country's number one team totally annihilated a team that had been ranked in the top twenty all year. Within the first few minutes, Louisiana Tech's unyielding frontline crushed Arizona State and its sophomore sensation, Kym Hampton. By halftime the score was 50-18 and Coach Hall decided we would return to the hotel to get rested for tomorrow's final against the Lady Techsters.

In the final two minutes of the game, the crowd erupted when the results of the East Regionals were announced. Kansas State had upset Old Dominion, the only team to have defeated the Techsters this year. The only thing stopping Louisiana Tech from reaching the Final Four and the first NCAA national championship? The University of Kentucky Lady Kats.

"What could the Lady Kats use today? A miracle" was the headline of an article in one of the Lexington newspapers on the day of the game. Thank God we didn't have access to Lexington's newspapers. Coach Hall was quoted as saying that we would need a miracle to upset Louisiana Tech. It infuriated PJ, Lea and me when she made desperate comments that seemed she didn't have faith in our ability. We entered each game believing we could win but Coach Hall always looked at things in a pragmatic way. Louisiana Tech hadn't lost a game in 58 straight games in Memorial Gym. They were ranked number one for 35 consecutive polls and had a formidable team with four players over six-feet tall. They were second in the country in scoring with an average of 88.3 points per game and were second in the nation in defense, allowing opponents only 54.2 points per game. In their last 12 games they had surpassed the 100-point mark seven times and had won by an average of 45.3 points. They had a deep bench, using a nine-player rotation.

No other UK team had ever gotten this far. One more step and we would walk into the Final Four. Miracle or not, win or not, we would be part of history and PJ, Lea and I believed anything was possible if we played together and fought.

Unlike the game against South Carolina, when we entered Memorial Gym and felt the awesomeness of women's basketball, in the finals of the Regional, as we took our final step toward reaching our dream of being in the Final Four, this time we felt like the sacrificial bull being led into the bullring. The emotionally-charged deranged spectators sensed a killing in the air and cried out to their matadors knowing they would be victorious. PJ and I connected in warm-ups with our universal, non-verbal sign that no matter what, we would go down fighting, giving everything we had. We had nothing to lose and we would play with reckless abandon.

The Lady Techsters started out fast and aggressive, building a 46-32 halftime lead behind senior All-American center Pam Kelley's inspirational play. This would be her last game in Memorial Gym and she would make it a memorable farewell. Kelley put in 19 first-half points, hitting nine of nine shots from the field. Coach Hogg rotated fresh players in as we continued to be worn down.

In the locker room at halftime, physically tired and wounded, we expressed our determination to fight back regardless of the score; we were the Lady Kats and would stubbornly fight for our dream. We made a second half comeback, pulling within six points with 16 minutes left in the game; this caused the agitated crowd to cheer more boisterously for their team. Louisiana Tech continued to rotate players as fatigue set in for us. With the final saber thrust deep, Louisiana Tech posted an 82-60 victory but we had held them to less than their average.

Kelley finished by leading all scorers with 29. I had 20 points and 10 rebounds and PJ finished with 16 points and 9 assists. Janice Lawrence, the Lady Techsters' other center, scored 17 points. PJ and I were named to the all-Midwest Regional team. We had been selected to every all-tournament team Kentucky had played in this year. In the locker room, as tears flowed, we all knew that if we had been in any other region, we would be heading to Virginia for the Final Four. We would have to wait another year, our final year, to get our chance at a national championship.

*****

With both UK's basketball teams making it to the NCAA tournament, the comparisons began. While we beat Illinois in the first round, the men's team was eliminated in the first round by Middle Tennessee, 44-50. One of the local newspapers put the women's game article on the top of the front page of the sports section. At the bottom of the page was an article by D.G. FitzMaurice with the title "Joe's Gotta Go!" The men's smaller article chastised UK's men's dismal performance against Middle Tennessee and early exit from the tournament. I never thought I would see the day when our coverage would mask that of the men's.

I was recognized as one of the best players in the nation, if not the best. Awards included Kodak, American Women's Sports Federation, Street and Smith All-American selections, and finalist for the Wade Trophy awarded to the nation's top collegiate female player. I ended the year nationally-ranked 5th in rebounding (14.3), 6th in scoring (24.8) and 13th in field goal percentage (58.2%). At UK I set the records for single game points (41), most rebounds in a game (27), most field goals made in a game (18), most rebounds in a season (457), most points in a season (794), most field goals made in a season (329), and most field goal attempts in a season (565). With one more year to play, I held career records for most points (2,063), most field goals attempted (1475), most field goals made (845), most free throws attempted (554), most free throws made (373), and most rebounds (1189). I was riding the wave.

That wave, however, couldn't make up for my dismal grades. Some professors were understanding while others gave little consideration to the fact that we basically had little control over our schedule or lives. I was behind in credits needed to graduate and hadn't taken and couldn't take any of my animal science afternoon lab classes because of a conflict with our practices. I would not graduate in four years, disappointing Mom, and there was no scholarship to stay for a fifth year.

*****

I was selected for the USA national team, returning to Taiwan for the Jones Cup. It had been two years since the last experience in Taiwan that nearly killed me but that didn't influence my desire to return. I had kept in touch with all my Chinese friends with letters.

My roommate for the trip was Sheila Foster from the University of South Carolina. She was a sweetheart but one of the craziest and most fierce players I knew. Sheila was quiet and fun but temperamental and stayed in the hotel room during free time. Now, thousands of miles away in another country, Sheila and I were still witnessing the secretive side of women's basketball that no one was willing to confront and expose – intimate relationships between coaches and players. We talked about some of the drama with the USA team, how some players and coaches tried to conceal their sexuality and attraction to each other. Sheila had had hands-on experience with this issue. Her former coach, Pam Parsons, had recently been released because of a scandal involving an intimate relationship with a player. With the homophobic and paranoid lens the women's basketball world was under, we knew this type of controversy could set women's progress and advancement back quickly. Everyone in women's basketball was talking about Parsons' scandal.

The USA breezed through the tournament, winning all seven of our games easily except for a 65-62 win against Australia. We fell short to Canada,70-67 in front of a capacity crowd of 10,000 to earn the silver medal. I returned to Lexington and prepared for UK's Japanese tour.

I loved travelling to Asia. I wasn't sure what it was but I felt at home in Japan and Taiwan. Our UK entourage had changed a little with the addition of two freshmen, Leslie Nichols and Karen Mosley. UK's First Lady, Gloria Singletary, joined us again. She was a gracious Southern Belle who sat courtside at our home games (sometimes with the Rowdy Bunch). Last summer in Japan, she sat on our bench fanning herself at overheated, no air-conditioned are-nas looking poised and polite. The Japanese male executives were smitten by Mrs. Singletary's genteel manners, beauty and Southern drawl. I could easily envision her in a hoop skirt, corset, pantalettes, a wide-brimmed straw hat and gloves, carrying a parasol umbrella and hand fan. She had become an intricate part of our group of wild young female athletes travelling across Japan, and remained com-posed even in the midst of the rowdy bus rides with Tanya blar-ing out sexually explicit songs through the speakers such as George Clinton's "Atomic Dog" or Marvin Gaye's "Sexual Healing."

We played six games on the tour, three against the Japan Nation-al team and three against Chanson, Unitika, and Kyodo Oil (Japa-nese women's professional teams). Unlike the previous summer, we only lost once, against Kyodo Oil. I led, averaging 25.8 points and 11.3 rebounds per game. We visited Tokyo, Nagoya, Kobe, Ham-mamatsu, Funabashi and Odawra with special excursions, dinners and events. I fell in love with Nagoya; it was one of the most beau-tiful seaside towns I had ever seen or felt. The authentic Japanese inn where we stayed with traditional tatami-matted rooms, Japanese gardens, and communal baths felt like home to me while my team-mates preferred western-style rooms with beds. At night I pulled open the sliding door to look at a breath-taking view of the sea. The lullaby of waves splashing on rocks freed my mind and lulled me to sleep. This was not an unfamiliar place for me.

Our planned event included dinner in small boats with the president of Panasonic. After each game we had dinner with the op-posing team and learned more about each other. Most nights ended with shots of Sake. We visited Shinto shrines and Buddhist temples, were pampered like queens with blind Japanese masseurs who could release any stress with their magical touch, and we giggled like little girls in communal baths as naked Japanese men and women paraded around.

The team had a four-day vacation in Hawaii after the tour but I didn't go. I couldn't afford it and had already spent too much time away from home. I wanted to visit Mom. I missed her.

*****

Patti Jo, Lea and I had made it to our final curtain call at UK. We had had our share of obstacles, but overall, I was blessed and following my dream. Tanya, our lone senior, had been sent out victorious with a birthday SEC championship win against Tennessee. She couldn't join us for our Japanese tour; she had played most of the year pregnant. If anyone could do that without anyone knowing, it was Tanya. Lori, who hadn't played a game after being re-instated, decided to leave Kentucky. Dissention between her and the coaches became too big a distraction. Kathy also decided to leave. Not many people believed her story about inappropriate behavior from a member of the men's coaching staff. I thought anything was possible, and believed her, but in Lexington, these men were considered gods. She never told me where she was going.

Although we had lost a few Lady Kat sisters, we added a few as well. The upcoming year, we became international. Mie Nishigori, the 18-year-old daughter of the president of Japan Amateur Basketball Association became a team manager. Coach Hall had recruited a 6'4" center from England, Sally Loughton. No one knew anything about Sally but she would arrive in Lexington for fall semester. Completing our new family of course were our freshmen, affectionately nicknamed "Lester" and "KMo."

Chapter 8

Breaking The Record

I headed back to the tranquil suburbs of Kansas City with a new perspective and mindset. Dad had finally decided to move to the Midwest with Mom, Wendell, Gary and Jackie but living in a custom-built beautiful home on a few acres in a secluded area didn't change what was going on within those walls. They had transitioned from our no-heat/no-air matchbox public housing in Camden to the suburbs of Cherry Hill, finally settling in a sprawling, spacious two-level house in the Midwest, but the edifice couldn't change the dysfunctional domestic situation within those walls. After travelling the world and experiencing what I thought was normalcy, and connecting in Japan on a deeper spiritual level, returning back to Mom's and Dad's turmoil confused and frustrated me. I couldn't understand how they remained together.

Jackie wore white dresses and a hat all the time and spent most of her time in her room with our old West Highland terrier, rarely coming out. Mom and Dad fought and then seemingly made-up and then fought again and then made-up. After being away for three years, I understood that their behavior wasn't "normal" and I hated both for the craziness. Who were these insane people? I definitely didn't consider them my parents. Parents were supposed to love and support their children and each other. I was tired of trying to figure out their relationship and Jackie was trying to escape as well.

Barry was now an NFL star with the Kansas City Chiefs. With the Chiefs he had been selected on the NFL All-Rookie, All-Pro, All-AFC teams and selected to play in the Pro-Bowl three times. Dennis was playing professional basketball overseas but had had a physical exchange with Dad on his last return trip from France, when Dad had insulted Mom verbally. Now Dennis would not return to visit. Wendell, Gary and Jackie lived with Mom and Dad. Wendell had sucker-punched Dad, nearly knocking him out earlier in the year after getting into a fight with Mom. I wondered how we could continue with such abuse even as we transitioned into adults. The boys seemed to have anger issues that may have originated from childhood issues that they were unable to release or resolve.

Jackie was a six-foot beauty with large breasts and curvy hips. She had torn her Achilles' tendon in a freak accident in Camden. Unlike me, she was extremely feminine and wasn't interested in sports. She was intellectual and just graduated from high school. We decided it would be best for her to move to Lexington with me. I was a senior and would have the possibility of moving off campus for my senior year. We could get a small apartment and she could finally break free of the madness. Jackie and I packed up all her belongings and headed back to Lexington together. We got on Interstate 70 East with Jackie navigating, music blasting, and heading to what had been an oasis for me, Lexington. We were young and immature and clueless about life, but we loved each other; we would always have each other and we would finally be free of this nightmare.

We rented an apartment. Coach Hall wasn't thrilled about my living off campus, but I loved it. I bought a ten-speed racing bike. I worked a few hours a week with a veterinarian, Dr. Lynch, one of the sponsors of the team. He gave us a white poodle we named Ivory. We decorated the house in a Japanese motif with many of the things I had brought back from Japan and I continued with meditation every day. I had a boyfriend, Ken, a Japanese student I met the previous year. Paul, whom I met playing basketball at the Seaton Center, and I had become good friends. Jackie landed a job as a receptionist at one of the most popular radio stations in Lexington while I prepared for my final season at UK. Each day I rode my bike to work, classes and practice then back home.

I began to feel that normalcy I had been craving and I loved having my little sister with me, but none of it lasted long. First, my bike was stolen, and then Ivory was killed by a car. What upset me the most, Jackie met a much older man while working downtown. She had never had a boyfriend nor dated. Neal was from Lexington's inner city. As an UK athlete I had had little interaction in Lexington's Black community. Lexington was racially segregated with most Blacks living in the northern inner city.

Despite the dissention between my sister and me, the Lady Kats prepared for a much-anticipated season. It began with the ABC affiliate, Channel 36, "The Terry Hall Show."

We started the season hot with four wins in Memorial Coliseum in front of record crowds. The first on November 19 was an exhibition game against the Chinese National Team. On December 5, in the third home game of the season against Miami of Ohio, after I scored my 21st point, the game was stopped and I was recognized for becoming the University of Kentucky's all-time leading scorer, surpassing UK men's basketball icon, Dan Issel. Coach Hall handed me the game ball as I reached 2,138 points in just three games into my senior season. I was totally unaware of the significance of breaking UK's record as I sheepishly stood at half court basking in a standing ovation. We blew out Miami 90-61. I finished the game with 42 points. I wish Mom could have been there to witness the achievement of her little girl from Camden.

We finished December undefeated with a 7-0 record. UK reaped the rewards of my success with national recognition for the women's basketball program. Paul Harvey featured me on "The Rest of the Story" segment of his popular national radio show. During the segment, Harvey nicknamed me "Shorty Still" and introduced me as the runt of an exceptional athletic family, who broke UK's scoring record, eclipsing any of the other outstanding athletic feats that were achieved by older and bigger brothers. Harvey ended the segment with, "By the way, Shorty Still's real name is Valerie Still. Valerie? That's right, the girl player who eclipsed the men's record...and now you know the rest of the story."

By the end of December Jackie moved out, and in with Neal

and I returned to live at Blazer Hall. When she announced she was pregnant, we didn't return home for the Christmas break. All of my success on the court didn't make up for failing to protect Jackie. Family was always first for Mom.

For New Year's eve, Rena, our assistant sports information director, invited the team to her house. When I arrived, Patti Jo, Lea and a few other Lady Kats were already sitting, eating and talking with a few people having drinks. I picked up a bottle of Jack Daniels whiskey, filled a shot glass and chugged it down swiftly on an empty stomach. Leslie and KMo watched in shock. I swigged the second glass-full and another and another until the bottle was nearly empty and finally began to feel numb. My teammates couldn't believe I had just drunk nearly a whole bottle of whiskey. The room filled with blaring music and laughter as the party continued.

"Hey Val, whatcha doing?" PJ asked me inconspicuously, trying not to bring attention to the situation. "Ya may wanna slow down with Jack."

"Yeah, Val...I don't think you want to be drinking like that," Lea chimed in.

"I'm good...I'm good...I'm real good..." I sputtered, patting Lea on the head.

It wasn't long before I began feeling queasy. I asked Rena where I could lie down. She put me on her bed, turned out the lights and left. The motion of the waterbed mixed with the liquor and food I had eaten caused me to projectile vomit. I barely made it into the bathroom, and ended up passed out on the floor. As everyone was counting down the final seconds of 1982, Rena banged on the locked bathroom door.

"Val...what's going on? Val! Val! She hollered. "Open up the door!"

"I'm not feeling well," I hiccupped as I crawled across the slimy floor and slightly opened the door.

"Ah Val...you drank too much," she said while cleaning me up. "You may be a superstar Wildcat, but you're a kitty cat drinker."

While she was laying me in her bed again, Leslie and KMo tried to come in, wondering what had happened to me.

"I'm okay..." I muttered as Rena blocked the door.

*****

On the flight to Memphis, for our first game of 1983, guilt swept over me; I thought I was becoming my father. It wasn't the first time I had consumed alcohol, but it was the first time I was drunk. We lost to Memphis State 71-75.

Back in Lexington, my insecurities and fears seemed to be caving in on me, but no one knew. A day later after practice, Ottie, wearing the USA national team warm-up jacket I had given him from the World University Games, told me he was having chest pains. I took him to the hospital emergency room. Ottie had suffered a heart attack and would have to remain in the hospital. He didn't have anyone so I stayed with him as long as I could but I had to be back in the dorm for curfew check. Our first home game of the year was the next day and I had to calm Ottie because he was upset about having to miss the game. I told him we would win for him and he just needed to focus on getting better. I would return after the game and tell him all about it.

We beat Middle Tennessee by only five points. Heading to the locker room I spotted Ottie sitting in a chair next to the hallway leading to the locker room. I hugged him tightly. After Coach Hall's post-game talk, I sprinted out the locker room and reprimanded Ottie for being at the game and took him back to the hospital.

We breezed through our games in January, winning them all going into February with an overall record of 16-1 and the highest ranking ever – 4th in the nation. Mid-January I was featured in two national magazines, Sports Illustrated and Newsweek. At the end of January, DG Fitzmaurice wrote an article, "Lady Kats make basketball fans pay attention." Coach Hall thought I had more of an impact on our program than any other player on any other program with the exception of Nancy Lieberman at Old Dominion University. Fitzmaurice's article pointed out the increased interest in the girl's game and the public's perception changing in a positive way. DG always had a witty way of making his point. I chuckled to myself reading: "The exposure that once was the domain of Playboy and Penthouse is now being given to the ladies in SI and Newsweek. Pictures of Still and Lea Wise now adorn the walls of little girls' rooms all over the Commonwealth, and the only stripping they do is in wresting the ball away from opponents."

Lea, PJ, and I had one month left of our college career and then the national tournament. February was one of the toughest series of games of the entire year; eight of the nine teams we played were ranked teams. We beat South Carolina 89-77 at home on February 2nd, in preparation for one of the biggest games of my career. February 5th pitted #3 powerhouse Old Dominion against #4 Lady Kats in Memorial Coliseum. Old Dominion was one of the teams picked to win the national title. Ann Donovan and I would face off again on my home floor.

As I shook Ann's hand before the tipoff, I had a flashback of young Ann and young Val four years earlier at the New Jersey High School All-Star game. This time we were in a madhouse of fans and the strangest thing was it didn't feel abnormal. This was how I had always imagined women's basketball would be. David against Goliath. Ann was one of the best, if not the best player in the nation and towered over me by six inches. I had dreamed of this moment and it had arrived.

In front of a record-breaking crowd of 10,622 fans, we brought down perennial power Old Dominion 80-66. In front of the largest crowd ever to watch a female basketball game we rendered ourselves a ferocious contender for the national championship. The tomboy, bedwetting, insecure, poor little girl from Camden, New Jersey was on the biggest stage of women's sports and making history.

We finished February with a 9-2 record and ended the regular season 23-3. On February 18, 1983 we played our last home game in Memorial Coliseum, and broke the record for attendance for women's basketball. UK paid tribute to Lea, PJ, and me with a souvenir program that listed our accomplishments. We had come a long way from those first games at UK when we barely got 300 people in the gym. It was odd to think it was our last home game. When the final buzzer blew, and the fans cheered, we had beaten Auburn 77-55.

After the game, two foreign men with heavy accents approached me. We sat in the Arby's next to Memorial Coliseum while Guido Bagatta, a tall Richard Gere look-a-like and his short-stature, curly-haired associate with dark intense eyes, Federico Buffa, tried to convince me that I should play basketball professionally in Italy. The Italian women's professional league had been around for years and since the WBL no longer existed, many American female basketball players now played in the Italian league. Now I had two opportunities to continue playing after I finished at UK, either in Italy or Japan, but before I could make a decision, we still had three more regular season games and the NCAA tournament.

We finished the season and my last collegiate regular season game in Knoxville, Tennessee. Our 81-69 victory against Pat Head and her Lady Vols sealed a successful and impactful collegiate career. My last three-hour bus ride from Knoxville to Lexington seemed to breeze by in minutes.

We lost in the second round of the SEC tournament against Auburn and were a 3rd-seed in the NCAA Midwest Regionals held at Notre Dame in Indiana. Tennessee was the first seed in the same regional but we wouldn't get another opportunity to play the Lady Vols. We suffered a first-round upset by 6th-seed Indiana, 76-87. Although it was devastating losing so early in the tournament, Patti Jo, Lea and I had accomplished what needed to be done without winning a national championship. The future generations of women to play at UK would inherit a respected program and could demand more. We were trailblazers of the program and set an example that would not be forgotten. I remembered as a freshman flipping through the UK 1979-80 women's basketball media guide and looking at all the records. Pam Browning's name was listed more than anyone else's but not many people knew who Pam Browning was except UK women's basketball fans. I wanted to have my name printed in the back of the media guide among the record holders. I didn't know how I could do that or if I would do it but the Still name needed to be remembered in Lexington.

Post-season accolades poured in. I was named as one of the ten semi-finalists for the first annual Naismith Trophy and for the second year in a row, I was a finalist for the prestigious Wade Trophy. I was named to a few All-American teams but with all the athletic honors nothing had had a more profound effect on my life than the near-death experience after my freshmen year. I had arrived at UK only seven years after the legendary, beloved Adolph Rupp had retired and the men's program was at its height, fresh off a 1978 NCAA championship. No one had expected a poor Black girl from Camden, New Jersey to become the face of UK basketball and own its most prestigious records. At times I had been easily distracted by my ego and lost sight as I followed my heart but in the end the Ultimate Source, God, always revealed Himself.

PART TWO: The Quest

"It was my good fortune to lend a helping hand to the weary travelers flying from the land of bondage... They were determined to have liberty even at the cost of life."

William Still

Chapter 9

Underground to Freedom

Against Mom's wishes I decided to play professional basketball in Italy. She had already nearly lost me twice with my illnesses in third grade and after my freshman year in college. She pleaded with me to stay and finish my degree but would support me regardless of my decision. I knew that if I returned to UK to finish, she would not be able to support me financially and I couldn't afford it. My eligibility was up and I would have to pay for the costs of finishing my degree. Italy was an unknown land, a strange land, but I believed it was part of my destiny and I was willing to take the first step into this new world. I wouldn't discover true opportunity until I escaped the boxes of race, gender and class in the USA. Italy would provide me that opportunity.

Mom couldn't believe I was actually going, but I assured her that I would go for one year, save some money and return. My contract included a $30,000 salary for 7 months, housing and transportation, and covered travel expenses to and from Italy and a return trip for Christmas break. Playing one game each weekend was a big change from my hectic collegiate schedule.

I didn't know anything about Milano. Mom and I packed like I was heading to a third-world country. Packing made me apprehensive but my desire to continue playing basketball overshadowed my fear of being by myself in a foreign country. I had reached my limits in the USA as a basketball player. Unlike male players who became more visible and popular and much wealthier by playing in the NBA, I would have to go underground in a sense, out-of-sight to fulfill my dream. I would have to take a risk into the unknown, a Still family trait.

My great-great granduncle William Still (the youngest brother of Levin Jr., Peter and James), a significant figure in the Underground Railroad, was a risk-taker. Before the Civil War, he illegally assisted enslaved African Americans in their pursuit for freedom and documented their stories. After the Civil War, in 1872, he published his records so that Black families could be reunited. He recognized and valued the courage, devotion and intelligence of the freedom seekers who chose the perilous and risk-taking Underground Railroad as their passage to freedom. Their craving for obtaining their dream outweighed any fear. William's passion outweighed any fear. He encouraged and inspired that determination and drive. My Uncle William would definitely embrace, understand and encourage my passion to obtaining my dream.

Mom took me to the airport. I hugged her tightly, holding back tears as I told her I loved her, and then shuffled down the jetway to board. Mom knew I was a survivor. I knew she would be praying for me.

On the flight from New York to Malpensa, I pulled out a notebook alongside my Bible and a few favorite books, and began writing. I didn't know why but I had to write. I had kept a journal periodically during college but it had been some time since I wrote in it.

We finally landed on a runway amidst trees and farmland. The airport was filled with semi-automatic machine gun-carrying soldiers in full combat-gear. I definitely wasn't in the USA. After I passed customs, tired and hesitant, a handsome soldier with dark curly hair and beautiful hazel eyes approached me.

"Buon Giorno, senorina...benvenuto in Italia," he said with a smile.

I felt like a little girl again, reminded of the dangers of talking to strangers.

I returned his smile and stepped out into a new world and adventure alone as the automatic-sliding doors closed behind me. I was a tall athletic, attractive, "exotic-looking" girl, who was also a naive young, vulnerable, dream-filled American in unknown territory. Mom had taught me not to talk to strangers but here everyone and everything was strange.

Four men and a woman rushed toward me grabbing my bags. The short woman with black wavy hair and large eyeglasses embraced me and gave me two kisses on each cheek as she began speaking to me in Italian. Silvana spoke no English. She lit a cigarette as Mr. Monti, the team owner/president kissed me next. He was a short, thin man with a really bad hairpiece. Mr. Ciocca, the team manager, a distinguished-looking man with graying thick short black hair combed back and a mustache that he continued to twirl, welcomed me with his broken English. Finally, Manuel Campiglio, a young, tall man with jet black wavy hair, an aquiline nose, strong long square chin and under-bite, along with Antonio, his assistant coach, kissed me on both cheeks and directed me to our transportation. I wasn't used to being kissed by strangers but I would soon discover those kisses were the same as a handshake in the USA. We hopped in a mini-van and headed to Mr. Monti's house in Monza, a small town northeast of Milano.

I didn't understand much of what was being said during our drive, even when Mr. Ciocca tried to translate in his broken English. I wondered how I would survive. At Mr. Monti's house, his family and maid greeted me warmly. I smiled, feeling a sense of belonging. Italy wouldn't be a strange place for me; it would be a new one. I felt a warm inviting energy, a familiar vibe as if I had already been to this place.

That night, after a delicious meal, I slept soundly and peacefully in this new land.

Chiming cathedral bells resounding from Monza's Duomo built in the Middle Ages gently awoke me. After a few minutes, disoriented from jetlag, I gained consciousness and scrambled to my feet in the pitch-black room. I reached the window trying to figure out how to open the roller shutters that sealed out all light. When the shutters were fully retracted, I put my head out the window, breathing in the melodic sounds of the church bells as I took a panoramic look at the breathtaking view from my window. I had never seen, heard or smelled anything like this before. Earth-colored terracotta-roofed villas and buildings covered the entire landscape and the smell of fresh-baked bread made my stomach grumble.

For the next few nights we gathered with Mr. Monti's family and friends for dinner. Dr. Buratti, a middle-age man with thinning hair and a beautiful smile, was one of Mr. Monti's best friends and kept everyone laughing. His six-year old daughter played with Mr. Monti's daughters. We spent hours at the table laughing, eating incredible specialty foods cooked by Mr. Monti's Sardinian maid, drinking wine and communicating without speaking the same language. I asked Mr. Monti to find me a language school so I could learn to speak Italian and communicate with everyone.

Initially, I was to stay at Mr. Monti's house for three or four days but as the weekend approached he invited me to Como with his family. Dr. Buratti joined us. The hour-and-a-half car ride was breathtaking. We drove a scenic route to avoid the autostrada. Como was beautiful and the view from the lake picturesque. Dr. Buratti offered to drive me back to Monza after the weekend. We enjoyed being together. The extra time allowed us to know each other better. The following week, he came over every night for dinner until it was time for me to move to my apartment in Milano and start training.

I shared an apartment with Bianca Rossi. She was quiet and reserved, and one of the best Italian players. She was tall and muscular with brown hair in a pageboy haircut and had light brown eyes. Although a newlywed, her redhead husband, Vittorio, lived three hours away in their hometown of Treviso. I loved Bianca's delicious Veneto dishes. We became friends quickly. Her best friend on the team was Michela from Gorizia who everyone called Mikki.

Mikki was the opposite of Bianca. She was outgoing and funny. She had an olive complexion and jet-black hair with beautiful light-gray eyes that changed color depending on what she was wearing. She lived with her sister in Sesto San Giovanni, on the outskirts of Milano. Mikki and Bianca had played on the national team together and were the captains of our team.

Practices began with morning training sessions, sometimes at Milano's historical Parco Sempione next to the 15th century Sforza

Castle. It was surreal working out near such historical landmarks. Kentucky's horse country was spellbinding, but here I felt I had fallen into a time machine. Who would ever believe I was training here? For evening practices, Bianca and I picked up Mikki and drove to our two-hour practices at the Palazzetto dello Sport in Cinisello Balsamo, a small town about 10 miles north of Milano. The traffic was chaotic, congested, and stressful. After a week of strenuous practices and not seeing Dr. Buratti, reality hit: I was a professional athlete and not on an Italian vacation.

Physicals were scheduled for Bianca, Mikki, and me. Sitting in the waiting room of a medical office, Bianca spoke just a few words of English and Mikki spoke only marginally better. Finally, a man dressed in a white lab coat came and led us back to another room. He spoke to Bianca and Mikki; I understood nothing. Once he left they began stripping off their clothes and I followed. I had already been shocked by my Italian teammates as we took showers together after practices, but I still felt uncomfortable standing in only my bra and panties.

At Kentucky, many players didn't shower at the gym and if we did, we had our own individual, private shower stalls. Players were very discrete when undressing and taking a shower. In Italy, after practices, players stripped down and walked around talking to each other, joking around and showering all together in a communal shower space. It took me some time to get accustomed to uninhibited players parading around naked, conversing and even washing each other's backs. Nudity wasn't taboo in Italy as it was in the USA. Topless women were on large public billboards in the cities and on primetime television.

Once the medical assistant returned, he said something to Mikki and Bianca and they took off their bras as he waited. There was no way I was exposing my breasts to a strange man. After some convincing I relented. We lay on a table and the assistant placed little suction-cupped electrodes around our breasts. I tried not to make eye contact with anyone. It was even more embarrassing when we began the exam by stepping up and down on stairs to the beat of the monitor. With our breasts bouncing up and down with each step, Bianca, Mikki, and I held back laughter. I needed a speed course in

Italian.

Learning Italian was important if I wanted to adjust quickly, so I enrolled in a language school a few subway stops from my apartment. Il Duomo, Milano's Gothic cathedral at my stop in Centro was the most magnificent building I had ever seen. It inundated everything else around it, including the hundreds of pigeons that scrounged in the massive plaza in front of the building. My fifteen minute walk from the Metro stop to school passed through the Galleria, then La Scala, one of the world's most historic opera houses, and down cobbled-stone roads. It was a mini-tour of one of the world's most historic cities. As I gazed in awe at the sights, people stared at me curiously. Once in class, no one spoke English, including the teacher. I understood and spoke the least Italian.

For the first few weeks in Italy I had been confused as my coaches had shouted, "die, die, die" constantly at me on the court. Did they really want me to die? And everyone continued to reference a Louie, I wondered who this famous Louie was. After a few lessons of Italian, I learned that *dai* was a way of saying "give more" or "let's go," it was an idiom used to encourage or motivate. And there was no Louie but *lui* which was the pronoun for "he."

By the time October arrived I had done numerous photo shoots, interviews, articles and even a magazine cover. The team's media relations person, Sergio, was always in search of publicity for the team. He was creative and pursued any and all interests in GBC's new "bella pantera della parquet." I was an anomaly in women's basketball, a great American athlete but also beautiful, exotic, and feminine. At UK, Lea had garnered all the attention for beauty and sex appeal. She was an All-American beauty, white with blue eyes and long flowing blonde hair. Most requests for photos were for Lea and not me. As a child I wasn't told that I was pretty. Now, I was being recognized for my beauty. For one provocative photo cover and article, I only wore silk black-laced lingerie and fishnet black stockings.

Adjusting to Italian lifestyle was a process. I was a goal-driven, impatient, competitive American in the fast food generation where everything happened instantly. Life dealt me a couple of major lessons that included appreciating every moment and patience, but the

Italian lifestyle would test those lessons. In Milano, the entire town closed down for lunch from around noon until about three in the afternoon, including banks and stores. Typical Italian meals never included the word "fast;" most lasted at least two or three hours. My patience was tested even more with household problems. It could take days, usually weeks before a repairman would come to fix something. Although it seemed Italy was regressive in some respects compared to the USA, it was progressive in providing professional opportunities for female athletes.

It was unthinkable that basketball was invented in the USA and American men and women began playing the game about the same time, but there were no professional leagues for women in the USA. Yet, the Italian pro basketball league for women provided valid opportunity for a playing career.

Each team had a sponsor. GBC, an electronics company that also sponsored soccer, cycling and men's basketball, was the sponsor for our team. The women's team lost the championship the previous year and had high expectations with my arrival. Practices and training were intense. I didn't understand most of the coach's shouting and yelling. His system was built around an aggressive, physical defense and he was demanding. After a few weeks of his tactics, I was mentally, physically, and emotionally drained.

I hadn't seen Dr. Buratti for awhile. When he and Mr. Monti arrived unexpectedly after practice my heart fluttered. After we ate together, Dr. Buratti drove me home.

"You are always on my mind," he said after gently kissing me, as the small elevator doors closed.

"Ho bisogno di verderti," I replied in my newly-learned Italian, hoping he knew how much I had needed to see him.

The night before our first game, I tossed and turned thinking about the game and Dr. Buratti. I wanted to start my professional career well and needed to sleep. I wanted a good strong start with GBC. Losing wasn't an option for me.

The first game of the season was a derby, a cross-town rivalry against Sesto San Giovanni another small town on the outskirts of Milano. Sesto was one of the most storied organizations for women's basketball in Italy. When I arrived at the Palazzetto dello Sport, the arena was packed with screaming and singing fans, standing-room-only. The concrete floor covered with a rubberized material was like playing on an asphalt outdoor court. Susanna Padovani, Bianca, Mikki, Suzy Cornelli and I took the floor to start the game. We stomped Sesto 109-60. I scored 36 points. Manuel was happy, Mr. Monti was thrilled, and the fans loved us. After the game Mr. Ciocca gave me an envelope with my salary in cash as I headed off to spend the weekend in Monza.

I spent Sunday with Mr. Monti and his family and Dr. Buratti and his daughter. On the drive back to Milano, Mr. Monti talked about Dr. Buratti. He was in the middle of a divorce. I just wanted to spend more time with him. He was 42 and I was 22.

Thea Gwyn, who played in the WBL but was now playing in Cesena called me. She and Sharon, her girlfriend, were in Milano and wanted to hang out. We met up with Jimi Gatlin who played for Sesto and hung out for the weekend exploring Milano. Jimi had a car. Sharon cooked American food and we enjoyed hanging out, speaking English, talking about our crazy Italian experiences and eating American food.

My next game was against Avellino. I was warned the South was much different than the North. Avellino was a ten-hour bus ride. Some players, coaches and managers smoked, which was a big surprise for me, and we always had wine during meals, even pregame meals. After eating, Bianca and Mikki usually smoked and sometimes at halftime of games players smoked in the locker room.

I met a UK fan at our hotel in Avellino. He was from Louisville and knew me and my brother. Small world. The game against Avellino terrified me. The gym was a small inflatable tent-like structure with a locker room that consisted of a few broken wooden benches and an old, dirty shower and bathroom area without doors. The seating around the court was close to baskets and the team benches. Fans could actually reach out and touch us if they wanted to. The portable baskets were surrounded by screaming fans, causing them to shake. The crowd was extremely hostile, and many fans who couldn't get in pressed up against the doors to watch or hear the game from the outside.

We got off to a great start, which seemed to quiet the crowd, but with a few bad calls I was on the bench. I stood to cheer-on my team after scoring a basket and some fans started making obscene gestures, yelling at me and throwing coins. In fear I sat down quickly, and quietly watched the game. In the second half as our lead grew, a foul was whistled against Avellino. The crowd exploded and began throwing coins. One hit a referee in the neck, causing him to fall to the floor. The game was stopped for a few minutes. A few plays later while I was shooting a foul shot, the fans standing behind the basket grabbed it and began shaking it. Despite the interruptions and distractions, we ended up winning the game by 15 points and sprinted off the court into the nasty locker room.

Players began undressing and showering when we spotted a few men peeking in a broken window at us. Mikki ran to the window with a bottle of water and threw it on them while yelling at them. This was the first time since arriving in Italy that I actually feared for my life.

We drove all night and made it back safely to Milano early Sunday morning. Sunday evening I was scheduled to go see the Simac Milano game and meet their star player, Mike D'Antoni and famous coach Dan Peterson. Cedrick, an American player with Varese, called around noon and asked if I wanted to go out after his game. I needed some relaxation after the Avellino experience and told Cedrick to pick me up after the Simac game.

Cedrick arrived at my house with a gorgeous Italian shortly after I returned from the Simac game.

"Hello, I'm Francesco," he said to me while leaning over to give me the Italian salutary two-cheek kisses. "I'm Cedrick's teammate," he continued in his sexy accent while opening the car door.

Francesco, 6'4" with curly dark hair and light eyes kept a meticulously "five-o'clock shadow" beard. His thick Italian accent along with his GQ attire and cologne swallowed me up. This guy had to be a model. We eventually ended up at a club in Milano. Cedrick and I had a few drinks and danced for awhile. When I sat down, Francesco came over and sat close to me.

"Would you like to dance?" he asked as my heart pounded wildly.

Of course I wanted to dance with this gorgeous sexy Italian. We danced for a while then sat down to have drinks. He told me he had dated the most famous Italian female basketball player a couple of year ago. Oh no, I thought. Mikki and Bianca had warned me about him. He was a "playboy" and caused trouble on the team. He was in a serious relationship when he began seeing the American player on the same team. He couldn't be trusted.

We exchanged numbers and left the club around three in the morning.

The next evening my teammate Suzy invited me out with two friends, Walter and Alberto, who picked us up in their silver Ferrari. Alberto was about my height, had long shoulder-length curly black hair with a mustache and trimmed beard and beautiful playful eyes. His full lips, luminous smile and gregarious personality were infectious. He was from a family of nobility. We danced and laughed and enjoyed each other's company until two in the morning.

After two nights of partying, Tuesday morning practice nearly killed me. After our evening practice, Francesco called me and asked if I wanted to go out the next day. Of course I did! Wednesday could hardly go fast enough for me, but finally practice was over and at last I would get to go out alone with Francesco.

I learned that Mikki and Bianca were right about Francesco after going out with him once. We drove around for a while and talked. Francesco joked a lot. I didn't know when to believe him and when he was serious; even though I liked him, after a while he began to get irritating but I didn't know what to do. It didn't seem that he had any plans when he suggested we go to his house.

When we arrived I began to feel a little apprehensive. I was at someone's house I didn't know and in a foreign country. Francesco spoke good English but we passed the time with idle talk until he pulled me to his room and we kissed. Before I knew what happened he was on top of me, telling me how much he wanted me. I shouldn't even be in his room, I thought. As he attempted to unzip my pants I insisted that we should get to know each other better. He assured me he didn't want to have sex with me but just wanted to cuddle and that we would be more comfortable without clothes. Sex hadn't crossed my mind. I was still a virgin and wanted to wait until I met the person I would marry. Francesco tried to convince me, with no success, to have sex with him. Finally, he asked me if I would at least kiss his penis. I had never done anything like that before. I didn't even know people did that. He told me he would talk me through it but I couldn't imagine having his penis near my mouth. After a few failed attempts with me gagging, Francesco became frustrated and irritated. American girls were supposed to be less inhibited than Italian girls, he said. He had spent nearly four hours in vain. Dejected, I sat on the side of the bed putting on my bra, panties, shirt and jeans. I liked Francesco so much and I thought he liked me too but I had disappointed him and now he was upset with me. He drove me home. As I shut the door to his car and headed up the elevator lift in my apartment building I was thankful that I hadn't had sex with him. Even though I had been stupid, I was protected.

I called Francesco a few times after that night but never got a response from him.

As the weeks passed, I began seeing Albert regularly and connected with Guido Bagatta as well. I met more American and Italian players and Suzy introduced me to more of her friends. She was a tall, long-blonde-haired, blue-eyed, attractive Italian woman and very sociable. Most of her friends spoke English. Suzy introduced me to Monica also. When our coach found out that I was associating with Monica and her young male teenage basketball player friend Riccardo, he informed me that Monica was a lesbian and I shouldn't hang out with her or her friends. He wanted to know every person I was going out with from this point on. I thought he was crazy and nosey.

By November I understood Italian pro basketball. The American player was always expected to do everything and do it well. When the team played well and won, that was great, but if the team lost, the American player was usually going to be responsible for the loss. The style of play was extremely physical.

Playing professionally was not difficult for me; we were undefeated and I was the league's leading scorer in our division and second overall behind Latauyna Pollard. Manuel continued to berate me in practices and games, insisting that I was not playing defense. Off the court, I was enjoying the Italian lifestyle. Bianca invited me to her hometown near Venezia. For a young girl from Camden,

New Jersey, I was astounded with Venezia's canal system, gondolas, buildings, art, Piazza San Marco and its overall beauty. In the few months that I was in Italy, I began to realize that this would be my wonderland. I found friendship, culture, sexual awakening, independence and confidence, all while doing what I loved – playing basketball.

Although we were undefeated and I was enjoying Italy, I was ready to return home to visit Mom by Christmas. I had had a few clashes with Manuel, and Mom had helped me work them out over the phone. I wasn't sure why the coach was never satisfied with my performance and I was tired of the mental stress. My return home recharged me. Everyone loved hearing about my Italian adventures and all were impressed when I spoke in Italian. I didn't tell Mom about all the new male friends or all the clubs I had begun to frequent.

After two weeks at home, I was ready to return to Milano. I was young and adventurous and Italy allowed me to just be me; to the Italians I was a beautiful American athlete. I had never felt beautiful in my life and all the attention and opportunities seemed to build my self-esteem.

Chapter 10

Giro d'Italia

On returning to Italia I was invited to a few popular sports shows on Italian television. One was La Domenica Sportiva, the most popular. After the show, Sergio rushed me backstage behind the set.

"Buona Sera, Ms. Still, I'm so glad you could come tonight. I'm Adriano De Zan," a small elegant man standing next to Mr. Castelfranchi, the owner of GBC, said in a deep, sexy Italian accent.

Adriano couldn't have been taller than 5'5." He was impeccably dressed in a classic dark tailored designer suit and elegant tie with striking silver hair, each strand perfectly combed backward. As he reached out to kiss the back of my hand, his flirtatious asymmetrical smile revealed a small gap between his front teeth. His gold-rimmed Cartier eyeglasses and watch were perfect accessories to his polished appearance. I didn't think Adriano was handsome, especially compared to the men I had met since arriving in Italy, but everything about him, his look, smell, sound and energy was tantalizing.

As our conversation seemed to be ending, Adriano told me an off-color joke. I didn't fully understand it but chuckled. He smiled.

"May I telephone you?" Adriano asked as he gave me his phone number. "I live near you; if you need anything, please call me. I will be out of town this week but in February I want you to be my guest at the biggest cycling event in Milano, Sei Giorni di Milano."

Adriano was the most popular cycling sportscaster and one of Italy's famous sports personalities. He was a well-respected and cultured TV celebrity. He called every day while he was away and had gifts and flowers delivered to me. I couldn't stop thinking about Adriano. When he returned to Milano we began seeing each other regularly. He travelled extensively, usually with his favorite driver, Gambino. The three of us spent lots of time together. Gambino drove, Adriano sat in the passenger seat and I sat behind Adriano with my arms locked around his neck. I loved and trusted Adriano. We explored every inch of Milano. Everyone recognized him as we walked the streets arm-in-arm. We were quite a sight. People stared at us as we entered and while we dined in restaurants. Adriano would request things that weren't on the menu. Often we would have seven- or eight-course meals. He showered me with jewelry, clothes, bikes, food and books. He was a human encyclopedia of Italian and world history. Often we met for an afternoon apetitivo at the Piazza del Duomo. On Sundays we enjoyed the theater, concerts or opera. Adriano lived with his elderly mother and twenty-one-year old son, Davide, from his first marriage.

Mikki, Bianca, and other people on the team were concerned about my relationship with Adriano.

"Perche, you are so fast to go home?" Bianca questioned me one night after practice.

" I need to get home," I replied hastily hoping, Mikki would stop talking in the locker room so we could head home. Until I had met Adriano, we would eat with Mikki and her sister often after getting extra shots in after practice but that had changed.

"Valeria, attention with De Zan," Mikki chimed in. "He was also like this with another American player on our team and I believe he is married."

"I don't think so Mikki," I responded, offended, not sure if he was or wasn't.

"Sei, giovane, bella e forte...he has at least fifty year...be careful," Bianca insisted. "We have the championship to win."

"I will, I will...adesso andiamo!"

Adriano had made reservations for us at Milano's Grand Hotel after he had come back from a trip. Mikki and Bianca chastising me didn't help the stress I was already feeling. I wanted to be with him but was still a virgin. I wasn't sure how this night would turn out. Mom had always said "sex outside of marriage is wrong." Although surprised when I told him I was still a virgin, he respected my position and we shared an intimate night together talking and cuddling. They were wrong about Adriano.

We began seeing each other as often as possible and he spent many nights at my house. The nights Adriano spent at my house he arrived late after Bianca was in bed and left early before she was awake. The more I was with Adriano the more I believed that we would be together forever and if that was the case I reasoned that making love to him would be okay even if we weren't married; but for now, we had only been together for a couple of months. We may not have had sexual intercourse due to my principles, but I was a willing participant of all of Adriano's foreplay ecstasy and my new found orgasmic pleasure.

"Devo parlarti, amore," Adriano whispered one night as he gently kissed me behind my ear, moving his tongue softly and slowing down towards my breast.

"I have never loved someone as I love you," he continued as I breathed deeply with each stroke of his tongue.

My body quivered as he slid his head between my legs. "You're so wet," he moaned. "Mi fai impazzire."

I enjoyed this new feeling but was conflicted. I wanted Adriano totally but I had never done this before. As he quickened the motion of his tongue, my body convulsed in ecstasy. He moved up on top of me and pressed his lips against my gasping mouth.

"No, no...no Adriano," I softly gasped, desperately trying to reason out the situation as his body pressed against mine.

"Amore, let me pleasure you," Adriano pleaded.

*****

"Stiamo sempre cosi, AD?" I asked Adriano in the morning as we awoke, and every day after this night.

I needed to know that we would always be this way. Absorbed

in love.

"Si, Amore, yes, my love," responded Adriano. "Non ti lascio mai."

Adriano promised he would always be with me.

I loved these new sensations and being with Adriano. People from my team became concerned that I had lost my focus on basketball.

*****

The regular season ended with one loss against Vicenza heading into the playoff. We won the quarter- and semi-finals. A rematch of last year's final against Vicenza would determine the champion. We had home court advantage for the best-of-three games.

The first game was a sellout crowd with fans packed into our gym. Adriano sat with his best friend and sponsor of our team, Mr. Castelfranchi, as we beat Vicenza 66-61. We lost the second game of the finals 74-59 as thousands of screaming fans packed the Pallazetto dello Sport di Cinisello. The game was recorded to be televised later on the second most popular sports show, Mercoledi Sport on RAI national television. Adriano sat courtside.

The third game was one of the most competitive finals played in the history of the Italian women's professional league. It ended in regulation, tied 57-57. In overtime, we lost 65-63. I was devastated. After everyone cleared the locker room and gym, I sat crying, not wanting to leave. My dream of winning a championship was so close and I had let it slip away. Adriano entered the locker room and put his arms around me and sat quietly as tears streamed down my face.

"Sei sempre the best," he said as he kissed my tears.

Bianca returned to Treviso the following day. Adriano made reservations for us to go out to our favorite restaurant. He was ready for a serious relationship with me and wanted me to return for the summer if I didn't make the Olympic team. Although it concerned me that he was 52 and I was 22, I was in love. His desire to be with me made me feel valued, protected and loved.

By the time the meal was over we both could hardly contain

ourselves. In the taxi ride back to my house, I clung onto his hand, never wanting to let go. Once home, he led me to the bedroom.

We gently explored a new world for me. I ran my fingers through his hair, feeling his tongue stroke me rhythmically. I had never felt such intense physical and emotional excitement as my strong, athletic abdominal muscles tightened. His fingers tenderly explored me as he kissed the inside of my thigh. He lay on top of me. I was finally going to make love. This was scary and exciting for me. I didn't want to surrender myself to anyone. How did I know Adriano wouldn't discard me or neglect me or leave? I didn't want to allow myself to desire a relationship but I knew I wanted him as he entered me and I lost my virginity.

We spent the night in each other's arms. In the middle of the night I awoke to Adriano's deep breathing. I felt vulnerable but safe; yet a feeling of rejection never left me. I had never trusted anyone with my heart. Why would I trust Adriano to hold it? He said he loved me. He validated me. And he enjoyed being with me but I wasn't sure. I didn't want to totally let my guard down just yet. This was all new to me. I would have time to think about it while in the USA.

I flew to Kansas City for a day and then headed to the Olympic trial. I made it to the final group of players, but Pam McGee, one of the famous McGee twins from the University of Southern California, was the last selection to the 1984 USA Olympic Basketball team. I was disappointed a little but excited that now I could spend time with Adriano.

Once back in Kansas City, Dad and I clashed. It seemed my emotions were over sensitized since being intimate with Adriano. I was excited and frightened by my feelings. I wanted Dad to know the pain he caused in my life, but I couldn't express my feelings. Adriano and I wrote each other every day. Sometimes he called. He suggested I return to Italy. Mom was surprised I was returning to Italy so soon. I left Kansas City, hoping to never return.

*****

Adriano and I spent a tantalizing summer together. Sardegna was one of the most beautiful and romantic places I had ever seen. We stayed at a seaside hotel near Alghero with our suite facing the sea. Each day Adriano had us picked up by his boat and we went scuba diving and underwater fishing. During the day we played tennis, enjoyed the spa, and were pampered with manicures, pedicures, and facials. In the evenings we ate at restaurants that served local specialties. After dinner we enjoyed Mirto. It was a delicious, sweet after-dinner liquor made from berries from the island. The first night, I walked out on our room's balcony and gazed into the most star-filled sky I had ever seen. It was spectacular. I asked Adriano if we could sleep under the stellar sky. After making passionate love, we fell asleep in each other's arms and the following morning awoke to a beautiful sunrise and continued enjoying each other.

After Sardegna we began Adriano's summer schedule of bike races in Venice and Tuscany. We breezed the canals of Venice on his friend's motorboat after a race in Carole then retracted back in time to the Middle Ages for the Palio di Siena at the town's annual horse festival. The leaning tower of Pisa was more massive than any of the pictures I had seen: Montecatini's spas, massages, grottos, and medicinal spring water invigorated my body: Viareggio's fresh seafood cuisine was delectable and Florence was magical. Tuscany was definitely for lovers and I was falling for Adriano.

Back in Milano, if we weren't together he would call two or three times a day. I watched his TV broadcasts when he was away. Adriano sent postcards from all the places he visited. I kept those postcards and letters he wrote and re-read them when he wasn't around.

The basketball season began in August. Mr. Monti had convinced me to return without raising my salary even though I had had an unbelievable year and was considered MVP of the league. I wanted to stay in Milano because of Adriano and the team knew that. Basketball was becoming a job. When things weren't going well with the team I got the blame. Expectations were high for the team since we had reached the finals the previous year. Although basketball was important to me, I was consumed with Adriano.

Two months before the playoffs I scored 88 points against Roma. We won 125-53. I was ejected from the game with two minutes to play for retaliating against Roma's players after they became violent. In the national newspapers, my picture with a black eye and scratches on my neck made the headlines. Although I had a strong year, averaging 34 points and 17 rebounds per game, the team finished in fourth place. We were eliminated in the quarter-finals.

I returned to the States for June, visiting Kentucky, Missouri and New Jersey. Mom wanted me to finish my college degree but I wanted to get back to Adriano. My sister P-Nut decided to return to Italy with me. She wanted to see and experience the enchanting land that had me beaming and glowing and meet Adriano. Italy was part of my future but I believed it was also part of my past, similar to what I had felt about Japan. I had come to Italy following my passion and had found my treasure. My heart was in Italy.

*****

My love and dependency on Adriano was both invigorating and scary. While he professed and demonstrated his love for and commitment to me, many people were skeptical. I had totally fallen for him and believed that we had a unique bond. I was only 23 and that frightened me. Adriano had helped me uncover a world I had never known, emotionally and physically. We explored and experimented. Adriano loved every inch of my 6'2" body. I learned to love my body and that it was possible to be pleasured and pleasure myself. After passionate nights of exploring each other, I held onto Adriano, confessing my love. I grew up always sleeping with one of my siblings. I loved waking up with Adriano next to me. When he was not around I felt incomplete. Hopefully P-Nut would be able to help me decide if I should trust this man who had turned my life upside down.

In Italy my agent and I negotiated a contract with Sesto San Giovanni to get my last payment from Mr. Monti, and I moved out of my apartment in Milano. Sesto, promoted from Serie B to Serie A, was willing to pay me more but would expect me to carry their young and inexperienced team.

*****

P-Nut and I returned to Italy. We travelled to Firenze and Roma with Adriano before heading to Sardegna for a week. We stayed at Adriano's house near the beach in Stintino, enjoying every moment before heading back to Milano.

I was faced with contractual conflicts but eventually worked out the terms of the contract, signed it, moved to Sesto San Giovanni, picked up my last payment from Milano and fired my American agent. P-Nut returned to New Jersey and Adriano and I headed to the last stage of the Tour de France in Paris.

Adriano loved France and was the perfect tour guide. After the race, we had dinner and a show at Moulin Rouge. I was shocked at women performing topless. We returned to the hotel and then went for a late night walk down Champs-Élysées. The more I was around Adriano the more I fell in love with him. Walking down one of the most romantic, beautiful streets in the world with the person I loved...life couldn't be better.

We flew back to Milano and left for Africa. Leopard Beach Resort in Mombasa was beautiful. There we met up with Adriano's friend, an important Italian Football Federation executive, for dinner the first night. He arrived with three women: Anna, an Italian, and the other two German. Anna was much younger than Adriano's friend. The older tall blonde German woman informed us that her daughter was a former Miss Germany. After dinner we headed to the casinos. Adriano became upset when I talked with other men at the Blackjack table.

Back in our suite, Adriano told me that Anna was his friend's mistress and not his wife. His wife owned a major clothing company in Italy and was at home in Tuscany. Many married Italian men had girlfriends or mistresses.

We all spent a few more nights dining together and finished the trip with a safari. The trip to Africa expanded my view of the world. There was so much more I wanted to see and experience. The month of August was spent travelling around Italy, returning to places we had already been and visiting some new ones. Soon practices began for the start of a new season and a new adventure for me.

Sesto San Giovanni's team, GEAS, had a new sponsor, a new president, a new coach, and a new American player. There was excitement in the city about the team. I lived in a small studio apartment and was given an old mustard-yellow Fiat 127. It took me some time to adjust to living by myself and in such a tiny space. In small Italian towns, it was difficult to go unnoticed. Townspeople all knew each other's business; most everyone in the small town knew who I was and everyone knew Adriano.

I met the Grossi family who owned a bakery. They became my family. Deborah, the daughter, spent lots of time with me. I eventually introduced them to Adriano and we ate at their house often. Adriano loved the Grossi family; they were honest, hard-working, good people. We nicknamed them "La Famiglia." Giorgio worked for a manufacturing factory. Adriano always came with gifts of food, wine or other things he thought they might like.

Deborah and I became inseparable. She sometimes skipped school to hang out with me. She was a pretty girl but slightly overweight and lacked self-esteem. She confided in me that she had been sexually assaulted. Her parents adored her and spoiled her but she didn't have friends. They attended every home game and any games that were in the vicinity of Sesto.

The president of the team was married but took interest in me right away. He came to my house to "discuss team matters," as an excuse to see me. Adriano wasn't happy about this. My broken Italian didn't help explain the situation. I always had problems with the conjugation of "to like."

"Lui mi piace."

I tried to explain that the president liked me but actually said that I liked the president. The more I tried to correctly conjugate the verb, the more infuriated Adriano became. He thought I was breaking up with him.

Adriano was one of the hosts for a popular sports television program, Il Processo di Lunedi. Often we ate with his guests after the show. They included soccer players, coaches, owners, presidents, celebrities and politicians. One night I met the president of the AC Milan team, Adriano Galliani, and Silvio Berlusconi. Berlusconi had started his own media group, with private TV stations that challenged the state-owned RAI network. His was the first and only Italian commercial TV organization and associated with the Italian Socialist Party. Adriano had many political friends I met. I wasn't sure who either of these men were, but Adriano loved AC Milan. A few months after our dinner, Berlusconi bought the AC Milan team; years later he would become Italy's Prime Minister.

During the winter, Adriano and I went to his house in Trentino on the weekends for skiing and relaxing. I loved the quiet and snow-covered Alps atmosphere. When we needed to get away from confusion and wanted solitude, we headed there. Adriano loved skiing so I learned to ski. Life was perfect when it was just Adriano and me in the middle of the majestic Alps. We were away from the public eye, isolated from all the chatter and gossip about our relationship. Getting away by ourselves gave us time to reconnect.

Rumors began spreading that Adriano was seeing other women while he was away on trips. My heart ached thinking that Adriano could cheat on me, but I masqueraded my insecurity and hurt. I wanted to trust Adriano but it was becoming more difficult, especially after finding pornographic magazines at his house. Finding those magazines made me sick to my stomach. For me this was clearly a sign that he was cheating. I began going out with my friends in retaliation.

One night we ended up at Hollywood International Club while Adriano was on a trip. Hollywood was where many of the American players partied after games. In bathrooms people snorted cocaine or smoked hashish and most were willing to share. It was always packed with out-of-control partiers and a long waiting line outside. Inside, the club's deafening music blared and strobelights lit the completely-dark dance floor while dancers became crazed with techno, house and underground music. I hopped onto the dance floor after a few drinks and let the music consume me.

When Adriano returned from his trip I searched his bags.

"What are these doing in your bag?" I fumed, pulling out a strand of condoms from a zippered pocket. "Noi non usiamo questi!"

The porn magazines in his bag were bad enough but finding the condoms set me in a fit. Adriano and I didn't use condoms.

"Che schifo! You're sick! You make me sick!!! Basta! Basta!

I retreated as Adriano stepped towards me to explain.

"Ma, it does not mean a thing amore...perche..."

"Tutti sanno...everyone, everyone knows...sono stupida!

"Ma, no...you must calm down... e niente... calma ti...dai...it is nothing."

His denial made me more enraged.

I needed Christmas break. Although I couldn't talk to Mom about what was happening in my personal life, at least I could curl up with her at night and feel like her baby. Mom and Dad had moved to a small isolated town in Missouri near Barry. She would do anything for Barry but missed being in New Jersey around family and friends.

As I was going through customs at Malpensa, one of the guards searched my bags. I had become the highest paid female player in Italy and usually transported my dollars back to the states, and I was carrying too many dollars. The custom patrol confiscated all the dollars I had saved from the beginning of the season. I was furious. I would probably never see my hard-earned money again. I called Adriano. He assured me that he would take care of it once I returned.

*****

When I returned Adriano had arranged for me to meet with his attorney. The offices were in the center of Milano in a historic building on the mezzanine floor overlooking a meticulous garden and inner courtyard. The elegant vintage 18th century building and landscaping were spectacular. I had met Adriano's attorney once before. He was a distinguished, stout, middle-age man with graying hair. I was shocked when a young, tall, gorgeous, well-groomed, model-like man entered the room and introduced himself to Adriano.

"Buon giorno, Senor Dezan, sono Stefano Maci, molto piacere conoscerla," he greeted Adriano in formal Italian.

The handsome Italian with dark sexy eyes and short-cropped jet-black hair, high cheekbones, Roman nose and chiseled jaw line couldn't have been more than thirty years old.

"Hello Ms. Still, it is very nice to meet you," Mr. Maci addressed me in a sexy Italian accent.

Our eyes locked briefly as his vibrations engulfed me as he shook my hand. Yes, he was beautiful. Mr. Maci, a new partner in the firm, turned to Adriano again to explain that he would be assisting me in recouping my money from Italian customs.

For the next few weeks Stefano and I met regularly until we were able to recoup my money. Not only was he good-looking; he was smart and funny. He explained to me that everyone in his office warned him not to get involved with me personally because of Adriano's association with the law firm, but we already knew that that would be impossible. After my issue with Italian customs was resolved we began seeing each other.

Despite all the off-court escapades and drama, I had an impressive season with Sesto. The team finished in fourth place heading into the 1986 playoffs. This was more than anyone expected. I was again the top player in Italy and Sesto wanted me back. Regardless of the outcome of the playoffs, I had secured another season with them. This year would be tricky for me in terms of contracts because I didn't have an agent.

We won the first round of the playoffs and faced Vicenza in the semi-finals. Vicenza had won the last four championships and was favored to win this year. We lost game one at Vicenza. In the second game, at Sesto, the gym was packed with screaming fans hoping for an upset. After six minutes we were down by only four points and making a strong comeback when I received the ball at half-court and turned to score on a fastbreak.

Catarina Pollini, the league's top Italian player, was the last line of defense standing at half-court as I charged forward to score. I faked one way and sidestepped her as she extended her arms with a clinched fist and connected with my face. I collapsed to the floor. The crowd initially erupted shouting at Pollini and the referees but silence filled the gym as I lay unconscious at half-court. An ambulance took me to Sesto's local hospital where I was transferred to one of Milano's major hospitals. I stayed overnight but in the morning, with my eye swollen shut, I called a taxi, left the hospital, went home, packed and left for Kansas City. We had lost the game 62-72. My mysterious "escape" from the Milano hospital without permission made national headlines.

Mom was horrified when she met me at the airport with my discolored and disfigured face and swollen-shut eye. She feared I had suffered permanent damage. It was time I returned to the States and stop putting myself in danger. I hadn't told her I was planning on changing my nationality and becoming an Italian citizen. Against her wishes, I returned in July at Adriano's request for me to go to the Tour de France with him. I watched as American Greg LeMond became the first non-European professional cyclist to win the Tour de France.

After the Tour de France, Adriano and I, along with his son Davide, left for Stintino. By the end of the summer, I bought a Porsche 911 Targa and Adriano and I began renovating an apartment in Milano and a farm house outside of Milano.

There were major changes when the basketball season started. Sesto had a new president, a new sponsor and a new coach. I signed a six-figure contract including bonuses and incentives, the best since I had been in Italy. Seven games into the season we were in first place in the league and I was the league's leading scorer, averaging over 30 points a game.

Basketball was going well but my personal life continued to become more complicated. I continued to have doubts about Adriano. I loved him but I didn't know how to make our relationship work.

My younger sister Jackie was also having problems in her marriage. I rented an apartment for her and her daughter, my Goddaughter, Hannah, in Sesto for a month. With Adriano travelling so much we began spending time with Davide, who was only a year younger than me, going to jazz clubs and dancing.

For Christmas I was surprised with a Giant Schnauzer puppy from Stefano. I named the puppy Benjamin. I loved animals and he thought I was lonely and confused. Stefano couldn't understand why I was still with Adriano. It seemed the more uncommitted and unattached Adriano was, the more I was attracted to him. I had met many available men but I couldn't think of not being with Adriano.

The season ended with us losing to Vicenza in the semifinals: another season of getting close to a championship but never winning one.

A few weeks later Davide and I recorded "Inside of Me," a song I had written. We tried to get a recording contract before I returned to the States with Deborah. Late summer, still waiting for a record label, Adriano and I vacationed at Gabbice Mare on the Adriatic Sea.

It was near an area famous for its elaborate mega discothèques that included swimming pools, Roman gladiators, barely-dressed performers and fireworks. We spent lots of time with Adriano's friends. One night we went to an invite-only outdoor jazz performance at a castle. The pianist was Romano Mussolini, the son of Italian fascist dictator Benito Mussolini. I met and talked with Romano after the concert even though I barely knew who he was. Adriano had told me the story of Mussolini, Il Duce, when we were in Milano standing in Piazziale Loreto where he was shot, kicked and spat upon then hung upside down on meat hooks from a gas station. Imagine meeting Mussolini's own son! He was a talented pianist. The evening was mesmerizing.

David, Adriano and I ended the summer in Stintino with Benjamin.

*****

I held out of preseason training for a third season with Sesto while negotiating the terms of my contract. Magenta offered me more money and a recording deal but Sesto owned my nulla osta, my "rights." Teams owned players' rights for trade and were compensated for players. Sesto eventually offered me more money and agreed to give me my "rights" for trade if I signed with them. This was the first time a player would have ownership of her "rights." This would also be the first year each team was allowed two foreign players. I accepted the offer, had Stefano write up the contract, signed it and began practicing.

The Communist national newspaper, L'Unita, asked me to write a weekly guest column on the women's professional league for the entirety of the season. The league was attracting the best women basketball players in the world and fan support had increased but there was still little media coverage and no television exposure. When we craved media attention out first year at UK, I never thought that one day I would be playing professionally and writing about the game I loved so much.

In our first preseason tournament in Ancona the big news was that LaTaunya Pollard was pregnant. This was always a concern for teams and players. Teams even included terms in contracts that voided a contract in cases of pregnancy.

We started the season with four losses. Losing was dreadful but some of the on-court drama was comical. Cynthia Cooper, who had played for the University of Southern Cal, was one of the best players in the Italian league. "Coop" played with Parma and was noted for her hot-tempered tactics, threatening and cussing out whoever irritated her, regardless of whether it was an opponent, her own teammate, a coach, or management. During our game against Parma she knocked out one of our players after my teammate threw a ball at her face during a dead-ball situation, and then ran. Watching Coop chase down my teammate across the court and deliver an Ali-like jab for the KO became a story we re-told when we needed a laugh. It wasn't funny when it happened but we always got a laugh retelling the episode.

A serious problem for the league was American players leaving before the end of the season. Some were homesick and returned home. Some opted for Japan. The Japanese season was much shorter and teams paid much better than most Italian ones.

The league's lack of respect for its players and their contracts was also a problem. Some teams cut players to save money once they knew the team would not qualify for the playoffs or because they wanted to bring in a new player. Some players left without being paid.

During a practice at the beginning of March, I broke my hand. Surgery was done under local, ineffective anesthesia; it was a nightmare. I cried during the entire agonizing procedure. The sound of the drill, the feel of the pin being inserted into my bone and not being completely numbed was torture. After the surgery I lay on La Famiglia's couch and suffered in pain.

I begged the team to allow me to go home so I could have my hand examined by an American doctor. With the possibility of going to the playoffs the team wanted me to return before two weeks.

Mom, as usual, remained calm when she picked me up from the airport on a Saturday. I was scheduled to see a KC Chief's team doctor on Monday. I returned every year from Italy with a new injury. When I exited the gate of the Kansas City airport terminal with a pin protruding out of my hand that was wrapped like a mummy for protection, Mom could only hug me and shake her head. I had to be careful not to hit the pin.

"Valerie, maybe it's time for you to come home permanently. You're getting a little old for this, don't you think?" She snarled. She knew my dream and passion and had supported me but her patience was "wearing thin," as she would say.

Monday the doctor examined me and scheduled another appointment the following week before I left for Italy. P-Nut flew in from New Jersey the following day. She unpacked her bags and we sat at Mom's kitchen table talking when the phone rang. It was Eric, my oldest sister's husband.

"Bonnie's in the ICU," he worriedly blurted out without saying hello and unable to hide his panic.

She was bleeding internally and in critical condition. They had two young children. Rodney was nine years old and Theresa only seven. Bonnie had been an elementary teacher for years but quit after she had her children so she could be a stay-at-home mom.

P-Nut and I booked the next flight to New Jersey. Mom would head to New Jersey once I returned to Italy. My broken hand was no longer important.

My heart dropped as we entered the isolated ICU room, with Bonnie bloated beyond recognition. She was attached to a myriad of machines and was receiving blood and IVs. P-Nut and I spoke with her briefly, assuring her we would be taking care of Rodney and Theresa. They had found her on the bathroom floor unresponsive. As we walked outside her room we collapsed in each other's arms and sobbed.

The initial diagnosis was that she had had a molar pregnancy and was losing blood, but needed surgery to determine the source of the bleeding.

Sesto had begun calling me to confirm my return flight to Italy even though they were aware of Bonnie's critical condition. They wanted me back.

Bonnie had exploratory surgery. Eric's call informing us that the surgery was successful left me with an intense joy I had never felt before. P-Nut and I grabbed each other, jumping up and down ecstatically while crying. I flew back to Kansas City that evening happy that Bonnie was recovering.

When Mom and I received the call from Eric the next morning that Bonnie had died in the middle of the night we were distraught. March 28 would never be the same. Mom showed no outward signs of emotion, so I internalized my pain and suppressed my emotion. It had to be unbearable for Mom that she would not see her young daughter alive again. Mom flew to New Jersey for the funeral while I prepared to return to Italy.

On March 30th, I flew over New Jersey on my flight from Kansas City to Italy as my sister was being laid to rest. As my plane headed out across the Atlantic Ocean, thoughts of Bonnie flooded my mind. Pangs of guilt grew stronger as I realized I should have stayed for her funeral.

Back in Italy, I sat in my small studio apartment alone, sad, and confused. Sesto didn't qualify for the play-off. Bonnie was dead. I missed her funeral. Basketball over life? Who was I? How did I end up on this path? I over-analyzed Bonnie's death. A young, healthy thirty-six-year-old woman should not be dead. Someone had to be at fault. I needed answers to calm the pain I was suppressing.

Less than a month after her death, she came to me in a dream. She wanted a memorial. All the sisters gathered in a room as she informed us she didn't need help now and we should go on with our lives. A month later I saw Bonnie walking toward me in a hallway in my dream. I touched her as she entered a room where my siblings and I sat. Her eyes were crystal blue, but became paler as she spoke. She said the only discomfort she had was the tubes that were placed in her.

While awake I went through the motions of everyday life, but in my sleep I enjoyed the interactions with Bonnie in my dreams.

Chapter 11

"It's Not Your Time to Go"

My interactions with Sesto became strategic and tense. They did not want to trade me but playing for Sesto was not an option for me after my sister's death. The two teams I was most interested in were Como and Magenta. Pool Comense was one of the best organizations to play for in terms of contract, playing, and management. Magenta's president, Massimo Porrati, a young businessman who owned a women's clothing manufacturer, was willing to do whatever needed to get the players he wanted. He was a fun-loving, chain smoker with a silver Porsche. His offer included procuring a recording producer and topping any offer Como made.

I returned to Stintino with Adriano and P-Nut hoping to relax, grieving Bonnie's death and needing to fix my relationship with him. Normally, Stintino was our paradise; instead there was tension between us. P-Nut and I enjoyed sunrises on the beach, explored and hiked and sunbathed in the nude at a secluded spot. At night we drank more than we should.

One night I dreamed of Bonnie. She told me that they had found a cure for her and I shouldn't worry. She wanted me to walk closer to her. The dream was comforting and I could feel her calming presence as I awoke. I enjoyed that peace.

Back in Milano, I signed a contract with Magenta and moved

into a two-bedroom apartment there. Porrati introduced me to Marcello, a local producer with a recording studio. We began working on my first single. Marcello wrote the music and I wrote English lyrics. P-Nut suggested I use the name Ishnar for my singing career. She believed that was my name from another life.

I was determined to fix my relationship with Adriano, so we headed to Stintino by ourselves. It was a difficult, painful week. Our relationship was beyond repair. We decided to give each other space. My heart ached. I did what I had always done since I was a child when I was hurt or in pain; I put on a strong facade, an impenetrable exterior, and pretended all was well. When I was a child, after Mom disciplined us, she would never allow us to cry. It was difficult initially but after constantly being hurt and told not to cry, it had become second nature to me. I no longer needed someone else to abuse me and discard my feelings; I did it to myself.

I met a young, striking model in Magenta and began drinking more. One night he introduced me to smoking cocaine. Putting cocaine in cigarettes made my lips tingle and then go numb. The high was immediate, short, but intense. When I wanted to escape my inner madness, the numbness and tingling sensation of my lips and the high left us both giggling and problem-free. If I couldn't cry outwardly, at least I could silence the hurting child inside by deadening her feelings and voice. Normally, basketball pacified me but Sesto had traded my nulla osta to Faenza, making it impossible for me to play for Magenta even though I had signed a contract with them. Magenta started preseason without me. That gave me more reason to drink and smoke cocaine. Recording and preparing for the release of my first single distracted me, but I loved playing basketball. I was at the peak of my career but wouldn't be playing. Bonnie's death overwhelmed me at times, Faenza would not release me, and Adriano and I had disconnected.

I was ashamed to talk to Mom about what was going on. I wasn't in control.

Marcello released my first single, "M.U.S.I.C." under the name "Ishnar." While promoting it in Roma, I was asked to be a TV analyst for the 1988 Summer Olympic men's basketball semi-finals, USA against USSR. The Russians beat the Americans by six points.

After this loss, NBA players were allowed to play in the Olympics. Watching the women win the gold medal was bittersweet. I had missed the tryouts with a broken hand.

Stefano and I held a press conference in October announcing my forced retirement. I was featured in newspaper articles and on magazine covers, and on national television shows. My photo on Italy's most-read basketball magazine's cover, topless in cycling racing shorts with only a basketball and my arms covering my breast, garnered needed attention for the league but negative publicity. Women's basketball was growing, I was the most popular player in the league, and now because of the scandal with Sesto, I would not be playing. After Panorama, an Italian news magazine and its most prominent weekly, featured me in a story, I began receiving more requests for appearances and interviews. Insonnia, a club in Pavia invited me to be one of their weekly performers. The manager introduced me to sniffing cocaine.

In November, Domenica In, a popular TV show, contacted me to perform. Roberto D'Agostino was the witty and colorful host of the show, a big-time celebrity. I was shocked to see the black curly-haired Roman with big designer black-rimmed stylish glasses at my dressing room door after the show. He wanted to see me while I was in Roma. We exchanged numbers and kissed. We partied the following night at his friend's massive Roman villa with drugs freely available.

By the end of November, Faenza finally released me; now I could officially play for Magenta. I played my first game with Magenta at Como. We won 80-78. I scored 28 points. The debate continued in the league as to whether I should have been allowed to play for Magenta. Regardless of the controversy and my drug use, I played well and continued to be a dominant player, and the most celebrated one.

P-Nut returned after a short break in the USA. Jackie arrived in early December with her son Levin. She was having problems with Neal. In mid-December he arrived with their daughter Hannah. I rented an apartment for them. Adriano and Davide came over to visit on Christmas eve. I pretended everything was good but was keeping secrets from everyone now.

My dreams of Bonnie became more frequent. They were vivid,

powerful, colorful and admonitory. It was time to stop destroying my life with drugs. I became friends with Andrea, one of the young players from the boy's team that practiced against us. Andy and I became inseparable. He was 16 years old and I was 27. The adorable, quiet 6'7" teenager with big light-brown eyes and short, spiked, blonde hair was extremely shy. He didn't talk much but we enjoyed being together. I just needed a safe place. Someone I could trust. Andy was uncomplicated, pure and loving. He was gentle, laid back and unassuming. Our love was intense but innocent.

I was named MVP of the All-Star game in Firenze and met Gerry Scotti. He was a well-known TV presenter and politician. Many speculated that he would become the next president of the league in hopes that he would resurrect the women's league. A crew from ABC television taped interviews with American players and took footage of the game. This was the first time ABC had been in Italy to cover women's basketball.

After the season, Adriano and I spent nearly a week together for the Paris-Roubaix bike race. I headed back to the States still confused about our relationship.

While I was staying with Jackie in Lexington, Neal came over and began a confrontation with Jackie about the children. I threatened to call the police as he continued his rage and came toward me. I was strong and athletic and never backed down from anyone. I braced myself in a fighting stance thinking I could defend Jackie. Neal's force hit me so hard, I knew that I was in trouble. I crouched my arms in front of my face trying to protect myself as he continued to punch me. I slumped to the floor, losing control of my legs and bladder, wetting my pants but still covering my face. I'm going to die, I thought with Neal straddled over me and pummeling my head. Jackie jumped on him from behind with her arms around his neck.

"Stop...stop...you'll kill her, stop....stop...Neal...let her go!!"

Neal let up, and then grabbed Hannah and Levin and headed out the door.

"Help, Val...he's got the children," Jackie yelled at me as she headed out the front door.

Still dazed, I stumbled to the front door in time to see Jackie in the middle of the street as Neal's truck came charging toward her.

Everything seemed to be happening so fast, yet still in slow motion as I pushed myself to run to the street. I snatched her out of his path as the truck sped away. Shaken and dazed I called the police against Jackie's wishes. An ambulance came and took me to the hospital.

"He tried to kill me, he could have killed me," I continued to mumble to the EMT.

Neal was later arrested and put in jail for the night. I called Barry to tell him what had happened. Barry and Sparky arrived the next day. Jackie decided not to press charges. Frightened, I returned to Missouri with Barry and Sparky.

It seemed no matter where I was, I was not able to find peace. Adriano called. He wanted me to return to Italy. It seemed that he always knew when I needed him. I returned to Magenta in July hoping to find peace. I began to fast and meditate. At the end of the summer Adriano and I returned to Stintino before heading to the Adriatic coast. Rimini, Riccione and Cattolica were famous for their elaborate discotheques. I loved to dance. Byblos, Baia Imperiale and Peter Pan were just a distraction for me and my quest to find inner peace.

*****

Magenta started the 1989-90 season replacing the other American player with Theresa "Spoon" Witherspoon, a guard from Louisiana Tech who had won the1988 NCAA championship. She was a spitfire on the court, never backing down from a challenge and fun to be around off the court.

Spoon and I provided our fans with an exciting brand of basketball. We had a fun team with great team chemistry and spent lots of time together off the court partying. In November after going out to a Mexican restaurant in Milano all together, I got smashed drinking "Tequila boom-booms" until early in the morning. My teammates dropped me off at home drunk. I had locked myself out of my house and tried to climb up to my second-floor apartment balcony only to fall and nearly impale myself on the wrought iron fencing around the building. I ended up in the hospital after puncturing my butt. I was the lead story and made the front page of the local newspaper along

▲ Me as a baby

▲ Front step of
813 Ferry Ave with Gary,
Mom and Jackie

▲ Mom, Me and Jackie circa 1969

(1848 - 1919)
Cousin Caroline Still,
William Still's oldest
daughter and one of the
first African American
female physicians in
Philadelphia ▶

died April 23, 1857
▲ Great-great-great
grandmother Charity
(formerly Sidney)

(1812 - 1882)
▲ Great-great grandfa-
ther Dr. James Still

(1821 - 1902)
▲ Great-great grand-
uncle William Still:
named "father of the
Underground Railroad"
in his obituary

Brothers Barry (Art), Dennis, Gary and me with cousin Shemiko at grandma and grandpa Still's house ▶

Oldest brother Sparky's (James) wedding, only one missing...me ▼

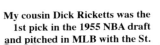

(1801 - 1868)
◀ Great-great granduncle Peter Still was sold to a man named John Fisher in Lexington KY circa 1809.
His biography "The Kidnapped and the Ransomed" was published in 1856

My cousin Dick Ricketts was the 1st pick in the 1955 NBA draft and pitched in MLB with the St.

Senior at Cherry Hill HS East

Freshman at UK

Grandma & Grandpa Still

▲ Mom Gwendolyn Alice Ricketts Palmyra High School 1949 yearbook picture

▲ Dad James Fleming Still: US Army mid 1940s

▲ Best friend Bonnie Hutton and I after a UK game in 1982

1982 NCAA SEC Championship in Lexington, KY

▲ Ottie Feedback wearing my USA National Team warm up jacket after his heart attack

▲ Simmons Family circa 1984 when I first met them

▲ Aaron and I during his 1st year at USNA

▲ * UK vs Charleston Dec. 19, 1982

* 1980 Lady Kat Invitational

* UK 1982

▲ Rob attending Aaron's graduation from the Naval Academy Prep School in Rhode Island

Adriano Dezan and I in 1991

▲ In 2001 visiting the Grossi Family after Adriano's death

◄ Stefano Maci and I: 1988 press conference announcing my forced retirement

▲ Mom & Dad

▲ Mentor and friend Dr. Charles L. Blockson

▲ Mom picking out the car I won for the 1997 ABL championship MVP

▲ Signing with the ABL in the fall of 1996 with Head coach and General Manager Brian Agler

▲ With Jackie Joyner-Kersee during a game against the Richmond Rage the inaugural ABL season

▲ Tipoff of the 1998 ABL championship series with the Long Beach Stingrays

WNBA 1999 Washington Mystics▼

▲ **Featured in an Italian magazine

▲ **Italian Basketball Magazine Super Basket

Promotion for release of my first single, M.U.S.I.C. ▼

▲ NAPS Graduation Ball in RI, Aaron with Captain Monagle and Uncle Barry (Art)

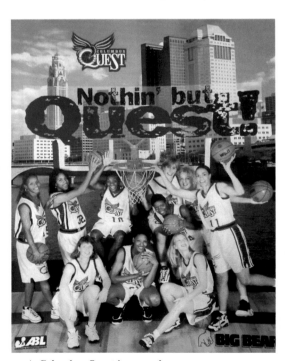

▲ Columbus Quest inaugural season program cover

▲ Mom and I a year before her death

▲ Aaron and John Schultz, childhood best friends,
born one day a part, my twin sons

▲ 2014 Aaron's graduation from VFMA

▲ 2016 visiting my Italian sister
Deborah Grossi in Milano

▲ Autographed Photo in Italy

◄ 2012 Women's Hall of Fame with legendary coaches Billie Moore and Pat Head Summitt

▲ 1997 Official White House picture: The first professional women's team honored, the ABL' Columbus Quest, visits with Hilary Clinton

▲ Best friends Sue Rogers and Cathy Shultz.

▲ Playing in the R. Williams Jones Cup with USA National team

▲With my Godfather Dr. Clarence B. Jones

Dennis and Aaron

▲First year in Italy with GBC Milano

▲ 2016 spending time with Zio Maurizio at Hotel Noris in Schio

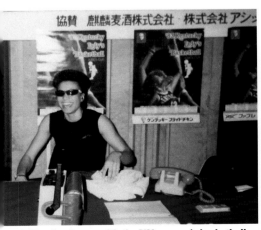

▲ Touring Japan with the UK women's basketball team in the 1980s

▲ Mom's brother Kenny, Aaron and myself

Rob, Aaron and myself ▼

▲ Aaron and I

▲ Mom visiting me in Italy 1991

▲Me with Hall of Famers Alex "A-Rod" Rodriguez and Nikki McCray

Aaron, me and Tubby Smith,
UK Jersey retire ▼

▲ Adriano and me at Stintino

▲ Visiting my great-great- grandfather's property that is now an historic site in New Jersey

▲ The Ohio State University graduation in 2007

Mom's Got Game Promo

A salute to the Seniors of '83

V.A.L

LEA

P.J.

They came to Kentucky in 1979, a trio of young girls who shared a common love for basketball. Their goals were high, but reasonable. None had enjoyed phenomenal success in high school. None were famous. They all hoped to win, but a 13-16 record for the Lady Kats the year before kept them from expecting too much too soon.

But much did happen. And soon, too. Only nine games into their collegiate careers, Val, Lea and PJ led the unranked Lady Kats to a stunning 97-78 victory over 7th-ranked Rutgers. That vaulted Kentucky into the Top 20. The Lady Kats have been there ever since. Now Kentucky is one of the most feared programs in the nation. This is a tribute to our seniors, who are a major reason Lady Kat basketball is what it is today.

We will never forget Valerie, the first Lady Kat All-American. She was our beautiful, gracious star, who will forever be remembered as one of the all-time greats in the game.

And PJ, possibly the most exciting individual to ever play the game. For four years she made us go. And go and go and go. She may have been the best-kept secret in America.

And finally, Lea, Lexington's own. Her contributions to the team's success, as well as to its image off the court, may have had more impact than any other single person's.

Together, the three combined for some of the most memorable plays in UK basketball history. So here's to Val, PJ and Lea. We'll always remember them.

There will never be another group like them.

◄ * Concept, design and photographs by Tom Moran

▲ Dr. James Still Medical Office and Residence in 1886

▲ Myself with Davide Dezan

▲ 1994 playing for Schio last Italian team

◀ Aaron and I cut down the nets after the historic 1st ABL Championship

▼ 2010 living in Kansas close to Dennis

First Italian Championship series with GBC ▶

2012 Time Warner Cable TV Show Our Season

▲ My son Aaron

Italian All-Star Game

◀ Post game interviews ▼

▲ Best friend Tammy Robb at UK
football game

*University of Kentucky Special Collections
**J and J Company SRL Superbasket / Giganti del Basket

GiGANTI
DEL BASKET
I PALAZZI DEL DUEMILA

ANNO XXIII - N. 17 (283) - 15 OTTOBRE 1988 - L. 4.000 - QUINDICINALE - Spedizione in abb. post. Gr. II

DONNE
Parte
il campionato
manca
la Still

OLAJUWON:
Il n. 1
sono io

SERIE B
Al via
aspettando
lo straniero

with a big photo of me as the team struggled to win. The headline, "Valerie Still rischia una fine atroce." I had risked a terrible ending.

At the end of the season, Magenta decided to drop to A2 and I signed a lucrative contract with Como, which included a beautiful flat in a massive old villa on a mountainside overlooking Lake Como.

*****

Since Bonnie's death, Mom and Dad seemed to be getting along better. My visit home included seeing a holistic practitioner, getting colonics, fasting, doing iridology and reflexology, being with nature, training for the season by running the hills and having good talks with Mom and Dad. While I was getting myself together physically and mentally, Dad and I began getting to know each other better. He surprised me with a basket of fruits and roses delivered to me for my birthday. I hugged him tightly and told him how much I loved him before leaving for New Jersey.

P-Nut, Jackie and her two children returned to Europe with me to visit Austria. We were going to the Grail Foundation for their "Sealing," an initiation ritual for members making a personal commitment to adhere to the principles of the Grail Message. The mountains of Tirol were magical. We enjoyed hiking and the tranquility of the environment. P-Nut no longer wanted to be called P-Nut but Francina and Jackie no longer wanted to be called Jackie but Jacqueline.

Como was heavily favored to win the championship and also do well in the European Cup, La Coppa Ronchetti. Olympic gold medalist and two-time NCAA champion with Tennessee, Bridgette Gordon would be my American teammate. The big questions were, did Como have too many prima donnas and could we all get along. Those questions were answered in our first game with a 102-70 win against Schio at home.

The Coppa Ronchetti started at the end of October. We played teams from Spain, France Moscow and Milano. Our first game was against CBN Pamplona. Bridgette and I watched televised bullfights in our hotel room in disbelief. We beat Pamplona 102-82 and started league play strong with a 121-117 victory at Schio followed by wins against Ancona and Parma before playing Spartak Moscow at home in the Coppa Ronchetti. We beat Spartak 88-66.

Being in Como was good for me. I still partied and got to Milano whenever possible but I had a goal. I was on a mission to win a championship. I continued to get publicity off the court and requests for appearances on TV shows and radio interviews. Gerry Scotti, now president of the league and also a member of the Italian Parliament, invited me to be one of the guest celebrities on Il Gioco di 9, a game show he hosted similar to Hollywood Squares in the USA.

Mom came to Italy in December. Everyone was shocked she had travelled that far to see me. We had an awesome time, sightseeing, shopping, and hanging out with my neighbors, Italian teacher, La Famiglia, and Adriano. We didn't talk about my relationship with him. After she left I found sexually-explicit Polaroid pictures of Adriano with two girls. I was devastated. I never told him about finding the pictures but when I returned home I burned all his letters and postcards to me. Our dysfunctional relationship was over.

Early February we travelled to Russia to play Spartak. I couldn't believe I was in the USSR. While visiting the city, one of our players was surrounded by a group of young gypsies. They snatched her purse and ran, passing the purse to each other. I took off and caught the one who ended up with her purse; before I could do anything the police honed in quickly, beating the guy and dragging him away. We watched the impressive changing of the guards in breathtaking Red Square. I made friends with a couple of the Russian players. After shopping for an ushanka and matryoshka dolls for me, we visited their home. We advanced to the semi-finals of La Coppa Ronchetti. One step closer to winning a championship.

March was the start of the semi-finals for La Coppa Ronchetti. We played Dorna Valencia with Kym Hampton as their American player. We lost in Spain 70-57. In order to advance to the finals we would have to beat them by at least 14 points at home. We beat them soundly, 73-56 at home to advance to the finals. We lost the finals to Milano despite my 26 points and 17 rebounds in the final game; now we had to recuperate and pursue the league championship.

The league play-offs began at the beginning of April. We had slipped to second place in the final regular season rankings behind Cesena. We played Pistoia in the quarter-finals, beating them in two games. The semi-finals against Bari would be difficult. Not only did Bari have a scoring machine in Lataunya Pollard but they also had the biggest player in the league, Razija Mujanovic, a 6'6" massive Yugoslavian player. She wasn't agile and didn't run well but she was a big body with a soft-touch shot and could alter the shot of anyone who got close to the basket. We beat Bari in the first game at home, 97-59. I led all scorers with 32 points, with the local newpaper's headlines, "Still perfetta." Our next game was one week later. Usually we would fly to Bari with it being far south but the team decided we would take the long train ride instead.

Halfway through the trip, my teammates informed me that a "cute" guy had boarded the train and was sitting in another compartment. I snuck a peep. Wow! They were right. He was bellissimo; tall, blonde, dreamy blue eyes, drop-dead gorgeous with neatly trimmed facial hair. Bridgette asked him to sit with us.

"Roberto Battoia," he held out his hand introducing himself as he sat right next to me. "Molto piacere." Ghost was my favorite movie and I was speechless looking at this Patrick Swayze look-alike.

When his stop came, he shook my hand and said good bye.

We beat Bari 90-77 and advanced to the finals. Two days later after returning to Como, Roberto called me at eight in the morning. My heart sang. We talked for a long time and from that day on we talked every day. He was sensitive, intuitive, spiritual, gentle and in tune with himself. He was a basketball player also, playing in southern Italy.

The finals began April 28th. It would be a rematch of the previous year's finals – Como versus Cesena. We beat Cesena at home, 83-68, the first game of the finals. I led all scorers with 24 points. The next two games would be at Cesena. May 2nd we lost the second game of the series 77-64. Cesena's Clarissa Davis led all scorers with 27. Even though I was battling the flu, I led Como with 21 points. Roberto came to the game. I was able to see him for about 15 minutes before we hopped on the bus and returned to Como. We lost the game but I was excited to see Roberto.

Three days later we returned to Cesena for Game 3 of the series. In front of nearly 5,000 fans, we started the game with a new starting five: three guards, Bridgette and me. Bridgette hadn't played well in the two previous games but she came out like a person on a mission. At halftime we led, 43-38. We came out cold for the second half and was whistled for four fouls in the first minute and a half. After regrouping we added to our lead, 66-52. The last few minutes of the game all hell broke loose. With less than a minute and a half to play, we were up 81-72 when the crowd erupted and began throwing coins. The situation got so bad the referees sent both teams to the locker rooms and ended the game. We won 81-72. I was one game away from finally winning a championship.

On May 8th in front of over 5,000 raging fans, I finally won a championship. We beat Cesena 73-68 at home. Two days later, the team had already announced in the local newspaper that they would be replacing me with Daedra Charles from Tennessee. The headline "Alla sera campioni, alla mattina leoni: Un futuro di voci: un nuovo tecnico (Corno) e una compagna di Gordon (Charles)." I was shocked. Bruce Levy my former agent was thanked for providing the new American. Winning the championship was fantastic but the fact that the team had already decided to replace me was hurtful and smothered the thrill. Finding out about it in the newspaper was insensitive and cruel but this was professional sports.

Roberto came to celebrate my championship and birthday before I left for the States. We enjoyed Como and Switzerland and visiting with La Famiglia in Milano. Although our physical and sexual attraction was strong, we connected on a more profound spiritual level. Roberto calmed me. He was secure in himself and provided a tranquil atmosphere for me. After a week with him I headed back to Kansas City and then New Jersey.

While in New Jersey, Francina and I began searching for a house for Mom. She wanted to return to New Jersey so she could take care of her aging, sick mother. After a few weeks we found the perfect sunny three-bedroom house with a basement and a big fenced-in backyard with a swimming pool. It was in the town where Mom had gone to high school and in a quaint neighborhood on a cul-de-sac.

I also bought a car, my first in the USA, a 1978 classic 450SL red Mercedes Benz convertible, and shipped it to Italy.

In July I returned to negotiate a contract with my new team, Alzate Brianza. It was my best contract ever, making me the highest-paid player in Italy. Although I had a Porsche and Mercedes, the team provided me with a luxury Audi sedan. They also signed Vickie Orr, a 6'3" post player who was the 1988 SEC Player of the Year with Auburn.

The day after signing my unbelievable contract, Roberto and I, along with Benjamin drove to his home town, Udine, to meet his family. We vacationed on the Adriatic coast for a week. Many evenings we went to the beach to enjoy the sunset. Roberto was gentle, kind and giving as a lover. Each night was paradise filled with captivating and stimulating dialogue, tantalizing foreplay, passionate love making, wild, passionate, euphoric sex and affectionate after-sex affirmations until we fell blissfully asleep intertwined. Throughout the night we enjoyed each other and regardless of what was planned for the following day, the night was always limitless for our pleasure. Nothing was off limits for us. Our nights were times I was able to forget the world, release and enjoy. He had a positive energy force and a philosophy of life that was passionate, engaging and enlightening. He wrote me poetry.

>Buttare via tutti i pensieri per il tuo sorriso
>Canta la gioia di ogni momento della vita condivisa
>Guarda un uccello per capire che la libertà 'e' amore per
>tutto cio 'che vi circonda.

After the week was over, Roberto and I returned to Como for a week. Before he left, I bought commitment rings for him and me.

I returned to the States and closed on the house in New Jersey. This would be a homecoming for Mom and Dad. Dad was having medical treatments, and would arrive shortly after Mom. Although I didn't get to enjoy all the fun and excitement of Mom's return to New Jersey, I knew this was a significant time for her and I was happy she would be back in her own environment. It wasn't long before she moved Grandma in with her as well.

Through all our conflict and dysfunction, the family had a foundation of love and now it seemed to be manifesting in a healthy way.

We had learned some unhealthy lessons about love from Mom's and Dad's relationship but we also learned that marriage meant staying together and working out issues, even those that seemed insurmountable. Regardless of disagreements, clashes and conflict, family was most important and we could work through anything as a family.

*****

Things were going well when I received a call from Mom in October.

"Your father has cancer," Mom confessed as I absorbed the dreaded "c-word." "He's receiving radiation and chemotherapy treatments."

Mom was always blunt about things but I wished she would have eased that news to me. It took my breath away. She had always been the strong one, the one who kept the family together, the one who cared for and nurtured Dad even when he was abusive and mean to her. They loved each other in a way I couldn't understand, and she was trying to process this as well.

Dad and I were finally establishing a father-daughter relationship and now I would have to deal with the idea that I might lose the father I had finally gained. After all the years despising him, I needed time to forgive him and know him and he needed to know me.

I spoke to Dad briefly, got off the phone and wept. I would be home for Christmas but until then I would have to quiet the frightened, hurt little girl and pretend that everything was okay. I put up my invincible persona, stayed busy, and found ways to suppress the pain but needed someone to put their arms around me and tell me everything would be okay.

Nine games into the season, my new team Sireg was at the top of the rankings with powerhouse teams Como, Cesena and Vicenza. Everyone associated with the team was ecstatic. We were playing much better than anyone expected but the news of Dad's cancer and my disassociation with Adriano ripped my world apart, weighed heavily on me and scared me.

Dad was dying and I couldn't let go of my love for Adriano; I just tried to cover the pain with an attitude of indifference. I was losing the two male figures that I believed could provide authentic love, support and validation. My persistent thoughts insisted that I should push through the brokenness of my heart, which cried silently as my mind plowed forward in a self-destructing mode. The little hurting girl inside me was frightened and hurt but Valerie would not allow the pain or any signs of vulnerability. Little did I know my internal, self-destructive struggle would soon manifest itself like an out-of-control, speeding force smashing into an unyielding, impenetrable reality causing a pause in the movement.

I was the most recognized female athlete in Italy but I still did not know who I was. I had filled the hole of not knowing who I was with men, drugs, alcohol, fame, sex, money and whatever else could numb the pain. I had searched and prayed and meditated and read tons of spiritual teachings but had become sluggish and unconscious, searching for external stimulants to heal an internal abrasion. I wanted someone to give me an answer when the answer was within me. I wanted someone to heal me when the healing would have to happen from within.

After our big win on Sunday, November 24, Vickie and I met up with Reggie Theus and a few basketball players at Hollywood, which as usual, was wild and out-of-control. Someone ordered me a drink. We all laughed, drank and talked about our games that night. After I finished on the dance floor, I picked up my unattended drink and joked with Reggie. Around 3 a.m. Vickie and I got in my Audi to return home. It was nearly 4 a.m.; after dropping off Vickie, I made my way through downtown Como. As I came around a curve everything went blank.

*****

"It's not your time to go, it's not your time to go, it's not your time to go..." the faint familiar female voice seeping out of the blinding, intense, light-bluish white light seemed like a thunderous echo, yet soothing and comforting. Where was it coming from? An overall sense of well-being permeated the atmosphere. Was someone watching me, maybe two? Bonnie? Bonnie? Bonnie? Who are you with? You...you? Can I stay? It's so peaceful here. No pain.

Can I stay?

"It's not your time to go, it's not your time to go, it's not your time to go…"

*****

As I laid motionless, the pain in my completely disfigured and swollen face became unbearable. Gianna, my Italian teacher, held my hand, and later painstakingly explained to me how I ended up in a hospital in Como two weeks earlier. Ironically the tree my car collided with was located just beneath her second-floor flat. In the days following the crash, neighbors shared stories of what had happened.

She told me that in the quiet early morning darkness, the loud screech of tires and a thunderous crash of a car colliding with a massive old oak tree resounded in peaceful Como. Startled by the loud noise, a teenage boy delivering freshly-baked ciabatti, panini and loaves of warm bread, tossed a bag full of baked goods to the ground and ran toward what once had been an Audi sedan; now it was just ripped, mangled pieces of metal scraps wrapped around the tree. With his heart racing and having witnessed the crash, he prepared himself for the worst. He reached the car, which had engulfed the tree as if the bark was part of the front seat and made the sign of the cross with his hands while saying a prayer. Through the shattered windshield glass he peeked in the front door window and to his amazement spotted a pair of women's shoes on the driver's seat. Quickly but unsuccessfully he tried to open the front driver's side door, which was jammed shut. He peeked in the backseat window. On the back seat lay a person completely immobile and unrecognizable from splattered blood, fragmented glass and a nose that had been nearly torn off. He frantically made the sign of the cross again, believing that he had witnessed a fatal accident.

"Chiamma l'ambulanza, chiamma la polizia," he shouted at people in their nightwear on balconies who had been awakened by the loud nocturnal noises. As he returned to the car, he could hear faint moans and groans.

Confused, with his heart beating rapidly and trembling hands he tried to open the front door again with no luck then grabbed the backdoor handle. The agonizing cries of a person in tremendous pain filled the air.

As Gianna recounted the story while her daughter Chiara brushed back tears, a tear formed in the corner of my eye and streamed down the side of my face. I vaguely remembered the boy.

"Stai ferma, stai ferma," he said to me, not believing the terrible condition I was in and also noticing that I was actually trying to move out of the car.

"Stop," he shouted at me, as if rebuking a zombie rising out of a tomb. I tumbled onto the grassy area next to the mangled car.

With a towel that someone had tossed from a balcony, I wiped my face and discovered that warm substance covering my face was actually blood.

"What happened? Why is there blood all over me? Why do my nylon stockings have tears and holes in them? Where are my shoes? Who is this person talking to me now? Where is Bonnie?" Thoughts raced through my shaken and confused mind.

"Devo prendere la mia borsa e chiavi," I informed the boy with a heavy American accent. He ran back to the car and grabbed my purse and keys and brought them back to me. Still not understanding exactly what had happened and with the Italian boy watching in astonishment, I pulled out my cell phone and called La Famiglia. Giorgio answered the phone with a sleepy but alarmed voice.

"Giorgio, sono stata in un incidente...dov'e Deborah?" I explained.

Deborah was on the phone quickly. In my confused state, I tried to explain to her what had happened, while sirens blared though the air. I knew I didn't have much time to talk but wanted her to know that I had heard and seen my dead sister. Deborah hung up the telephone, got dressed quickly and took the 40-minute drive to Como, hoping I wouldn't repeat the last comment about my dead sister to anyone.

At the accident scene, a police officer took the eye-witness account from the delivery boy while the EMT struggled to keep me calm.

"Come ti chiami?" asked the EMT.

"Valerie," I responded, trying to get to my feet.

"Stai ferma, non moverti," he insisted as he and his assistant retrieved a stretcher from the ambulance.

Before the EMT got a stretcher I had stumbled to the ambulance, each step taken in excruciating pain. In my heavy American accent, I joked in Italian about my appearance. I needed to go home to clean up and rest because I had a basketball practice scheduled in a few hours. After a few minutes of resistance I allowed them to transport me to the hospital but only if I could climb into the ambulance. With help from the EMT, I painfully climbed into the ambulance and sat on the stretcher, trying to make sense of what was happening. The ambulance sped off in the still of the cool winter morning to Ospedale S. Anna in Como with sirens screaming. Finally, I collapsed on the stretcher, going in and out of consciousness, still consumed by that soft voice…it's not your time to go, it's not your time to go, it's not your time to go.

*****

At the small provincial hospital, I was bustled around in a panic. There were multiple severe injuries including head and neck injuries. My face was punctured with pieces of glass from the windshield, which also broke my nose, nearly ripping it off. I didn't have a seatbelt on so the impact from hitting the tree initially caused me to hit the windshield, jamming my legs and body forward then violently throwing me to the back of the car, where I eventually regained consciousness. My right wrist was swollen like a balloon. Glass fragments were also in my legs and one piece was lodged in the left-side of my chest above my breast, cutting through my blouse. X-rays of my head, neck, chest, and arms were taken. Deborah arrived and in between procedures I called Francina. She was a nurse and I was hoping she would be able to come help me. I didn't call Mom because I didn't want to upset her. Francina said she would be on the next flight to Milano. I was taken to a large room with five other ladies. Deborah stayed with me.

I couldn't walk without excruciating pain so I asked for a wheelchair. At night one of the old ladies began screaming out for her son. I was scared and alone and couldn't believe what was happening to me. In the morning, a large white-plastered cast was placed on my right arm from my fingers to my shoulder with a piece attached to my ribs that held my arm up parallel to the ground. It reminded me of the casts seen in cartoons. A plastic surgeon examined me because of the severity of my nose and face injuries. My abdominal and pelvic area continued to be painful but the doctors disregarded my complaints.

Francina finally arrived. We cried and laughed as she hugged me. My face and eyes were swollen with both eyes badly bruised and discolored and my face was covered with cuts from the glass fragments. She couldn't imagine how I would recover from the facial injuries. After getting over the initial shock, Francina told me that I smelled really bad. I hadn't been washed for two days. Deborah went to my house to get my toiletries and Francina bathed me. We laughed about the huge comical cast that was on my arm for a broken wrist. I insisted on brushing my teeth and Francina combed my hair. News of the accident was released. Once the hospital discovered who I was, I was moved to a private room.

After three days of complaining about my stomach hurting and pelvic pain, more tests were done on that area: x-rays and MRI. I had broken my pelvic area in six places. The fracture of my first vertebrae was treated with a removable neck brace to immobilize it. A plastic surgeon repaired my broken nose and the laceration from the corner of my nose to my mouth. Nothing was done for my cheek or pelvic fractures.

Adriano arrived and was visibly shaken when he saw me. We hadn't seen each other for quite some time. I was unrecognizable with my disfigured, discolored, and swollen face filled with punctures and cuts. He made sure I was getting the best treatment and visited often.

My severe head trauma left me delusional. I was never alone; either Francina or Deborah was always with me. They took turns with night and day shifts. Night shifts were difficult because I couldn't sleep and became extremely confused. I'm not sure what would have happened to me if Deborah and Francina weren't there to care for me. Even in what seemed to be my most tragic time, God always provided and protected me.

After a couple of weeks, I began to feel better and I wanted to go back to the USA for treatment but with the injuries I risked more damage with additional movements and would have to wait until I was fully recovered.

Rudy Tavana, the team doctor from AC Milan, arrived one day. He lived near Como, had heard about my accident and wanted to know if he could help in any way. As soon as he saw me, he told me that my nose was crooked and would need to be reset. He would also help me with my recuperation and rehab once I was out of the hospital. I was in the hospital for nearly a month. Roberto came up to visit also. The second time he came to visit he brought his friend. Francina told me they were just hanging out, driving my Mercedes around and not helping out. I confronted Roberto about the accusations and things between us changed. I saw less and less of Roberto once I was released from the hospital and began rehab. Rudy developed an extensive rehab program including swimming and advanced technology. We spent lots of time together once Francina left. I also began doing rehab at AC Milan's training facility.

Deborah and I visited the scene of the accident and saw the remains of the car. After seeing the damaged tree and the mangled car that was at the local junkyard, I wept, knowing that I was blessed to be alive. Between that fact and my near-death experience with Bonnie during the accident, I knew it was time for a change. I had lost my way somewhere and this was a sign that I needed to find meaning for life.

I was given a second chance.

It wasn't my time to go. I wasn't sure where or what would happen but I was thankful to be alive. I vowed I wouldn't go back to Hollywood. This wasn't my first brush with death; I had nearly died when I was at UK. Like that time, I was thankful for and aware of what most people took for granted: being able to walk, feeling the warm sun and knowing that I had people around me who loved me. This was a new beginning for me.

*****

Mom's heart was broken when she finally saw me. I was so emaciated and barely able to walk. This was another return with me

168

injured but this was the worst she had ever seen me. I had lost a lot of weight and was just starting to regain muscle tone. Mom fought with me about eating as I insisted on fasting and meditating. She saw my physical deficiencies but I knew I had spiritual and emotional deficiencies that needed to be mended. I was still searching.

Against Mom's wishes, I decided I would return to Italy to play another year. I needed to play one more year to prove that I had recovered. Cesena offered me a good contract, including stipulations for the following two years if I wanted to stay.

I heard Adriano was living with someone now and Roberto and I had grown distant. I would be starting new by myself. I drove past Adriano's house in Milano, wanting to see him and say goodbye but too frightened.

Tears streamed down my face with Brian McKnight's "One Last Cry" playing as I drove south down the Autostrada with Benjamin in the front seat. I mourned the death of my relationship with Adriano and the death of a dream. I had my last cry before putting it all behind and getting it out of my mind for the last time during my over-200-mile-drive to Cesena. The words and music expressed my feelings perfectly.

I played that song over and over, feeling so alone as I exited the highway and arrived in Cesena.

*****

After a few preseason games with Cesena, everyone knew I was back in championship condition, scoring points, grabbing rebounds and playing aggressively and passionately. I had been given a new chance and I was enjoying every moment.

Andrea Lloyd, along with Catarina Pollin and I would make up one of the strongest front courts in the league. It was exciting and strange to finally have the chance to play with Catarina after years of battling against her. Andy was an All-American from the University of Texas who had won the NCAA in 1986 before winning a gold medal in the 1988 Olympics. She had been with Cesena since arriving in Italy and won an Italian championship in 1990 and a European championship with Cesena in 1991. She spoke fluent Italian and drove around town in her Chevy.

In September, a local TV station asked if I would be interested in hosting my own TV show. It would be the first of its kind; the first time an American athlete would have her own show and it was the first show that focused on women's basketball. I accepted and we began taping STILL Basket, a weekly sports show that previewed upcoming games and reviewed previous games.

The show was doing well when I found out that Darryl Dawkins played for Forli, a town less than 20 miles from Cesena. He was one of my favorite players when he played with the NBA 76ers after being drafted straight out of high school in 1975. "Chocolate Thunder" was known for his powerful dunks, which he named. Now he was playing with Forli in the Italian A2 League. I was thrilled when he accepted the invite to be on my show.

I arrived early to film Darryl's practice and then conducted an interview. As my crew set up cameras for the taping, a guy standing under the basket walked toward me. He introduced himself as Sean, Bret Bearup's younger brother. Bret played for UK when I was there. I had had a little crush on him. We were good friends but I didn't remember his brother being this good-looking - about 6'5,"close-cut dirty blonde hair with a mischievous smile.

"Do you know Rob Lock?" he asked, signaling a guy running drills before I could answer.

The tall, strawberry-blonde, pale blue-eyed sweaty player with a trimmed mustache and goatee made his way over to us. Although he was mammoth in size he had a clean-cut, all-American adolescent face. Sean was talkative and outgoing while Rob seemed standoffish.

"Rob, remember I was telling you about Valerie Still playing in Cesena," Sean said as Rob approached. "She's here to interview Big D."

"He's always the last one out for practice," Rob warned. "I'm Rob, I remember meeting you briefly in Rena's office while I was still playing for UK."

Darryl finally came out. After taping our segment, Rob, Sean and I exchanged numbers.

*****

It wasn't long before Sean called asking if Andy and I wanted to go out with him and Rob. We all went out together. Sean was Rob's "personal assistant" and tons of fun. They lived like typical American bachelors, stocking up on American food and drinks from the US military base commissary. They had an American satellite dish and could get some American and English television programming. Rob's mom sent him videotapes of his favorite American TV shows. They kept their stash of porn magazines and videos around the house. Rob and Sean treated me like one of the guys and I loved that. It reminded me of hanging out with my brothers as a child.

Sean and I began going out. He was multifaceted; childish, crude, and juvenile while also witty, creative, engaging, artistic, and truth-seeking with a philosophical edge. Our physical attraction was powerful and magnetic. It wasn't long before we began a salacious relationship. It was unrestrained and uninhibited. Being in this type of sexual relationship helped to keep me unfettered.

Preparing for a Halloween costume party outside of Milano, Rob explained to me that Sean had informed him that he was in the process of training and taming me. My bad-girl, wild-girl reputation could be harnessed and he would do it. Once at the party, I spotted Spoon and introduced Rob, barely acknowledging Sean. I spent most of the night dirty dancing with a short Italian guy in a crazy metallic spiked wig, ignoring Rob and Sean until it was time to go. The car ride home was tense and quiet to say the least. After that night, Sean and I began seeing less of each other.

Rob sent Sean back to the USA for Thanksgiving and we began spending time together. He returned to California and I to New Jersey for Christmas break. We returned a couple days after Christmas. Rob's parents came back with him to spend the New Year. Sean never returned.

I met Rob's parents at a dinner at our favorite restaurant with Darryl and his wife, Robin. Although Rob and I had begun a relationship, he restrained himself from any signs of affection toward me around his parents. While they were in town, he slept at his house and I slept at mine.

Rob and I seemed to have completely opposite personalities. I was hardnosed and indifferent in regard to the media's assessment of my playing abilities and Rob was always under scrutiny and sensitive to all the backlash when he didn't perform well. I was the outgoing, wild, party girl, superstar basketball player and Rob was the quiet, conservative, mediocre basketball player in A2. At UK, I was known as the overachiever, a player no one expected much from but who eventually became UK's all-time leading scorer, and Rob was the underachieving post player who hadn't reached the expectations everyone had for him. I was in love with Italy and the international scene and Rob hated Italy and couldn't wait to get back to his small town, Reedley, California. I was from a large East Coast family and he was the "golden baby boy" in his west coast two-sibling family.

In our little cocoon away from everyone, we formed a solid bond. We had to go through our rough spot of accepting each other's personalities and quirks but we did so by ourselves and that made our relationship strong. In five months, I was in love again.

With a third of the season left, Cesena was heading for the play-offs. More importantly, it seemed I was finally settled into a good relationship. Rob and I were consumed with each other. I didn't have the desire to party but instead loved cuddling up with him and watching tapes of American TV shows I had never heard of or seen before. When we were not together, Rob spent hours reading airplane magazines and articles his dad sent him. He was obsessed with flying and couldn't wait to retire from playing so he could do what he really loved – fly biplanes. He was miserable playing basketball and being in Italy but the fact that he was making money so he could one day own and fly as many biplanes as he liked motivated him.

We were a tall beautiful couple that stood out in Italy. Heads turned wherever we went. Rob, 6'11", had a naturally lean, muscular, strong, sculptured body. His butt was tight, firm and well-defined. He walked with his shoulders back, chest held high, and slightly on his toes. I loved watching him run and jump. His athletic body was explosive. When he wore his designer, tailored suits or clothes he was striking. As a tall woman next to Rob I physically felt and looked small. I loved walking hand-in-hand. His oversized hands engulfed my large hands and made them seem tiny. Rob's facial features were strong and well-defined with imperfections that gave him character. The tip of his nose turned slightly to the right after being broken once but I thought that was adorable. His small, narrow mouth seemed out of proportion to his large head in proportion to his body. His smile was usually restrained but when he relaxed and felt safe and content it melted my heart. His pale-blue eyes seemed to express a hint of sadness but were intense and penetrating.

Our lovemaking was insatiable. Whenever we had time, we spent it enjoying the physical pleasure of sex. I was busier than Rob during the day with my TV show and usually needed to be out of the house early in the morning. Even after high-spirited, energetic, mind-blowing sex all night I would hustle out of bed happily while Rob begged me to stay. Going against the norm was thrilling for us as well; finding places to sneak in an occasional quick lovemaking session wasn't easy for two oversized people like us but it was fun whether on a beach, in a park or in a public bathroom at an Autostrada stop. Rob was 27 years old and I was 32; my sexual confidence was high and Rob was a willing and eager participant. Although I didn't like the idea of pornography, I knew Rob loved that and was open to joining him in watching and participating in some of his fantasies.

*****

After a fantastic regular season Cesena finished in second place behind Como going into the play-offs. We lost to Como in three games for the title. The team asked me to return as STILL Basket prepared for a second season. Forli, the team Rob played for, anticipating a promotion to A1, instead finished in 7th place after the regular season and was eliminated in the play-offs. The team renewed Darryl's contract but not Rob's.

Chapter 12

Back in the USA

"It's not your time to go. . ." It had been some time since I embraced those words but as I sat on my floor pillows in Cesena meditating in the midst of white candles and incense, they filled the room. I hadn't completely understood their significance when I initially heard them after the car accident. During my recovery, they had lost the impact they initially had on me. I figured it wasn't my time to die but Bonnie never told me why. Why hadn't she just clearly told me what I needed to do so I could do it? I was an elite athlete trained to follow instructions; that usually didn't take much thinking, just hard work. Now I was still struggling to decipher Bonnie's message to me.

Dad and I had begun to correspond with each other by letters and phone calls. Mom was happy to be back in New Jersey around her family, children, grandchildren and friends. And although she and Dad still had their clashes and disagreements, they were enjoying a life together without children living in the house.

Periodically, Adriano and I were in contact. Before our last split, he had proposed to me but I didn't believe we could overcome all the insecurity, hurt and pain we had caused each other. After I refused his ring and marriage proposal, he moved on with someone else. Now we could be supportive of each other. He had been through the crazy drug-filled period with me and was glad I had bounced back.

My main concern now was the uneasy feeling concerning my relationship with Rob. We had been best friends first, like two team-mates, but as the relationship transitioned to an intimate one, our conversations included loaded questions about former relationships and future aspirations. Rob didn't want children. I loved children and wanted a family. Rob's focus and love was airplanes and finding someone who would share that love. I became interested in airplanes and repressed my desire to have children; with time, I was sure Rob would change. I also thought time would change his parents' feelings toward me.

We joked about his parents' dislike of me and how they disregarded our relationship. I couldn't understand why they wouldn't accept me. They had only met me during their Christmas and New Year visit but I needed acceptance and approval from them. The thought of being rejected by his parents overwhelmed me. The frightened little girl in me was overreacting. I silenced that voice moving forward with Rob and our relationship. Even if his parents didn't initially like me, I was sure that once they got to know me they would embrace and love me. It seemed he wanted me to join him on his family's vacation to Mexico but there was some resistance. Regardless, I would retire and follow Rob wherever he received an offer. It seemed like a sporadic, unbelievable, un-thought-out decision by everyone who knew me.

We headed to California to spend time flying in his father's bi-plane. Reedley was a small rural town unlike what I envisioned of a California city. The initial greeting between Rob's parents and me was awkward but cordial. Rob and I trained every morning, even though I had retired. He spent lots of time with his father working on airplanes in their hangar. I attended my first air show at a small airport in Merced. Rob took me flying in an old Stearman. It was an exhilarating experience; slowly cruising in the low-flying vintage open-cockpit aircraft with a gentle breeze on my face, enjoying God's beautiful creation. Flying like this was a spiritual experience. After so many years of being autonomous, I now had finally allowed someone to be in the pilot's seat and take control and I was a content passenger.

Sadly, near the end of my visit, Deborah called me from Cesena. Benjamin had been poisoned. We had been together for eight wonderful years. I was crushed. Regardless of what was happening in my life, I knew Benjamin loved me. Now he was dead.

After California we headed to Lexington. This was the first time we were back at UK as a couple. We were well-known in Lexington but had had totally different experiences at UK.

Rob had received a scholarship during a period that could be considered the "dark-ages" of the program. It was a transition period for the program with a change of coaches, a drop in success and increase in scandals. He had tons of funny stories about Joe B. Hall's psychological warfare on players and Eddie Sutton's drinking habit and scandal-filled years at UK. Rob's senior year ended with the Emery envelope scandal, when an Emery Worldwide employee discovered $1,000 in cash in an envelope sent from a UK assistant coach to a recruit's father. I remembered hearing about that.

The following season, amidst the NCAA investigation of numerous serious violations, Sutton and athletic director Cliff Hagan were forced to resign and UK was placed on probation. The SEC title Rob won with UK was forfeited.

Returning as a couple, we would be UK's first illustrious basketball couple. I reconnected with Maryanne and Steve and Bonnie Hutton but couldn't find Ottie. I also reconnected with D.G. Fitzmaurice, who was working at the NBC-TV station in Lexington. They offered me a job. Rob had been offered a contract with Montecatini in the first division in Italy. I would return to Italy with him in the fall instead of taking the job offer.

Grandma Ricketts died and I returned to New Jersey for her funeral before returning to Italy with Rob. This was my first summer spent entirely in the USA since I had left college. We returned to Italy excited about our life together. This would be my first season not playing basketball.

Montecatini was the perfect opportunity for Rob. He would finally be playing in the first division. I loved Montecatini Terme. Adriano and I had spent lots of time getting relaxing and therapeutic treatments there with its health spas, natural grottos, and medicinal spring water. The Tuscan town was beautiful. Rob and I spent the first few weeks enjoying Tuscany and solidifying our relationship.

His parents stopped communications with him. He was visibly hurt by the alienation so I began writing letters to his parents. It was difficult for me writing to them, knowing that I was the reason they weren't talking to him, but I wanted them to know me and how I felt about Rob. I talked to Mom about it as well. As usual she had supportive and candid advice. I couldn't change them. Rob and I were adults, and a couple; his parents would have to live with our decision to be together.

When preseason began for Rob, I felt the pain of not playing any longer. It finally hit me that I would not be doing what I loved, playing basketball. Instead, during his free time we travelled; from Florence to Portofino to Como, Milano and Lugano, Switzerland. Rob bought me a promise ring and we decided in Switzerland we would find a church and make the commitment between us official. On the way we stopped in Como for a romantic dinner at Il Gatto Nero, a charming, intimate, romantic restaurant nestled in the hills with a spectacular view of Lake Como. After a candle light dinner Rob got on one knee, took my hand and asked me to marry him. I knew that Rob was the one and we would live happily ever after.

In December, I wrote Dad about Rob and our relationship and he began to open up to me about his struggles during my childhood. He would have loved to give us everything but he couldn't and that was hurtful to him. He was excited now that Rob would become his son-in-law and hoped we would start a family soon. I wanted Dad to walk me down the aisle at my wedding.

Rob struggled on the court. We returned to Lexington for Christmas together and stayed with Bret Bearup who convinced Rob that we should purchase a house there. They talked about Rob working with Bret in his newly-created investment business as well. I didn't think we should buy a home yet. I was still saving my money, wanting to be able to retire and live comfortably. I was probably the first female basketball player to make a million dollars. With my childhood I promised myself I would never return to Camden; I would never be poor again and I would never trust anyone fully to take care of me. Now, everything was happening so quickly for me.

We found a beautiful home, ten miles from downtown Lexington in the middle of rolling horse country. Rob's parents reconnected with him and tried desperately to talk him out of buying a house with me.

Back in Italy, I began working for a TV station. Each weekend I was at the league's "game of the week," doing courtside interviews. For Easter, I flew back to Lexington, put down $70,000 cash on the house and it was ours.

Montecatini didn't renew Rob's contract. We moved into our beautiful over-7500-square-foot home as a young, inexperienced couple with new responsibilities and both retired from basketball. Our contemporary white-stucco house sat on one of the highest points in Fayette County on a hundred and fifty acres of beautiful, scenic Kentucky bluegrass.

It seemed we were the perfect couple, in the perfect environment and in a beautiful, serene setting, but Rob and I were in very unfamiliar territory. I was no longer in Italy where I felt secure, was allowed to be me and open to a world of unlimited opportunity. Rob was back in the USA where he longed to be but he was also in Lexington where he had experienced frustration and insecurity. We were no longer in our Tuscany cocoon where we were a high-profile celebrity couple, but now we were an "interracial" couple in Kentucky. I never thought of us that way but Rob's parents' influence was a constant reminder. They warned Rob about the difficulties of having mixed-race children. They were concerned about the hardships our children would face. Rob's father knew of an interracial couple. He described their children as splotchy. When Rob told me this story, I didn't know whether to laugh or cry; it was so ridiculous. Splotchy?

*****

We stayed busy during the summer doing what we thought normal couples did. We bought a dog. We bought stuff for the house. We began decorating. We spent time together, hung out with friends and were invited to awesome events and parties in Lexington. Rob's old friends and teammates, including Greg, his best friend from college, began hanging out at our house.

Rob was a different person with his old friends. Most of them endorsed the double standard for men and women. Some of his friends were cheating on their wives and that was okay as long as the wives didn't know and weren't hurt. They all insisted on telling the same old stories about their college escapades as high-profile athletes. The sporting world is a sexist system but hearing about their degradation and exploitation of women as if it was a badge of honor to be rehashed, re-savored and a source of entertainment, irritated me.

Being one of the highest-paid players and longest-playing veterans in the league helped me accumulate a sizable nest egg. Although top female players were not earning nearly as much as some of the mediocre male players in the Italian league, I had always been frugal with money. Rob suggested I use Bret as one of my investors. I did.

I met up with Bernadette Locke in Memorial Coliseum. Rick Pitino had hired her as the first female assistant basketball coach for an NCAA Division 1 program in 1990. Pitino's controversial but ground-breaking decision made headlines across the country. Many wondered if it was a publicity stunt or really a sign that gender discrimination was beginning to crumble in sports. I was excited for Bernadette but proud of UK and Pitino for making such a bold move. Rob asked me to marry him again in Memorial Coliseum.

I stayed busy. WLEX-TV, Channel 18 offered me a position to be a celebrity reporter. I began my segment called, "Still on the Go." It featured former UK athletes and what they were doing currently. I began planning for our wedding . My wedding dress and Rob's tuxedo were made by our Italian tailor. Reservations for the church and invitations were made and I was enthusiastic about the wedding. Dad was doing fairly well but his health status was changing weekly. The more I talked about the wedding the more Rob became withdrawn. One day he told me he couldn't marry me. I was devastated and embarrassed but pretended it didn't really matter.

I had never imagined leaving Italy. I had never seriously dated American men, nor committed to anyone and now Rob had my heart. When we were in Italy he was totally committed: now back in the States he had doubts. His cancellation of the wedding and rejection of me forced me to deal with who I was. I had returned to the place where people had defined me and continued to define me as a Black female basketball player, but that was not who I was. Unknowingly,

Rob's rejection and his parents' rejection actually forced me toward my hidden treasure – to know who I was.

For so long I had fought against being placed into socially-constructed identification boxes, especially the race box. Italy had allowed me to jump outside of that box but I was back in the States now. The Black/White dilemma in the USA based on lies and tightly woven into the fabric of American culture is one steeped in a history of shame. Rob and his parents would end up being a catalyst, a painful catalyst that forced me to know who I was. Although they would do it in a seemingly negative way, based on the color my skin, the final resolve was that I would be moving toward my treasure and closer to understanding my purpose in, and meaning of, life. When I decided to surrender everything and follow Rob, it was similar to when I left the USA for Italy. Italy, an unknown place, had allowed me to explore opportunities unavailable to me in the USA; now it was time to move forward into the unknown again.

Italy was only part of the journey. I had had life-changing experiences there and now I was returning to the place where I started. I wasn't the same person. I had faced some of my fears and knew a little more about myself but was still in search of who I was. I was in the process of refinement, self-purification, shedding layers of mis-identification and contamination, burning off impurities in search of pure gold - my authentic self. Purification or refinement means going through the fire. This process is painful at times but necessary.

Chapter 13

Daddy's Little Girl

The summer of 1994 became more stressful for Rob and me. Rob seemed to be emotionally distant from me and the more he pulled away the more I pursued him. Regardless of my inner hurt I would be understanding and patient. Bret had decided Rob would not be working with him and now Rob's agent desperately searched for a team. I was still hurt that Rob had cancelled the wedding but stayed busy working at the TV station. I called everyone with the news of the wedding cancellation. Through the humiliation and opposition from his parents I still loved Rob. And I longed for him to love me.

Rob signed with a team in France and left for Limoge. I didn't know anything about Limoge but I was willing to join him. I gave notice to the TV station that I may be joining him. They assured me I would still have my position once I returned.

One of the last people I interviewed for the show was Dotti Berry, my assistant coach from UK. She was now "married" to another woman and living in Lexington. Her same-sex marriage would be an interesting story. Not many gay women were open about their relationships like Dotti. She was a successful businesswoman but we would discuss her fight against intolerance and discrimination. Terry Hall had left UK, a homophobic environment, as the winningest coach, amidst homophobic accusations. Lesbians, in women's basketball, continued to suffer from not being allowed to be their true selves.

A few days after Rob left, I found out I was pregnant. I wondered how he would take the news. He had been stressed about not working and also seemed to be having second thoughts about us. I interviewed Dwane Casey the day after taking a home pregnancy test. I was eager to see Dwane. We had dated a little in college. After being wrongfully accused of sending money to a recruit while he was coaching at UK, he had just won a significant settlement in his case and was being hired as an assistant coach with the Seattle Supersonics. He had been through a terrible time with the recruiting scandal at UK and now he was finally recuperating. After the interview we went out to dinner together. We exchanged numbers and stayed in touch.

I called Rob that night to tell him about possibly being pregnant. He wasn't playing well, didn't like the situation with the team, was already lonely and wanted me to come to Limoge as soon as possible. I nervously shared the news of my pregnancy. He was shocked. He wanted to know when Roscoe, our dog, and I would be coming to France. I told him I needed to see a doctor to confirm the test.

I scheduled an appointment with Reva Tackett, a gynecologist. I had met her and Mary Jane Lagrew, a pediatrician, after buying our house and we all had become good friends. MJ lived with Ingrid, who became my "other mother." Tears streamed down my face as Reva performed the sonogram. Although they all thought I should stay in the States to have the baby, I decided to join Rob in France and then return closer to the due date. Reva made me promise the first thing I would do once I arrived in Limoge was find a good doctor.

I called Mom to tell her about the baby and that I was heading to France. She suggested I stay in the States; instead I packed up my stuff and Roscoe and headed to France. I hoped that our baby would draw Rob and me closer together.

Rob was miserable and unhappy in Limoge. We found a veterinarian clinic for Roscoe a few days after arriving. The vet was French and his wife was American. They befriended us and we spent time with them at their beautiful French chalet, in a secluded wooded area, to help Rob de-stress.

Each day Rob returned from practice more and more discouraged and disgruntled. Rumors began circulating that the team was discussing the possibility of cutting him. By mid-October, things got really bad and Rob thought it was best I return to Lexington

We loaded nearly 20 bags and Roscoe on a train from Limoge to the Paris airport and talked sparingly during the four-hour trip. I was hurt that Rob was so miserable and also because we weren't able to enjoy the first months of our new baby's life. Even though Rob's situation was depressing, I loved being pregnant. Although I wasn't able to share my excitement with him, this was the most wonderful thing that had ever happened to me. I had been slowly dying spiritually for the last couple of years. The upcoming birth had breathed life into me.

Rob and I embraced and kissed at the gate. Tears streamed down my face as we turned in opposite directions.

I settled in on the airplane thinking about everything happening in my life, laid my head against the window and fell asleep. I awoke shortly after being in the air, feeling as though I had wet myself. I hurried to the bathroom. In the tiny, confined, isolated bathroom I panicked with the unexpected sight of blood. I hit the call button and exited the bathroom scared and frightened. The calming flight attendant assured me that everything would be okay as I frantically explained to her I was pregnant, bleeding and alone. She made an announcement, asking if there was a doctor on board as she cleared the last row of seats for me to lie down. A doctor arrived and informed me that bleeding during pregnancy wasn't necessarily a serious problem. He suggested I lie down, remain calm and try to sleep.

Lie down, remain calm and sleep? I thought. There was no way I would be calm or sleep. I had nearly 6 hours to conjure up the worst-case scenarios and plead to God to protect my precious baby. I cried.

After we landed safely in Cincinnati, police officers entered the plane. They questioned me. Once I was cleared, EMTs put me on a stretcher and rushed me to a hospital. Everything happening created more angst for me and I couldn't stop crying.

The motionless heartbeat on the ultrasound monitor in the emergency room and the silence in the ER doctor's stethoscope signaled the worst for me – the death of my baby. The ER doctor wouldn't confirm the baby was dead as he watched me break down and cry uncontrollably. I called Reva, crying hysterically. She would wait for me at Central Baptist Hospital in Lexington with MJ and Ingrid.

Reva confirmed that my baby had died and explained that miscarriages were common and normally not caused by anything done by the mother. I lay in an emergency room sobbing. I wondered what I had done to cause this, thinking about all the stress in the last few months, all the travelling, all the chaos, the rubella shot, all the training and not being aware I was pregnant. I couldn't believe it wasn't my fault.

I spent the night in the hospital. MJ and Ingrid took Roscoe to their house and when I was released I stayed with them until I recovered.

I called Rob and told him what happened. He would return once the team paid him.

The next months were like living in a fog. The loss of my baby represented the loss of what I believed would be a new birth for me. Now, I was confronted with the underlying tension between Rob and me and also being truthful with myself. How would I move forward honestly? I had tried to suppress my inner unrest and the pregnancy seemed to be a solution for my discontent.

After Rob was cut by Limoge, his agent found a team in Spain. In December, without my knowledge, Rob finalized a life insurance policy he had begun in September with Bret. He named his parents, sister and Bret as beneficiaries. He also had a will written up that excluded me.

With the start of a new year, I was unaware of Rob's dealings with his family and Bret but I knew things weren't going well for us. The call from my Italian agent at the beginning of 1995 about a fantastic offer to play in Schio was God's answer to my prayers. I would replace an injured American player for four regular-season games and the playoffs. Andrea Lloyd would be my teammate. Although Rob wasn't thrilled about my decision to return to Italy, and I was a little nervous, I knew it was the right one. I packed a few bags and left.

It was wonderful being back in Italy. I would only be in Schio for a short time, so I would live at Hotel Noris, owned by Maurizio and his wife Noris. The first night back, after a delicious meal with Maurizio and his daughter Erica, he brought out his best grappa. We sat and talked and laughed and enjoyed the grappa. I was back at home again.

Hotel Noris was home for the next few months and Maurizio affectionately became "Zio Maurizio." They were nurturing and loving to me. Unlike the previous years I spent in Italy, I didn't socialize much; instead I spent most of my time at the hotel when I wasn't practicing or playing.

Playing basketball took my mind off the miscarriage. Initially, my eyes were set on the six-week mark when I would be able to get pregnant again, but after being in Schio, I no longer discussed it with Rob. He decided to visit me in Schio. The small town was ecstatic about the team being in the finals. While Rob visited, we couldn't walk the streets without fans sharing their excitement about the team.

Rob didn't stay long. Before leaving he told me he missed me and loved me. He reminded me that in a few weeks, we would both be back in the States and we could try again to have a baby.

Schio lost the championship to my former team, Como. I said goodbye to all my new friends, Zio Maurizio and his family and returned home. It was strange; I wanted to return to Lexington but I knew I would miss Italy.

*****

On Thursday, May 11, 1995, at 11 a.m., the start of my five-day "fertility window," the period when I was ovulating, and the best time to get pregnant, I lit scented candles and put on Rob's favorite Luther Vandross CD. We shared the most intimate, cherished moment of our time together as we united to receive a special gift from God.

Later Reva confirmed that I was pregnant. This time instead of telling everyone, we decided to wait until after the first trimester. Mom called a couple weeks later and told me that Dad was not doing well. I flew out to be with him.

Jacqueline, Francina, Francine and Gary were at the house when I arrived. I stepped into his room and quietly watched him as he slept peacefully then gently kissed him on his forehead. For a moment, he recognized me and we carried on a conversation as I sat on his bed. Mom had been by his side since he had gotten bedridden, feeding him, bathing him, and loving him. She had contacted each sibling now that he wasn't eating and was not as lucid.

I spent the week talking with him, giving him foot massages and rubbing his hands with lotion. I had never realized how big my father's hands were. I'm sure that he had held my hand at some time while I was a child but as I gently caressed his hands now I felt like the little girl who had yearned for her father's love, validation and approval. Our conversations were coherent at times but eventually his rambling thoughts would become delusional, confused and unintelligible. Although I wanted to keep the news of my pregnancy a secret, I told Dad that I was pregnant during one of his clear-thinking periods. I wasn't sure if he fully understood but he seemed to be happy about the news of my pregnancy. The man who had caused me so much pain was dying, but I was the one in denial.

I booked a flight for Lexington to participate in a UK alumni event with a return after the weekend so I could get back with Dad. I kissed him, told him that I would be returning shortly. Mom assured me everything would be fine until I returned.

A few hours later at 12:45 a.m., Dad died at home with Mom by his side. She called me later that morning as I was rehearsing for the event at Rupp Arena. Dotti was with me when I received the news.

Rupp Arena was packed with all of UK basketball's elite for the grand gala as I stepped on stage and fumbled through the evening as Master of Ceremony with Dan Issel. No one knew my father had died. The following morning, I returned to New Jersey. As we buried Dad I caressed my belly that was carrying his DNA. I had had a tumultuous relationship with my father but in the last few years had a chance to embrace him for who he was. He was a complex man who loved his family but didn't know how to demonstrate that love. He was a carefree spirit who had been constrained with responsibilities and burdened with a family legacy of excellence. I didn't understand him fully but with the birth of my child, maybe I would have a chance to atone for the dysfunctional parent-child relationship I had with him and understand him better as well.

"Rest in Peace, Dad" I whispered as they lowered him into the grave. Mom remained stoic. We returned to the house where they had enjoyed their last years together.

"Valerie, I made my peace with your father. I told him I forgave him and it was okay for him to let go and I loved him," Mom shared with me about the last hours of my father's life.

Mom and Dad shared a love I couldn't understand. Although Dad never asked her for forgiveness, she never held any animosity toward him and loved him until he took his final breath. They had been together over 45 years. He was her first and only love. Together they instilled in us the importance of family and staying together regardless of the circumstances.

I didn't understand at this moment that my father's lack of commitment to me represented uncertainty, instability and insecurity. However, regardless of his commitment to me, he was who I am. I was a Still; his blood flowed through me. For my entire life I had chased after his approval, validation, and love because I thought it would give me security; instead, that pursuing of a relationship with him pushed me to discover who I truly was. Not being fettered to certainty and security was freedom. It was unpleasant at times but it kept me growing and moving. Once I loved him, I loved myself but now my relationship with him changed because he would no longer physically be on earth. I hadn't realized that all the years my mother insisted I love and respect my father, she was actually saying that when I love and respect my father, I love and respect myself. It would take me years and years before I understood this. My hatred for my father was only self-hatred and I would have to learn to embrace uncertainty, insecurity and instability to be my authentic self.

Ironically, I had chosen Rob and was willing to compromise myself because I thought he represented security, certainty and stability. Rob's seemingly rational, sensitive and reserved personality was the complete opposite of my father. Now that my father was dead, I had Rob and a child that would meet my need for the illusion of security. I didn't understand that pursuing the illusion of security at all costs would mean losing my authentic self to the point where I would embrace self-hatred. With my father dying, my sense of stability was shaken. My earth passage with Dad was a painful one but much needed on my journey of self-discovery. With Rob, I would continue on my path of self-discovery leading to awakened and conscious living. Dad wouldn't be there physically to walk me down the aisle on my wedding day and give me away but the symbolic exchange had already happened and Dad would always be close to me in spirit.

I returned to Lexington sorting out my thoughts and feelings. While I had been gone, Rob and his father, without my knowledge, had bought an airplane.

The first week of July Rob had a surprise for me. He told me to buy a nice white dress and pack my bags for a weekend get-away, just the two of us. We were heading to Martha's Vineyard.

The weather was gorgeous as we headed to Edgartown in a rental car from the airport. Our first stop was the nineteenth-century courthouse building. We met with the county clerk and filled out a marriage license. We were getting married! I was surprised.

Next stop was Vineyard Haven. We took the coastline to get a view of the ocean. The sights were breathtaking: miles of sandy beaches on one side and New England-style houses and trees on the other side. We pulled up to the Thorncroft Inn, one of the most beautiful bed-and-breakfasts on the island. Karl, the innkeeper, greeted us as though we were family visiting his quaint cottage home. Birds and wild little animals played outside along the trails lined with beautiful, colorful flowers and plants. Classical music filled the air inside the inn as Karl accompanied us to our suite.

Rob picked me up and carried me to the canopy bed. After enjoying the moment, we decided to drive downtown for a bite to eat. Martha's Vineyard was picturesque with its beautiful spacious beaches which were nearly empty except for a few people enjoying the breath-taking sunset. Back at the inn, we lay by the fireplace, holding each other and making silly comments about being Mr. and Mrs. Lock, even though I had not changed my last name.

The next day we had breakfast in bed and then headed out to check out the island and do some shopping. We found a small airport on the south side of the island in Katama then returned to Edgartown for lunch at The Wharf. Before returning to the hotel we stopped at a local florist and bought a small bouquet of white roses and white baby's-breath to put in my hair for the wedding. Wedding? Rob had made arrangements for us to be married at sunset on the beach.

In the little white dress I had bought at Dawahares in a Lexington mall a few days earlier, we headed to Menemsha Beach. John Alley, the local Justice of the Peace, met us on the beach. He arrived looking like Abe Lincoln, dressed in a long-tail tuxedo jacket and top hat. A few people sat on the beach and also in sailboats near the shore with a large burnt-orange sun drifting near the horizon. Rob and I stood hand-in-hand, gazing into each other's eyes as we pledged our love and commitment to each other. With the permission of the Justice of Peace, Rob and I kissed as he pronounced us man and wife to the applause of the few people on the beach and with boats' horns tooting. An older couple holding hands while watching approached us. They told us they had been happily married for sixty years and wished us the same.

We returned to our candle-lit suite, with a cozy fire blazing, rose petals spread throughout and champagne on ice. I would never forget my wedding. I had always longed for acceptance and family; I thought that would be my security. That night I had what I thought would bring me happiness.

Back at home, I called Mom and told her what we had done and that I was pregnant. It was odd being so excited during this time when Dad had died only a month earlier. My brother Wendell had moved in with Mom, in the basement. I was glad she had someone living with her. I began calling her every day to check up on her and also to get advice on being pregnant and giving birth. She was happy I had finally settled back in the States.

Rob still hadn't told his parents about our marriage or the pregnancy. Although I thought that was odd, I tried not to allow any negativity to invade our space. I had a new spirit that I was carrying and it was important to keep our environment as positive as possible. Talking to Mom every day helped me keep tapped into my spiritual awareness. Mom was my spiritual mentor and always provided positive reinforcement.

*****

Not long after getting married Rob re-signed with Girona. I wouldn't make a decision to move until I was sure my baby was healthy and safe. This baby was new life for me, a new birth for me from God that I would return.

Little did I realize my search for security, or the illusion of security, would cause me to lose my identity unknowingly. As a child, when my physical and emotional place was uncertain and insecure, I was more willing to explore and more open to everything the Universe had to offer without restraints. I went from a poor, uncertain, unstable little girl in Camden, New Jersey to unimaginable heights, thinking I was getting closer to obtaining security and certainty.

In Italy, I didn't own a house or car and my relationship with Adriano wasn't a possessive one. I had more freedom to explore, travel, and develop relationships and experience fully while attracting wealth. Uncertainty, insecurity, and instability meant freedom and growth for me. Now that I finally thought I was secure and stable with a big house, cars, husband and family, I was willing to do whatever to keep that illusion of security, including compromising who I was and eventually losing my authentic self.

Chapter 14

Dream Becomes Reality

Once safely past the three-month mark of my pregnancy I packed up our dogs, Roscoe and Gladys, and headed to Spain again. Rob and I enjoyed each other. We walked Barcelona's beaches with the dogs, visited historic Barcelona, played arcades and found a couple of wonderful local restaurants.

My Spanish obstetrician scheduled an amniocentesis test. While waiting for the results of the genetic testing, we had our first big conflict about the baby. If there was an abnormality, Rob wanted to terminate the pregnancy. There was no way I could abort my baby. As we waited for the results to return, I agonized about the decision. There was no further discussing our positions; it only caused me more angst.

In a private Barcelona clinic, after months of emotional distress and anxiety from the loss of my first child, I received the wonderful news that the baby growing inside me was perfect. This allowed me to close the door on the nightmare of my first pregnancy. I began writing a journal to my baby.

Rob was relieved that the baby was healthy and happy and that he was having a boy but he was still miserable playing. No matter what I did, nothing changed the situation and he refused to join in my enthusiasm with the pregnancy.

After a month of Rob's disinterest in me and my pregnancy, I returned home to New Jersey. I was excited about my baby boy, but we were constantly dealing with Rob's issues: his playing, his financial situation, his strained relationship with his parents and Bret, and his planes. I spent Thanksgiving with Mom. The first holiday without Dad. Everyone was curious to see me pregnant. I paid off the mortgage on Mom's house so she would never have to worry about a place to live.

After having ten children, she had learned the art of embracing each individual. We spent hours together quietly and introspectively, putting pieces of her puzzles together. She always had words of wisdom and reflection as we sat at her kitchen table with the sun beaming through the bay window filled with plants and flowers.

I left New Jersey energized and spiritually uplifted, ready to enjoy the last trimester of the pregnancy with Rob. While I was gone, and without my knowing, Bret and Rob hired an estate planner who had documents written up so I could not contest the will he had prepared earlier. The will excluded our baby and me. It would be years before I found out about this.

With Rob acting strange and after my Spanish doctor told me I was eating too much and gaining too much weight, even though I had only gained twenty-five pounds, I returned to Lexington before Christmas for the birth.

Rob quit the team and returned to Lexington in January. He was so despondent during the last few weeks of my pregnancy, that when I was diagnosed with preeclampsia and was placed on total bed rest, I called my sister Francina for help. Rob spent most of his time at the airport with his plane or hanging out with his best friend Greg who was also depressed and seeing a therapist.

*****

My due date was Valentine's Day, but Reva induced labor on February 6. We settled in the hospital that evening. I planned a natural childbirth without an epidural or medicines. Rob went home to get a good night's rest while Francina spent the night with me. With the start of the first contraction Francina and I joked as she viewed the monitor and talked me through it. As the second contraction came, she began her play-by-play analysis again.

"Okay, Valerie, the wave is forming...time to breathe," she chuckled while panting. "Remember your breathing."

I used the techniques I had learned in birthing class, thinking it would minimize the pain, huffing and puffing to her reading of the monitor.

"The wave is starting to peak," she smiled as I wondered why these initial contractions were so intense. I grimaced in pain.

"Wave crashing! Okay, you made it through another one! Way to go! It won't be long now."

Each time she walked to the monitor at the start of a contraction, I became more and more annoyed. This was way more painful than I had imagined.

"Could you just not talk during my contraction," I spewed after contraction three.

"Maybe you should get the epidural, Valerie...there's no need for you to suffer like this," she said after I nearly broke her hand and dug my nails into her skin during the fourth contraction. Her suggestion irritated me.

I couldn't imagine getting the epidural. I didn't want the drugs to get into Aaron's system and I didn't want to be a wimp. I was a professional basketball player; I could take these contractions; women did it all the time. What was wrong with me? The nurse had warned that if I waited too long before having the epidural it may not be effective, but I had seen that horse needle they would inject me with in one of my classes. I was miserable and didn't know what to do.

"Valerie, you know you can get an epidural and not go through all this pain," she said, as gently as possible.

"Francina, please, please, get the nurse and tell her I need that epidural, right now!"

The anesthesiologist came in smiling and whistling.

"Don't worry, this is gonna make you feel so good!"

Don't worry! I had to sit on the edge of the bed and bend over slightly, while he inserted a humongous needle in between my vertebrae. Don't worry? It was between this procedure or the next contraction that was on the horizon of the monitor.

"Okay, let's do it," I said. He inserted the needle and I felt relief immediately.

"I love you! Are you married?" I joked as he wished me luck for the rest of my delivery on his way out the door.

"Why didn't I do this earlier?" I said, smiling at Francina.

Francina and I laughed together as the next crashing wave came in. I was like a bleached-blonde California surfer enjoying the tidal wave. Throughout the night, with each contraction Francina held my hand. In between contractions she rested on the couch in the room. It reminded me of when I had been in the hospital after my car accident in Como. I was glad she was with me.

Rob arrived the next morning with Greg; they were heading out to breakfast. Francina phoned him as Reva and MJ prepared for the delivery. With the lights dimmed and Reva talking me through my last contractions, MJ read the sports section of the newspaper while Francina took pictures and Rob sat nervously. I pushed and pushed as Aaron's head crowned.

"Val, I'm going to have to cut you just a little..."

Reva barely got those words out as she turned and reached for her surgical scissors when I pushed as hard as I could. I couldn't think of her cutting me. Aaron spurted out like a missile as the nurse reached over Reva's shoulder, cupped her hands and caught him like a wide receiver catching a descending touchdown pass. Everyone gasped. Rob cut Aaron's umbilical cord. Francina continued taking pictures.

"He's beautiful, Valerie, " she said through tears. "Thanks for letting me be here for this special moment."

Aaron was born at 1:07 p.m. He was 8 lbs, 10 ounces and 21 and a quarter-inches long. My heart swelled when I saw my new-born son. I had spent the last nine months getting to know him, praying he would arrive safely in this world. He was a night owl like me, always getting active after the sun was down. Whenever I ate spicy food he got the hiccups. He loved classic music; it always calmed him down. We looked each other in the eyes. He was perfect and precious, even with his funny little cone head. I was blessed.

After two nights in the hospital we took Aaron home. On the way, we dropped by the vet to pick up Gladys and her pups. Overnight we had gone from being pro athletes to a family with a child, five dogs and lots of responsibilities. I wanted to be the best mom possible and a loving wife and I believed Rob wanted to be the head of the household and provide for his family. Rob, however, still had his dream and passion for airplanes and flying. I wanted Aaron to have a problem-free, stress-free childhood filled with love, but didn't realize I would have to navigate my relationship with Rob first.

We began experiencing subtle but real problems soon after Aaron arrived home and Francina returned to New Jersey. Rob was depressed about not having a job, having the responsibility of a baby, his uncertain finances and not getting enough attention from me. I was physically tired and overwhelmed.

One of the first nights we were home, Aaron wouldn't sleep. Rob was irritated as I picked up Aaron and went into one of the upstairs rooms. Nothing I did would quiet Aaron. Frustrated, I laid him on the bed.

"What do you want, Aaron? What is it? What do I do?" I asked my newborn son.

I was sleep-deprived and needed answers. I picked him up after a few seconds and rocked him to sleep. On April 12th, Aaron finally had his first full night of sleep in his crib. It was his first major milestone and one that I was excited about.

When Aaron was a little over a month old we travelled to California to visit Rob's parents. It was his first flight and a cross-country trip with multiple layovers that Rob planned. I was still recuperating from giving birth and visiting his parents always terrified me. I usually didn't associate with people who did not like me but these were Rob's parents. We hadn't addressed the issue and all pretended nothing was wrong. My mother told me it was important to get Aaron on a schedule. Rob's family constantly interrupted Aaron's schedule with visitors and visits. I was over-sensitive as well and took his mother's comments and remarks as negative and critical of me. Rob was happy to be back with his family and hanging out with his father. When we stayed at Rob's parents' house we never slept together, even though we were married.

A few days after returning from California, Aaron and I flew to New Jersey to visit my family. While there, UK won an NCAA national championship. Mom loved UK and it was fun watching the game with Barry, Mom and Aaron. Aaron was born during a year in which UK won a NCAA championship. Life didn't get better than that!

Back home in Lexington, Aaron was scheduled for surgery to repair two hernias. As they wheeled him to the operating room I was a nervous wreck. The day before we had celebrated Aaron's first rollover from his tummy to his back. Rob and I were in full parenthood mode in the hospital waiting room praying that our baby would be fine.

*****

By spring, Rob had decided that Greg was going to live with us because he needed help. He was suicidal. He had been seeing a therapist for a while, but the breakup with his girlfriend left him to be severely depressed. Putting Aaron in danger was the last straw for me.

"I know Greg's your best friend and I like Greg but he can't stay here. Find him a hotel and you two can stay together but I don't want something to happen to Aaron!"

"Aaron? Aaron? What are you talking about? Are you crazy? Greg's my best friend and I have to support him! Aaron will be fine. This is my house too!"

"How can you put your friend over your son? What if he does something? He's suicidal and seeing a therapist. You don't know what's going to happen. I'm not telling you to not help him but I know there's a better solution than having him stay here. I'm going to protect my baby!"

"I don't care what you say, Greg is staying here...period!"

"Well, Aaron and I won't be there."

After the heated exchange we decided we should seek counseling. We began couple therapy with Greg's therapist. Rob resented me for not letting Greg stay with us.

Regardless of the issues, I believed we could work through our problems. I asked MJ for a therapist. I began sessions with one she recommended, hoping to get some answers for myself. Each week,

Aaron and I sat in the therapist's office as I tried to figure out what I was doing wrong and what was wrong with me that I couldn't make my marriage work after such a short time.

Bonnie Hutton, my best friend from college, who was living in Florida, came to visit me with her two daughters a couple weeks later. We went out by ourselves. Although I was slightly embarrassed, I told her I was seeing a therapist. In all my playing days, I had never encountered a problem that I couldn't find a solution for and solve, but marriage was driving me crazy. Bonnie offered her advice over a good bottle of Merlot, "Marriage wasn't always easy but eventually it worked out if two people loved each other."

My relationship with Rob was confusing and unpredictable. For Mother's Day, he prepared breakfast and bought gifts and a card from himself and Aaron —maintaining the appearance of a happy family. MJ, Ingrid and I took Aaron golfing with us and sometimes Rob joined us as well. MJ taught him how to feed Aaron his first solid food. Some nights Rob bathed Aaron. We attended air shows together, which Rob loved, but there were times when he preferred Aaron and me not to be around. One of those times was in July when Sean came to visit him. I hadn't seen Sean since Rob had sent him home in Forli'.

Aaron and I flew to Buffalo to visit Barry and his family while Sean visited Rob. Dennis and his family were in New Jersey visiting Mom. We drove down to New Jersey and hung out with Barry's family, Dennis' family, Wendell's family, and Mom. I had so much fun with all the confusion and enjoyed some freedom. Aaron's first two teeth showed up while we were at Mom-Mom's. I loved recording all of Aaron's firsts in his journal. We all packed into a 15-passenger van and drove back to Buffalo.

Shortly after Aaron and I returned to Lexington, Pietro, a good friend of mine from Italy, and his family came to visit. Pietro and I had known each other since the first year I played in Italy. He was a journalist from Sardegna and we became best friends immediately. Pietro was fun-loving and adventurous. Pietro, his wife Kirsten and children arrived in a broken-down van he purchased for a few hundred dollars to travel across the USA. When they pulled up in our driveway, they reminded me of a hippy family as they exited the vehicle, happy and full of energy. I was happy that they were coming to visit but Rob didn't like me associating with my Italian friends.

*****

Back in Lexington, Channel 18 called, wanting to know when I would be returning as a sports reporter. The 1996 Summer Olympics would be starting soon and everyone was talking about the USA women's basketball team that had toured the world for a year before the Olympics and was undefeated. It was refreshing to see the positive change in America with regard to women's basketball.

After watching the Olympics, I registered to finish my degree at UK. With Aaron growing, I knew it would be more difficult to get my degree as he got older. I only needed a semester to finish. I would finally make a different dream come true for myself – getting that degree.

Aaron began crawling near the end of August as I was inducted into the Kentucky Athletic Hall of Fame along with William T. Young, Kyle Macy, Darrell Griffith, Paulie Miller, Don Fightmaster, Steve Meilinger and Jim Reid. M. J. and Ingrid helped Rob with Aaron as he crawled around their table. I was seated next to W. T. Young at the head table. His horse, Grindstone, had won the 1996 Kentucky Derby and his horse Editor's Note had taken the Belmont Stakes. We enjoyed the evening talking about athletes, horses, UK, and life in general. He invited me and my family to visit him at Overbrook Farm in Lexington.

Young took us on a personal tour of his meticulously kept horse farm. It was the quintessential horse farm – acres of rolling bluegrass with miles and miles of wooden horse fencing. It was amazing that the horses on the farm lived better than most people. Although we didn't see Grindstone, Aaron got a chance to pat Storm Cat. Storm Cat's breeding fee during the peak of his stud career was one of the highest in the world at $500,000.

It wasn't long after the Olympics and my induction into the Kentucky Hall of Fame that Dotti Berry began bugging me about the new women's professional league, the American Basketball League. We had begun working on Still Kids Improvement Program (SKIP) when her marketing company began working with the league. She wanted me to try out for a team. I said no. Aaron was only six months old. I was retired. I was 35 years old. I wanted to finish my degree. I hadn't played for quite some time; I was out of shape and my marriage needed work. She called again and I said no.

In her next call she informed me that she was able to get me a try-out with the team from Columbus, Ohio. It would be a short three-hour drive and I had nothing to lose.

"Dotti, I don't even have a pair of basketball shoes," I scuffed at her over the phone, tired of her bugging. "I'm nursing Aaron right now; can you call back later?"

"Val, we'll pick up a pair on the way to Columbus; there's tons of outlet stores," she replied in her heavy southern drawl, not acknowledging my annoyance.

"Dotti, I don't have anyone to watch Aaron," I said, knowing she knew I would never put my needs above Aaron's. I was no longer a basketball player; I was a mother. And mothers, especially old mothers like me, didn't play professional basketball.

"Val, I'm going with you and I'll take care of Aaron while you try-out," she insisted. "This could be a chance of a life time for you. You'll be making history. I know that you can do this and you'll be great once you start playing again."

Dotti was always a motivational, conquer-the-world type. She had been by my side when I had overcome my life-threatening illness at UK. I trusted Dotti and prayed about the try-out. I didn't tell anyone except Rob. We were planning to leave for California to visit his family. Surprisingly, Rob offered to ride up to Columbus for the try-out with us. Dotti, Rob, Aaron and I headed up I-75 North to Cincinnati. Dotti and I picked up a pair of shoes and socks at an outlet store and then we got onto I-71 North to Columbus for the try-outs. I nursed Aaron before getting off the exit for Columbus so that he would be asleep for the try-outs. We arrived at a big brown hangar/barn-type structure in a field. I had driven all this way and for what?

"Val, this is gonna be great. Just be you!" She said, reaching out to grab sleeping Aaron from my arms.

We entered the sweltering building without air conditioning

while sweaty players were already running drills. I didn't recognize anyone. It had been so long since I had played, especially in the USA. A blonde-haired familiar face ran over to me during a water break to say hello. Andrea Lloyd. I had played with and against Andy in Italy for many years. We had lost the championship together at Schio. The rest of the players looked so young, strong and out-of-control. What had Dotti gotten me into?

I slipped on the socks and shoes I had just purchased, discarded the box and checked on Aaron. Libby, a lady with the team, came over and introduced herself and asked if she could help with Aaron. An attractive middle-aged man who looked like he hadn't been sleeping well, with droopy eyes, large teeth, chipmunk cheeks and a strong country accent, walked up and introduced himself.

"Hello, Valerie, I'm Brian Agler, coach of the Columbus Quest. I'm glad you came. Get a ball and get warmed up. We'll get you in some drills but first let me introduce you to the team," he said as he whistled and the players slowly made their way toward us.

The two smallest players on the team were the most rambunctious. They were a comedy team, keeping everyone laughing, but were also very talented and full of energy. I warmed up and began drills. Although I was out of shape, I managed to hold my own. My heart raced, my chest burned and I was short of breath but my competitive nature wouldn't let me quit. What I lacked in skill and conditioning, I made up for in sheer determination. I defended, took an occasional shot, out-rebounded much younger and athletic players. I was always a rebounder; that instinct came back quickly. When it was time to pick teams for scrimmaging, the two small players, Pee Wee and Sonja, selected teams. I was one of the first players picked.

It was fun getting back to playing. It wasn't easy but this was what I loved doing. I was so out of shape but basketball would always be my passion and when I played, the world was always a much better place for me.

When I was done with the work-out, I headed over to check on Aaron, anxious to leave. Dotti and Rob were standing to the side; I mumbled under my breath to them. "Let's get out of here so we can get back home. Sorry this didn't work out."

Brian hurried toward us waving us into his office. He took a seat behind his desk and Dotti and I sat in two chairs while Rob stood near the door.

"Val, we'd love to have you on our team," he said. "I think you could really help us out and I think we're going to have a pretty decent team. Katie Smith isn't here yet; she's one of our top players and we had our number-one post player quit after seeing the team. I think you have a great opportunity here. I want to sign you right now."

I couldn't believe I was being offered a spot on a professional team in the USA. As a little girl, my dream was to play professional basketball in the USA and now, at 35 years old and with a baby, my dream was becoming a reality. I turned and looked at Rob who was in disbelief.

"Give us a few days, Brian. We're heading to California," I stuttered while my thoughts raced. "I really need to talk this over with my husband."

As I headed to the door, Pee Wee and Sonja ran over, hugged me and kissed Aaron. Sonja tapped Aaron's head.

"Hey big head 'lil man, we'll see you soon," she joked as Brian yelled for her to get back on the floor.

I had big decisions to make. On the drive back to Lexington we discussed every possible scenario of my decision to play professionally. I talked to mom as well before leaving for California.

*****

Rob and I sat in his parents' home in California, waiting for a contract to be faxed. I wanted to play but I needed Rob's approval. This would definitely complicate our transition from professional athletes to a traditional husband and wife scenario. I didn't think in terms of husband and wife roles. No matter what the circumstances or where he was playing, I was willing to follow and do what was necessary to make it work for us. Now I had a chance to help our family with an offer of a lifetime, but I would need him to play the supporting role. I didn't know what was going through Rob's mind but I was hoping he would be supportive. It would be his turn to play the supportive role but for a male athlete ingrained in the traditional roles of male and female, would he be able to adapt to playing the supportive role?

On top of the role reversal in our relationship, this meant redefining motherhood. Could a good mother be a professional basketball player? Could a mother pursue her career and still be a good mother? Could a mother pursue her career and be a good mother without the support of her partner? For an elite athlete, it was about getting the job done regardless of obstacles. But I wouldn't think of my son as an obstacle. As an elite athlete, mother and wife I would have to learn how to navigate the treacherous waters, ride the bumpy situations and avoid the pitfall of wanting everything to run smoothly. Male athletes who were fathers never had to question whether they were good fathers when pursuing their career. I had waited to have a child so I could be the traditional stay-at-home mom, but now I had the opportunity to be a pioneer for female athletes by being both a professional athlete and a mother.

The terms of the contract that were important changed because I became a mother-player. Yes, salary and training was important but could Aaron attend practices? Could he travel with the team? Would he be allowed to travel with us? On a personal level, I would have to decide if I wanted to continue breastfeeding and whether I could perform even after being up all night with a sick child. Should I feel guilty because I was playing and Rob wasn't?

Making the decision to play indicated that I was willing to give up the illusion of security. My marriage and family represented security. Deciding to play in the ABL, a concept that was uncertain and unstable, and one that would mean major unexpected changes, seemed illogical for someone who was always in search of security, but in my heart I knew I was supposed to take this journey. I knew that with my decision to play, Rob could easily become more irritated and our relationship could be destroyed. The decision to play would take all control out of my hands and put me in a position to fall apart. I was willing to take that chance.

*****

My decision to play in the ABL after being married for a year

202

and with a six-month old child challenged societal norms. Many, including me, believed that I had I become the rare quintessential ideal working mom when I began playing for the ABL Columbus Quest. That was far from the truth.

Although I didn't know about Caroline Still at that time, we shared the same DNA. William Still's daughter, my nineteenth century cousin, had already succeeded as a working mother during the oppressive Victorian era. She not only became one of the first female African American doctors shortly after the Civil War; she did so while mothering a small child. She paved the way for the positive changes that were taking place with regard to the relationship between women, motherhood and career that allowed me the opportunity to sign my ABL contract.

The old saying, "The pen is mightier than the sword," or "he who holds the pen controls history" was true. Caroline Still's working mother narrative was not one that was well known. She had broken down a barrier for women and African Americans. My decision to sign with the ABL was thought to be exceptional. A thirty-five year-old mother of an eight-month-old baby willing to sacrifice her family, marriage, husband, and child to be part of the anomaly of a women's professional sports league in the USA was unthinkable and noteworthy in the twentieth century only because the working women's narrative of the nineteenth century was rarely written about. The Still spirit continued to drive me on my new quest.

Chapter 15

Long Journey...Enjoy the Ride

1996 represented birth: the birth of my son, the birth of a professional league for women, and my rebirth as a person. Aaron represented my future and my legacy. By the end of the year, the ABL represented the future for women in sports and I would be a part of that legacy.

At the beginning of October, I packed my bags with just enough for Aaron and me to survive temporarily. We moved into a hotel, which would be home until I was able to find an apartment. I practiced with the Columbus Quest only twice before signing an ABL contract and heading to Springfield, Missouri with six other players for our first ABL exhibition game against the Colorado Xplosion. Andy Lloyd was recovering from knee surgery and Katie Smith's agent was negotiating her contract, leaving us with only seven players. The game would be an explosive start to a tantalizing life experience that Aaron and I could have never been prepared for.

The night before our trip, I sat in my small cluttered hotel room in Ohio, nursing Aaron, wondering what influence this would have on my son one day. Since his birth many had speculated on whether he would play basketball someday like his parents. I wondered how Aaron's view of women would be influenced by being in this environment of strong, athletic women. After laying him down to sleep amongst bags, I sat quietly, folded my legs, lit a candle and began a new meditation technique, focusing on being strong, stable, and unchanging like a mountain. Once done, I slept peacefully.

We arrived in Springfield the next day, settled into our hotel and later had practice. Dotti and Aaron attended. The exhibition game the following day would be part of history and although no one had much belief in the Quest's ability, Brian believed that if we would compete and execute, we could exit the game with dignity. It was a long night for me. Aaron had problems falling asleep in the small portable crib I had brought with me. Eventually Dotti walked him around the hallways so that I could get some rest for the game.

The Springfield game was the first official pre-season game for the Columbus Quest. We played at Southwest Missouri State University (SMSU), a hub for women's basketball. The fledgling ABL needed to develop interest in the league by strategic placement of teams and playing in markets where women's basketball was prominent. Although Springfield didn't have an ABL team, the game was sold-out.

Without Katie, many thought the Quest was definitely the "least likely to succeed" team and dubbed the "Questions." The fact that even I, an old retired player who had an eight-month-old child, was given the opportunity to try out and actually made the team was a sign that the team was doomed to fail. The Xplosion was favored to win.

The record crowd at SMSU watched in awe and excitement as the underdog and undermanned Quest entertained with meticulous execution of skills and played with extreme discipline, cohesiveness and a fearless attitude. With the final buzzer, the Quest's effort and victory over the Xplosion in that first preseason game could symbolize the plight of the ABL, an underdog league with a fearless attitude that had a chance to change women's professional basketball in the U.S. forever. Coming off the bench playing only 24 minutes, I scored 20 points, pulled down 11 rebounds and had 7 steals. We won the game 87 to 76.

Brian was thrilled about the win but more importantly he was excited about the way our team had come together. I celebrated on the court like a high school player and then returned to my hotel room to breastfeed Aaron and nurse my aching body. I was feeling pain in every muscle and joint. After I got Aaron to sleep I wrote in the journal I kept for him:

You won't believe the changes that have happened since I last wrote to you. You and I are in Springfield, Missouri, for the first official professional women's basketball league game. You probably won't remember any of this but you are a part of history. Maybe as you read this it will be hard to imagine that you were there from the start. Hopefully, the league will be like the NBA by the time you read this…

*****

At the Quest press conference I became the official "modern, working but nurturing mom" of the ABL. It was interesting that when I played in Italy I was known for my sensuality and wild, partying character while still being able to be a star basketball player. With the ABL, I was presented as a nurturing mother and wife who could play basketball. For marketing I would be a family woman with husband and child. The press release included Aaron and my husband. I was juggling the hectic schedule of being a mother and a professional basketball player at the same time, toting Aaron from practice-to-practice and event-to-event, nursing him along the way. I was also the veteran underdog who had waited patiently for my dream to come true in the USA. I was the hero who had returned home after the long journey.

The first few weeks weren't easy; Aaron and I lived by ourselves in a hotel in a place I was unfamiliar with and without family or friends. Rob stayed in California. Brian was understanding, and he told me not to put pressure on myself. After December, I would be ready. He and his loyal assistant, Kelly Kramer, were extremely understanding with Aaron as well. I wasn't sure how we would work it out but we all became accustomed to Aaron being with the team. He was at team practices, team meetings, and team events and travelled to games and scrimmages on the team bus and on flights. Typically, in professional sports, children of athletes were never seen; instead, with the Quest, Aaron changed the way professional athletes and coaches perceived team members' children.

Early morning practices were a real challenge for me. For the 7 a.m. practices, just getting through the two hours was an accomplishment, especially when Aaron was up until 3 or 4 in the morning. Unlike my younger single teammates, I usually arrived at practice with a load of maternal responsibilities while working through my domestic situation. I called Mom every night after bathing, nursing and putting Aaron to bed. She was proud of what I was doing and encouraged me to push through the difficult times.

My teammates became family. We were a unique blend of players and personalities. Andy and I were veteran players who had played many years overseas, winning championships but were now both married. Andy and her Italian husband were newlyweds and adjusting to his first time in the USA. We had mature players like Tonya, who had played in Turkey and Israel but had also coached high school and at a community college; Sonja, who graduated from Arkansas State in 1992 without the possibility of furthering her career; Cass who led Montana State to their first Big Sky Championship but had become a surgical nurse, and Carol Ann, the 1994 collegiate player of the year. We had players who had been out of college for a year. Nikki, our franchise player, was an Olympic darling with a diva attitude. La'Shawn Brown had postponed going overseas to play in order to finish her degree at Louisiana Tech. Lastly, we had talented rookies, arguably players with the most talent and potential on the team, Katie and Shannon. They were the first class of American female players who would never need to leave the USA to pursue their dream of playing professionally. Hometown favorite Katie was the NCAA Player of the Year and Shannon "PeeWee" was definitely the most athletic player on the team. Aside from athletic talent, the most important quality of the team was unselfishness. The team was deceivingly talented and uncannily amalgamated.

Brian's continuity offense was one that required players to make split-second decisions depending on the play of the defense. His defense was an in-your-face, scrappy, relentless man-to-man that relied heavily on help from teammates; his practices were brutal. His personality and system along with Kelly's demeanor and loyalty to Brian created the perfect spark to ignite the fire in each player.

On October 19, 1996 we played the first game of the season against the Richmond Rage in Columbus. Richmond was one of the teams favored to win the championship with stars that included Olympian Dawn Staley, Brazilian superstar Marta de Souza Sobral, and multi-sport Olympian hero Jackie Joyner-Kersee. Staley had celebrity status in women's basketball and Joyner-Kersee was one of the most famous female athletes in the world. Many would come to our first game just to see those two players. The last time I played against Jackie was when UCLA played Kentucky in Memorial Coliseum in 1981; since then she had become the world's greatest female athlete.

After introducing the Richmond team with cheers from the crowd, the announcer bellowed over the sound system, "And now, your Columbusssssssssssss Quest!!!"

The place erupted and with each player's name announced we took our place in history on Battelle Hall's court. I stood facing Jackie Joyner-Kersee, holding back tears with the national anthem booming over the loudspeakers. The announcer informed the boisterous crowd that this was the first official game of the ABL's Columbus Quest, women's professional basketball, and we were making history. Both teams stepped to half court to shake hands. Jackie and I hugged.

The Quest jumped off strong and never let up. Dawn Staley was stunned as we routed Richmond 101 - 76, becoming the first team in the ABL to break 100 points. I was the first sub off the bench and during a pause in the action looked at the scoreboard; the time – "8:13." It would not be the last time I saw those numbers.

*****

The day of the San Jose game, Aaron began climbing up the stairs. By December he learned how to climb downstairs, wave byebye and stand by himself while we were blazing through the season with a 14-1 record and undefeated at home, continuing to surprise everyone in the league. Though the team was having tremendous success, I suffered with aches and pains, adjusting to elite training and trying to navigate my relationship with Rob.

On our trip to New England, Aaron became ill. His temperature spiked and he began vomiting on the morning of the game. Leaving Rob and sick Aaron at the Hartford hotel was difficult for me. This would be Aaron's first time being sick and I wouldn't be there to comfort him. When we returned to Columbus, I had a meltdown. I couldn't do this anymore. My body was aching all over, my heart was hurting and I was overwhelmed. I called Dotti first to let her know; I was over my head and needed to call it quits. After talking to her I called Mom.

"Mommy, I can't do this anymore. I don't think there's a place on my body that doesn't hurt, even the soles of my feet ache, plus I'm having a hard time breastfeeding Aaron. What's wrong with my milk? I'm always tired. And Rob's not happy."

I began to sob.

"It's okay to cry. Let it out. Sometimes a good cry is just what you need."

"But...but...but... I love playing but I can't do this...it's too much."

"It's okay honey, you have to take one moment at a time. Get some rest whenever you can. When Aaron takes a nap, you take a nap. Things will get better. Call your sister Francina and see if she can come out and help you."

I called Francina. She came. We pushed forward.

In our first home game in December, La' Shawn, a reserve post player, grabbed Aaron sitting in his stroller courtside and began warming up by pushing him around the perimeter of the court. Aaron's first steps were captured by The Columbus Dispatch photographer after a practice in Battelle Hall, with Sonja and me celebrating him. The picture and an article about my juggling motherhood and a basketball career appeared on the front page of the Accent section. The picture spoke a thousand words of a mother's joy during a milestone in her child's life while expressing the support and love I had with my basketball family. Aaron helped diffuse the normal tension and stress of a pro athlete and basketball helped relieve the tension and stress of my domestic life.

The Quest continued to dominate the league, losing only one game in two months, and remained undefeated at home. The first ABL All-Star game was held December 15, 1996. I stopped breast-feeding Aaron at ten months even though I was hoping to at least get a full year. Before the Christmas break we were defeated in Richmond. Francina returned to New Jersey. We ended 1996 with a west coast trip and two wins against Seattle and Portland and the best record in the ABL.

In the Portland airport, as we waited for our red-eye flight back to Columbus with a layover in Chicago, I changed Aaron's soiled diaper before boarding. I loved playing practical jokes and decided Nikki would be my target. Nikki and I had become good friends. She loved singing to Aaron and he loved pulling her trade-mark golden braids. Nikki was the diva on the team, in an endearing way. When flying, she always sat in first class, while we travelled in the economy section. Usually she would bring free drinks back to us from first class and we would always tease her about being a diva. On this night though, while Nikki wasn't watching her bag, I slipped in Aaron's dirty diaper without her knowing. By the time the team boarded, we all knew about the diaper except her. We chuckled among ourselves as she placed her stinky bag in the overhead compartment, thinking about what the other first-class passenger sitting next to her thought about the strange odor. Throughout the night, Nikki brought drinks back to us as we wondered when she would realize her bag was stinking.

During our layover in Chicago, Nikki took Sonja to the airline's Red Carpet Lounge. When they exited, Nikki pulled me aside.

"Val, you're so silly, putting that diaper in my bag," Nikki laughed. "Don't worry, I slipped it into Sonja's bag without her knowing."

Sonja approached us, with a big smile, as Nikki boarded our next flight to Columbus. When Nikki had boarded, Sonja turned to me.

"Val, Nikki doesn't know, but that diaper is in her pillowcase," Sonja said as we broke out in laughter.

Nikki hadn't upgraded to first class for this flight but sat a row in front of the team. As she grabbed her pillow from her bag and fluffed it up before resting her head on it, we could barely restrain our laughter.

"Who letta air biscuit?" Nikki turned to the team and shouted.

"Air biscuit" was the term I used with Aaron for flatulence. Everyone burst out laughing, including Nikki, when she reached in her pillowcase and pulled out Aaron's little dirty surprise. After that trip, my teammates were always watchful for "gifts from Aaron." Although these acts seemed juvenile, part of the Quest success was the ability to work hard but have fun.

I had become a fan favorite even though I wasn't a starter. Older women loved me because I was proving that women were capable of maintaining a certain lifestyle as they grew older. Male fans loved my aggressive, all-out, fundamentally sound play, while girls loved me as a role model and I loved being a role model for them. In each one of them, I saw myself. Young fans were obsessed with the Quest; many were young female middle school basketball players. I always took time to talk and interact with all of our fans.

Arminta was one young fan who came to every game and always had special signs and surprises for me. Regardless of how much time I took to leave after the game, she would have her mom wait so we could talk and hang out. "Mickie," as she liked to be called, and I became really good friends. She became a little sister to me and a big sister to Aaron. Another young fan, Tiffany, also began helping Rob by watching Aaron during the games and whenever I needed a babysitter. Mickie and Tiff didn't miss one home game.

*****

The Quest clinched the Eastern Conference title on January 19 against the Atlanta Glory in Atlanta. We blew them out by 43 points.

We returned to Columbus and celebrated our Eastern Conference title at a gay bar downtown. It was not an unfamiliar place for us; we had had several events at a few of the gay bars in town. Columbus had one of the largest gay communities and the ABL embraced the gay community. It was remarkable that gay women didn't have the stigma of being gay with the ABL and our teams. Lesbians had always been a major support of women's basketball but they were always hidden from its history and tradition. This was no longer true in the ABL. Pee Wee and her girlfriend Jean had a wonderful relationship and openly shared an apartment during the season.

We celebrated Aaron's first birthday three times. The night before his birthday we had a home game. At the beginning of the third quarter an announcement was made that it was Aaron's birthday. Fans joined in to sing "Happy Birthday" to him while he crawled around courtside. Three days later Aaron and I headed back to Lexington to celebrate with MJ and Ingrid. And finally Mickie and her mom helped me organize an official party with the team at my house. They all came bearing gifts and toys and I had each person write something in Aaron's journal.

*****

Not many expected the Quest to pull off a clean sweep in the ABL standing and statistics. We led the league in both scoring offense and scoring defense. Sports Illustrated wrote a feature article about our incredible talent but the lack of fans. We weren't concerned about who was at our games or watching us; we played with unrestrained passion. We clinched home court advantage for the playoffs and I was placed in the starting lineup because Andy was injured. We easily beat San Jose 2-0 in a best-of-three series to advance to the finals. Richmond beat Colorado 2-0 to make the finals an All-East-coast one.

In Game One of the finals, we beat Richmond by one point with a bucket by Nikki with 39.7 seconds remaining. One down, two to go.

The second game of the finals we were ice cold and I was overpowered by a much younger, bigger, and stronger Taj McWilliams. I played only 16 minutes. Taj was a powerful player and in games one and two, she outplayed me. When the final buzzer sounded, we lost 75-62. Richmond had met their objective to win one game in Columbus.

At home I used my visualization of a mountain meditation to clear my mind. I had begun meditating again after the first month of playing with the team.

Our shooting problems continued in game three at Richmond.

We had several opportunities to win the game but as the clock ran down, Adrienne Goodson converted an easy basket as the nearly 7,000 fans erupted with the final score of 72-67. Richmond was one victory away from the first ABL championship.

In practice the next day we were relaxed and more confident than ever. Brian told us to make sure we got a good night's rest and not be up too late. Sonja and I couldn't sleep and turned on the TV. A replay of Game Three was on BET. As we watched the game, still fuming about the loss, an announcement was made that the MVP of the championship series would win a new Nissan Altima.

"Taz, that's my car...my mom needs a new car!" I shouted at Sonja. "I'm gonna win that damn car!"

"Yeah, right Val...Taj will give your mom a ride," she snapped back. "But you did kill tonight. If you play like that you may have a chance."

Whenever we were in critical games or situations with our backs against the wall, we always found a solution. After warm-ups, game four was delayed. Waiting for the scoreboard to be fixed, we interacted with our fans behind the bench who had travelled to Richmond for the finals, and teased Richmond's fans. With the start of the game, I won the tip-off and played possessed. I scored 22 points and grabbed 16 rebounds while dominating and frustrating Taj defensively in the paint. During a timeout in the second half, I looked at the scoreboard – "8:13." I kept seeing these numbers: scoreboards and clocks. My childhood address was 813 Ferry Avenue. Whenever I saw "813," I now felt Dad was watching. He had never been to any of my games or seen me play while he was alive but I believed he now was watching me and was proud. We beat Richmond 95-84.

The night before the final game, I called Mom as usual. She was excited about watching the game live and would be glued to the TV set. Everyone in the family was so proud. I promised her I would win her a car.

On March 11, 1997, we took the floor in front of our first sell-out crowd. I won the tip and made the first basket. The game was a classic Quest team effort with each player being significant. Players on the floor poured in every ounce of passion with each shot, rebound, loose ball and steal. Players on the bench exploded with support and enthusiasm after each action on the floor.

We went into the locker room at halftime with the lead. Brian didn't have much to say. Before returning for the second half he left us with his infamous, "You better hook up!"

The lead went back and forth throughout the third quarter. We built a ten-point lead with less than five minutes in the fourth quarter. With about a minute left in the game, we had a good lead. It was clear we had just won the first ever ABL championship. I hit another basket and celebrated down the court. With less than a minute, Brian pulled me out of the game with the crowd on their feet in a frenzy, showing their appreciation. I hugged Brian, Kelly and all my teammates and turned to find Rob and Aaron in the stands. Aaron was clapping as Rob pointed toward me. With the final buzzer, and the scoreboard reading 77-64, the arena exploded while the team celebrated on the court. I ran into the stands to get Aaron as the trophy ceremony began.

With Aaron sucking his right thumb and rubbing my ear with his left hand, I was named Most Valuable Player of the Championship series. The Nissan representative held an oversized cardboard car key in her hands as she turned to me.

"You've had a long journey here," she said. "And to enjoy the ride home, I want to give you the key to the Nissan Altima."

She was right; it had been a long and treacherous journey but I had arrived.

*****

At the end of March I travelled back to New Jersey with Aaron. Mom, Aaron and I went to the Cherry Hill Nissan dealership and she picked out her car. It was burgundy with leather interior, sunroof and a spoiler and was pin-striped. If anyone deserved a new car, it was Mom.

Aaron and I returned to Lexington in April, forever changed. The last year had been like a fairytale. Adriano had written me a few postcards and a letter. He had heard about the championship win. He was excited for me as well.

My high from our ABL championship didn't last long; during

a routine gynecological exam, Reva discovered a lump in my right breast. She did a biopsy and decided it was best to have the lump removed. The week waiting for the results was stressful as I thought about the possibility of not being around to watch Aaron grow. Once it was revealed that the lump was benign, I joked that while the younger players on the team were having knee surgery, I was having a lump removed from my breast. Getting old was no fun.

*****

Although Rob and I continued having relationship problems, I was the first Quest player to re-sign with the team. After signing my 2-year contract with the Quest we sold our house in Lexington and moved to Powell, Ohio, a suburb northwest of Columbus.

The Quest made history when we became the first women's professional team to be invited to the White House for a championship visit. It was during the Monica Lewinsky scandal and First Lady Hillary Clinton formally met with us. Sonja, who was from Arkansas, tried dancing with the First Lady. She turned and spoke to me while I held Aaron in my arms.

"I'm happy we have role models for our little girls," First Lady Clinton said while touching Aaron's face. "We need good role models like you for our little girls and boys."

Before we left, the First Lady kissed Aaron.

"Bye, bye little Aaron," she said to him as she turned and walked away with her secret service protection.

*****

At the end of June the WNBA began its inaugural season. Instead of having one strong, solidified league, the country would be divided between the ABL and the WNBA. And women would be in the middle of the conflict. We had fought hard for equality and now the focus was placed on which league would last. I didn't understand why the WNBA had begun a league when the ABL was a perfect solution for women's professional basketball. Why didn't the NBA partner with the ABL? Then we would have the best women's professional league in the world with the best players and the financial and marketing power.

I would become one of the loudest and most confrontational voices in the conflict between the ABL and WNBA. The NBA was a powerful entity and most were not willing to speak out against the NBA, but I was dubious about its intentions in women's basketball.

In its inaugural season, the slogans for the ABL – "Real Basketball" and "Little Girls Dream Too"– both seemed to denote a common mindset and values of athletes regardless of gender. The common dream of any athlete is to play a "real" sport. The primary mission of the ABL was to provide "real athletes" a "real sport" while capitalizing on the popularity of women's basketball; a subsequent mission was changing the ideology of female athletes in America.

Having the commitment of the premier players in the world was the ABL founders' first objective as they formed their "Player's League." Each team featured a 10-woman active roster. Average player salary in the ABL was $70,000 with top players earning as much as $125,000 and a minimum salary of $40,000. The players also owned 10% of the League in the form of a Players' Trust and had a voice in league management through participation on the Advisory Board.

The first season had been successful. Unfortunately, the biggest opposition would come from the NBA with the WNBA. It seemed the WNBA would be a bad and degrading imitation of professional basketball for women: a three-month summer league, which wouldn't pay players enough that they wouldn't need to play overseas still, and would always be considered a minor league to its Big Brother, the NBA, playing in NBA venues when the men weren't playing. I met with Gary Cavalli, Anne Cribbs, and Steve Hams, the founders of the ABL in California. I wasn't sure if they had the capability to sustain a professional league but they had done an awesome job the first season and I believed they had the best intentions for women's professional basketball.

*****

As a basketball player whose career was peaking at the age of 36 with a happy and healthy son, I could no longer deny my marriage was falling apart without anyone knowing. I thought success was arriving at the top, separating from the rest, where everything came together and problems were all resolved. It would take years before I understood that the objective shouldn't be to rise to the top of the mountain, getting away from my attachments, worldliness, people, suffering and chaos; instead I would have to move toward the suffering and painful relationships down the mountain until I reached the still, healing water at its base. That is where I would discover the love that would never die. The trek down the mountain would lead me to awakening and my soul yearned to be awakened. My experience with the Quest was an intricate part of my awakening process.

Chapter 16

Not Quieting a Voice

Opportunities poured in for me as the WNBA began its first season. Reebok signed me; this included being featured in Reebok commercials. I was also chosen as one of a few players to star in the ABL "Real Basketball" national ad campaign for the upcoming season. Being an outspoken skeptic of the NBA's motives for getting into women's basketball and its treatment of women, I was sought after by national newspapers, magazines and TV programs for quotes and comments about the status of women's basketball and the WNBA.

At the end of June, I was invited on BET Talk to discuss the two leagues. I was in the BET studios in Washington, DC with host Tavis Smiley and Ruthie Bolton-Holifield was via satellite from Sacramento where she played in the WNBA. After a passionate exchange between Ruthie and me, ESPN's sportscaster Robin Roberts called me before I left the station. She felt that creating tension and trying to discredit the WNBA would only hurt women's basketball. I felt that keeping the integrity of women's basketball and honoring the thousands of women who had sacrificed before the NBA decided that women's basketball could be a profitable capitalistic venture was important.

Nikki McCray and I had become good friends during the season and after the championship we hung out together. In July we headed to Miami. We were invited to the red-carpet-grand-opening event for an All-Star Cafe in South Beach. It was two weeks after Gianni Versace was murdered two blocks away and the organizers hired at least 12 security guards for each celebrity. We partied with Tiger Woods, Shaquille O'Neal, Pat Riley, Joe Montana, Andre Agassi, Wayne Gretzky, Ken Griffey Jr. and Alexi Lalas, all partners in the restaurant chain. Pat, a famous sportscaster, who had been drinking too much, was hitting on Nikki, and I met A-Rod, a handsome young talented baseball player with beautiful eyes, and who played for the Seattle Mariners. We laughed and talked and took some pictures together. Nikki said we made a cute couple but joked that I was old enough to be his mother.

Shortly before training camp, Nikki signed with the WNBA; Katie was holding out of training while negotiating her ABL contract and Tonya finally re-signed with the ABL. We had our core back: Tonya, Shannon, Sonja, Andy and me, believing that Katie would eventually sign. Five new players were signed. Brian's training schedule was grueling.

In our new home, Rob, Aaron and I adjusted to our suburban neighborhood in the northwestern suburbs of Columbus. Although Rob at times seemed to enjoy our new life, he still was unable to fully engage in our non-traditional, roll-reversed marriage. His dream was to have an airplane business with his parents. In Columbus, I was recognized and engaged in activities in the community. The Quest players and coaches were honored in City Council, and a victory celebration on the steps of City Hall and at City Plaza made us household names in the community. Unlike the beginning of last season, Quest fans anxiously awaited our first game of the season.

To start the 1997-98 season off, Dotti organized an ABL exhibition game in Memorial Coliseum in Lexington between the Quest and the Atlanta Glory. It was a homecoming for me. It had been fourteen years since I had played in Memorial Coliseum. Returning after winning the ABL championship was satisfying, playing in front of family and friends and having Aaron watch me play where I had set the records at UK.

The ABL tipped off its second season on October 12, 1997

in front of a record crowd of 12,623 at the Hartford Civic Center. Six days later, with a laser-light show and screaming fans we received championship rings at our season-opener home game against Richmond. We stood at half-court as our 1997 World Championship Banner was hoisted to the rafters while Tina Turner's "Simply the Best" played through the sound system. Aaron sat with Rob, Dotti and Maria, our nanny, a few rows behind our bench. We were defeated 86-87 and started the season 2-2. This was the first time we had not been in first place; some questioned whether we would be able to have another successful season.

On the court, the Quest continued to have a unique cohesiveness; part of that affection spilled over into intimate relationships between team members. Pee Wee and Katie became a couple during the season.

In December we had our first game in Philadelphia. I was excited about returning to the South Jersey area. It was my first time playing basketball where I grew up since graduating from high school and playing in front of childhood friends and family. Some of my teammates from Camden High and their families came to the game. Barry was on the East Coast with his family so they attended the game along with Mom, her brother Kenny and his wife. Uncle Kenny held a big party at his house for the team. After the game we drove to New Jersey. We beat the Rage 80-69 as the cherry on top of the cake.

By January I was among the ABL leaders in scoring, rebounding and blocked shots and was selected to play in the 1998 ABL All-Star Game at Disney World. The contest took place at Disney's Wide World of Sports complex. Rob, Aaron and I left a couple of days earlier to spend time relaxing and enjoying family activities; this was our first family vacation. It was stressful for me doing family activities while preparing to play in the All-Star game. On game day we had breakfast with Micky Mouse, Winnie-the-Pooh and Goofy, explored downtown Disney and had lunch at the Rainforest Cafe. After Aaron's nap we headed to the arena for the game.

Stepping onto the court, with the crowd cheering loudly as my name was announced during a pregame light show, was unreal. I soared for the tipoff and scored the first basket of the game with adrenaline surging. Less than two years earlier I was preparing to birth Aaron without a thought of playing basketball ever again and here I was playing with the best players in the world. In four months I would be 37 years old; I was well past the normal age for most professional athletes but excelling and at the peak of my game.

I met Reggie Williams, former NFL star and vice president of Disney Sports, at the reception. He was intense, engaging, intelligent and interesting. We promised to stay in touch. I was always in awe of meeting famous athletes and celebrities even though I was considered a noted athlete. My upbringing had left me with an inferiority complex.

I was exhausted by the time we returned to Columbus but didn't get a break. We were 32-7 and had twelve more regular season games. We beat Philly again 76-71 and won all 10 games in January, clinching the Eastern Conference title on January 28 against Seattle at home. We finished the regular season 33-8, only losing in Seattle at the beginning of February.

Our incredible 36-8 regular-season record included winning an ABL-record 13 straight overall and 21-straight home games. We had four over-100-point games, finishing the last two games of the regular season eclipsing the 100-point mark. The last game of the season we beat Atlanta 101-70.

We beat San Jose in the Semi-finals of the playoffs 2-0, as we had the previous year. Our opponent for the finals was the Long Beach StingRays. Long Beach had a great team, a big physical team, a smart team. They were strong in each position. I would be matched up against Olympic gold medalist Venus Lacy, a 6'4" aggressive, physical post player, but also would match up with the ABL's number one draft pick, Yolanda Griffith, who was also 6'4". Long Beach also had 6'4" Cass Bauer, who had played with us last year but was traded to Long Beach.

We lost the first two games in Long Beach and found ourselves on the brink of elimination heading back to Columbus. Long Beach only needed to win one of the next three games to clinch the title. In Game Three we returned to our unyielding defense, held Long Beach to 61 points and won 70-61. We beat them in Game Four as well.

In the locker room before the fifth and final game of the series, we laughed and carried on as usual with our typical pregame locker room rituals. Music blasted, Pee Wee curled her hair and we teased each other about the previous games. We joked about Venus Lacy's hot temper. If there was a way of getting Venus agitated enough, we might be able to get her ejected from the game, making it a little easier on us. We laughed about Maura McHugh, the coach for Long Beach, insulting Katie on national TV during the last game. The networks had placed wireless microphones on coaches during the game so spectators could hear what was happening on the benches and during the game. In a timeout near the end of the last game, while Katie was scoring at will, Maura shouted at her players in the huddle, "we've gotta stop Fatty." She was referring to Katie. Although we teased Katie about it, it was offensive and gave us even more incentive to win. I jokingly offered $100 dollars to any team member that could trip up Maura on the sidelines. She was always standing on the court or kneeling close to it.

The game started intense as usual. Venus was overly aggressive and physical. She set a moving screen on Tonya, pulled my jersey to stop me on a fast break and pushed Andy to the floor, trying to get around a screen while I scored our first four points of the game. Later Venus shoved Tonya in the face and turned on me late in the baseline corner in front of the Long Beach bench. I was open for a second for a three-point shot when Venus came barreling out to contest it.

As I released the shot and she turned to block me out, I continued my follow-through motion, forming a fist, and punched her in her back. With the ball going through the basket, no one had noticed my hand motion. Venus was in hot pursuit so I turned to run down the sideline toward the referee at half court, as if transitioning to defense along the Long Beach bench. I tried to brush up against Maura, who was on the court, but missed and headed past the referees before Venus could catch me. The referees intervened along with two or three of Venus' teammates and with her coach constraining her. They couldn't afford to have her ejected from the game. As the refs sorted out what happened I told Katie what I had done while we walked back to center court and the crowd cheered wildly. We got the ball back because of the technical foul and after setting a screen for Pee Wee, I flared to the three-point line at the top of the key, scoring another three-point shot.

We led after the first quarter 14-12 and the game was tied at 33 at halftime with me leading all scorers with 13 points. We beat Long Beach 86-81. I was named MVP for the second-straight Finals series as we repeated as ABL champs. Instead of a car, I was awarded with a nice cash bonus.

The Columbus Quest joined a handful of teams that had won back-to-back professional team titles. I was the second-oldest player in the ABL at 36, but led the Quest with 14.6 points and 7.0 rebounds per game during the series, including a game-high 25 points in the clinching game. Including the playoffs, we had won 25 straight games at Battelle Hall.

As a team, we set numerous all-time ABL records during the 1997-98 season. I had done all I wanted to as a player; this would be my final season.

During the post-game press conference, I announced my retirement. I would go out a champion but I would still support the ABL. Maybe now I could be a spokesperson for the league but as for playing, I had accomplished more than I could have ever imagined. Aaron and I retreated to New Jersey to visit with Mom. I needed to sit with her at the kitchen table and put puzzles together. Aaron would enjoy some of her fried chicken.

*****

As I enjoyed retirement, Brian visited me at home. He had called me a few times trying to convince me to return for one more season but my time with the Quest was done; I could leave on a high note and give a younger player the opportunity to fulfill her dreams. Brian suggested I needed to return to continue to be a role model for young girls. When that didn't work he begged me to return so that we could build a dynasty like the Boston Celtics. Just one more season we could three-peat and etch our names in women's basketball legacy. One more year, I thought. I could do it. I would return for .

*****

In June, I announced the founding of the Valerie Still Foundation, a non-profit organization to help young girls grow into confident, healthy women. It was a way I could give back to all the women and girls who had supported me and also help girls like myself who were dealing with challenging issues of discrimination, self-esteem, health and peer pressure. I had always wanted a daughter and now I would have the opportunity to have many daughters. VSF was my passion now. I was able to get sponsorships from local businesses and Nationwide Insurance, which was headquartered in Columbus. VSF held a charity game between the Columbus Quest and the local media for promotions and sponsorships. Programs began in local schools with the first HOOPS! event, an all-day basketball clinic and tournament for middle-school girls. The focus wasn't on basketball but about providing positive female role models for young girls and for their empowerment. A number of female business leaders, politicians and teachers attended the event as guest speakers and presenters. Each year we invited a local high school team, a small college team and The Ohio State University team to help with the clinic. An all-star basketball game between our female guests, who weren't necessarily basketball savvy, demonstrated to the young girls that being active and participating in sports was beneficial for girls and women. HOOPS! Eventually became the biggest basketball event for young girls in the central Ohio area.

*****

The first sign for me that the ABL was having serious troubles was after I was named to the ABL Player's Advisory Committee. We met at the ABL offices in California to discuss the status of the league. I was shocked to hear that the league was proposing to cut players' and coaches' salaries and couldn't get a TV deal with a major network. The ABL was in financial difficulty.

Preseason started with a cloud of uncertainty looming. Everyone knew the ABL was struggling but it was business as usual for the Quest. Once we were on the court, we had laser focus and our focus this year was on winning a third championship. Our core from the first year had dwindled down to five: Katie, Shannon, Sonja, Tonya,

and me. Andrea had retired. My life was busier than ever with raising Aaron, running the Valerie Still Foundation, still working on my
relationship with Rob and now another season of basketball.

I was glad when October finally arrived. Our first exhibition
game of the preseason against the new Nashville Noise team was
October 11, 1998 at home. The ABL had weathered the management
storms and with the toss of the ball, the Quest's season began. Our
loyal fans cheered as we played Quest basketball, fast-paced and
aggressive.

Early in the game I grabbed a defensive rebound, passed it out to
Pee Wee and sprinted down the court for what should have been an
easy layup. She heaved the ball long toward our basket but it floated
toward the baseline. I planted my right foot hard on the baseline,
trying not to go out of bounds, but the momentum carried my body
forward. My knee buckled and I collapsed. Anticipating a basket,
the fans grew quiet instead as Brian and our doctor and trainer ran
onto the court. I was in excruciating pain. A few minutes later I was
assisted to the bench.

An MRI revealed the worst for me. I had torn my anterior cruci-
ate ligament and my meniscus. After all the years of playing, I had
had many injuries but never one this serious. I would need surgery
to replace the ligament. I had had the perfect opportunity to retire
gracefully after our second championship; now I was determined to
return before the season was over, finish it with the Quest and retire
for good.

Tiff's mom, Tammy, began calling to check on me. If I needed
anything she would help and whenever I needed help with Aaron,
she and Tiff were available. Tammy had worked for her family-
owned daycare for over 25 years. Aaron would be in good hands.
After my surgery Tammy came over to my house to help. We became best friends as she checked on me every day.

The team started the season with a home win against New
England. In the second game of the season in Nashville, less than
a month after my injury, Katie tore her ACL. After the team beat
Colorado in the third game, Brian talked Andy into coming out of
retirement. The following game the Quest beat the Chicago Con-
dors, bringing our record to 5-0 heading to a four-game West Coast

trip. But before the trip Brian signed with the WNBA. Tonya took over as head coach/player until the ABL could find a replacement for Brian, whose abandonment of the team was shocking.

On December 24, 1998, while we were all home on Christmas break, the ABL filed for bankruptcy protection and ceased operations. There was no official notice to the players. Most of the players heard the news on ESPN's Sports Center or through calls from friends or family. The Quest was in first place in the rankings with an 11-3 record and on its way to a third championship. My heart sank as I frantically made phone calls to see if this was just a joke. Unfortunately, it was true. The ABL no longer existed. I cried. The anguish of my career ending due to an injury paled in comparison to the loss of a family, a dream for millions of little girls, including myself.

With no forewarning, the end of the ABL meant unexpected unemployment and loss of healthcare for players. It also meant an uncertain future for both ABL and WNBA players and caused tension between the two leagues' players. The WNBA players felt the pressure of an influx of talented ABL players that could potentially mean unemployment for them, and the ABL players felt uncertain about how the WNBA would treat them. No longer having health insurance or income, some ABL players filed for unemployment compensation.

The city of Columbus held a farewell rally for The Quest downtown. It was painful seeing all the young girls and mothers crying about the loss of women they had come to love and respect. Each Quest player addressed the crowd with remarks. Pee Wee, as usual, was able to put a funny twist on the situation as she shared her experience at the unemployment office in Columbus with Sonja.

The demise of the ABL was devastating to most players. One Philadelphia Rage player, Trina Price, committed suicide. Stories in the media painted a picture of a player whose passion was basketball. With the recent deaths of her father and mother, Price had used basketball to cope. She had ended up with The Rage after she was not drafted by the WNBA. At the beginning of the 1998-99 season she had been excited about her new opportunity to play professionally in the USA with the ABL; a few months later her love and hope were gone. The 23-year-old shot herself.

The New Jersey Sports Writers Association named me Female Athlete of the Year. WNBA president Val Ackerman also received an award. I was surprised that we were placed at the head table together. We were cordial with each other. I expressed to her that I hoped I would have an opportunity to finish my career playing with the WNBA after my injury.

I attended the 1999 WNBA Pre-Draft Camp. Everyone knew me as the WNBA critic. I didn't participate in the workout sessions but my new agent thought I should be at the camp. A few other ABL players didn't participate in the sessions as well, including Katie, who was still recovering from her ACL injury, and Andy. When I arrived to check in, Lynn Norenberg, the graduate assistant at UK when I played and now with the WNBA Basketball Operations Department, came up to me. She had married former NBA player Rick Barry and was now Lynn Barry.

"Hey Val," Lynn was abrupt and unfriendly. "You talk too much; you should learn to keep your mouth shut."

I was taken aback by her comment and moved away from her, trying not to allow her negativity to influence my experience.

Back in Columbus my agent had been in touch with a few teams on my behalf and thought that I would probably be drafted last in the first round as a sign of retaliation. We planned to meet in her office for the draft on May 4th.

Brian was the general manager and coach for the WNBA Minnesota team. We knew he would be picking most of the Quest players if he had the opportunity. The WNBA had assigned Pee Wee to Orlando and Katie to Minnesota with Brian; that left Tonya, Sonja, Andrea, and me for the draft.

Brian's first pick was Tonya as the seventh overall pick of the draft. I wasn't drafted in the first round. Brian picked Andrea in the third round. I wasn't drafted in the second or third round. As the fourth and final round was beginning I had a knot in my stomach. With Brian's final picks, he selected Sonja and Angie. I was not drafted in the 1999 WNBA draft. I was the ABL's two-time MVP of the finals series on the best team in the league, an All-Star, but I had not been selected by one WNBA team.

After all the years of playing basketball nothing had ever hurt me this badly. I had always been a fighter but I had finally come up against something I couldn't beat. Deep in thought and fighting back tears, I heard Aaron's little cheerful voice once in my car riding back home.

"Mommy, are you alright?" he inquired.

"Mommy's okay, Aaron," I replied, not wanting him to see me upset.

"You're wonderful, mommy," he said, trying to reassure me. He was in tune with me. "Are we going to the park? I want to ride my bike and play basketball with you."

"Yes, sweetie," I said.

An hour after the draft, my agent and I received calls from the Cleveland Rockers and a couple other teams wanting me to try out as a free agent. I refused.

*****

On June 6, 1999, I wrote an article for the New York Times. It was half of the front page of the sports section with the title, "A 15-Year Playing Career Is Quieted but Not Her Voice." I didn't come up with the title but it was a good one. Outside the women's basketball world, few people knew me, but after the New York Times article, written from the perspective and lived-experiences of a veteran player, the unappealing secrets of what was happening in women's professional basketball were revealed.

After giving a little history of myself I presented my theory on the NBA's takeover of women's professional basketball and why I felt it should be important to all Americans, especially women. This wasn't about women's basketball; it was about women and our role in society. It wasn't by chance that I wasn't drafted but an hour after the draft I was asked to try out for a few teams. The NBA was letting me know that a peon like me had no power over the paternalistic and powerful NBA.

My article went on to point out facts that would support my theory that the WNBA didn't have the best interest of women in mind in forming the league. I backed it up with facts about their derogatory ad campaign the first year, "We Got Next." We Got Next was not a positive statement on playgrounds where I came from. "We Got Next" meant waiting for the big boys to finish before getting an opportunity to play. I thought it was ironic that the NBA was actually accurate with this slogan for the WNBA, since the women would have to wait until the men were done with their normal, regular season before playing three months in the summer.

Although playing in the summer could be considered demeaning, the NBA's handling of women's professional basketball was problematic in more significant ways. The fact that women players still needed to play overseas because of the inadequate wages and a three-month season was scandalous for a professional league. Players were underpaid and overworked. The NBA also didn't offer healthcare or a retirement plan to the WNBA players.

The majority of the WNBA players were gay and yet the NBA insisted on presenting them as heterosexual, as if being homosexual was deviant and needed to be hidden. The ABL had at least begun educating the public in terms of acceptance of gays, deviating from popular ideology on sexuality, even at the risk of alienating itself from potential public support.

I also questioned the fact that Brian Agler, my former coach, who had talked me out of retirement only to quit the team for the WNBA, didn't draft one of his best players. He had drafted every Quest player, including Angie Potthoff, but not me. I had exercised my right, as an American, my freedom of speech, but was being punished for it.

My New York Times article sent shockwaves through the women's basketball world. Val Ackerman called my house and left a voicemail on my answering service, wanting to talk to me. I didn't respond. I had talked too much and didn't have anything to say to her. I would leave women's basketball, forced out, but at least I would leave with my voice still being heard.

I knew that there was a great probability that the ABL would be erased from the history of women's basketball. The Quest was one of the greatest sports teams of all times but with the ABL's demise, the WNBA would erase it from the annals of women's basketball and dismiss it from professional sport leagues.

After the article I received support as well. Reggie Williams, Vice President of Wide World of Sport at Disney, called and told me he had read the article and thought it was a bold and courageous statement.

*****

The ABL was a social movement, a spiritual movement that had the possibility of changing professional sports in a meaningful way. It was not about just physical prowess and attributes: who could throw the farthest, jump the highest, run the fastest, score the most points or which athlete was the strongest. It was a medium for deeper conversation, reflection, and understanding about women in sports. It was an ideal platform because it was able to attract women who wouldn't have necessarily had an interest in sports and men who wouldn't have necessarily had an interest in women in sports.

Things that were seemingly insignificant in sports, such as children or gays, became focal points in the ABL. The Columbus Quest's model of operations introduced a new way of how children and the interaction between players and their children were accepted. Today, children of athletes and coaches are regularly seen on the sidelines of football fields or courtside at basketball games. Gay female athletes in women's basketball are now more open about their sexuality, while homosexual male athletes are still stigmatized in men's team sports.

The ABL was the heart of women's basketball. Professional women's basketball was a public platform that could engage all women. The ABL gave birth to a new perspective, a new look at women and their role and value in society, demanding equal pay for equal work and fair treatment. This battle was between the mind and heart.

*****

When I wrote the New York Times article, I thought it was empowering and that I had made strong points about what I believed the WNBA represented for women, but the most revealing and powerful point I made was inadvertent. In the last paragraph, I expressed that regardless of what had happened to me with the WNBA draft and being forced out of pro sports, the most important thing was I was a mother and still had my son. Of all the degrading and demeaning things I thought the NBA was doing to women with the WNBA, causing me to think that being a mom was more important than being myself was probably the most paternalistic and sexist. I realized much later I had let their actions inadvertently color my own beliefs about self.

Usually, it is a small group of radical people that sow the seed for major social changes in American history . . . not the majority. The ABL was that small group. It put love into professional sports and turned love into a political force. At least the ABL served its purpose. I would have to pick up the pieces and move forward on my own spiritual journey.

Chapter 17

Loss of a Soul Mate

The initial shock of not being drafted into the WNBA eventually faded with my reality of mother-and-wife duties. Basketball had been my identity for so many years that I wasn't sure who I really was. I hoped the friends I had made through the Quest would remain. Tiff, Tammy and her husband Ansul had become close friends.

"Valerie, I don't like you because of basketball, I like you because of your spirit," Tammy reassured.

I had gotten to know Tammy indirectly through Tiff in the last few months. We were complete opposites. She was quiet and guarded and extremely religious. She invited me to go to church with her. Tammy became my spiritual mentor and best friend.

Life had settled into a predictable pattern, when just over a month after the WNBA draft, the Washington Mystics offered me a contract for the remainder of the 1999 season. I accepted the offer. Washington's coaches, Nancy Darsch and Melissa McFerrin, called me to calm any reservations I had about coming to Washington. They had a young talented team that needed experience, guidance and maturity.

Washington had selected superstar Chamique Holdsclaw as the first pick of the 1999 draft. It would seem that with Nikki and Chamique, their problems would be solved. Instead, they struggled with team chemistry. Unlike the NBA, where young talented players had the chance to develop with veteran stars, in the WNBA young players like Chamique would have to come into the fledgling league and be expected to carry the team. She carried the extra pressure of the Mystics and the WNBA even though she would not be compensated for that additional pressure.

Before the 1999 season, the WNBA signed its first collective bargaining agreement. Chamique signed for the maximum rookie cap salary of $50,000. The rookie minimum in the NBA was $248,000. On July 1, 1999 I signed a contract with the WNBA for the 1999 season for $17,809 that required my participation in league- and team-scheduled appearances and events until May 15, 2000. It was pro-rated for the minimum player salary of $25,000. I had been making a six-figure salary in the ABL before bonuses. The WNBA contract did not include health insurance nor any bonuses.

Michael Jordan had been named the president of basketball operations. At least Aaron and I would get an MJ spotting every now and then, a perk for playing in the WNBA.

My first game with the Mystics at home against the Sacramento Monarchs was unbelievable. First, running out to warm-up in the NBA Washington Wizards' MCI center was crazy. Second, looking up and seeing 14,178 screaming fans was bizarre. Third, scoring my first basket, making my first foul shot and grabbing my first rebound in the WNBA was unthinkable. Fourth, my son was witnessing all of this. I scored 5 points and grabbed two rebounds in 11 minutes as a reserve player. We lost 79-74.

We headed off on a six-game West Coast road trip starting in Minnesota where Celtic great Kevin McHale, who now was in the Timberwolves' front office, towered over everyone as he hung out in the hallways leading to the court.

It was mind-blowing playing in the America West Arena in Phoenix, the Delta Center in Utah and the ARCO Arena in Sacramento where all my favorite NBA stars played. Rob and Aaron met up with me when I got to California. Unlike the ABL Aaron wasn't allowed to travel with me or the team. Our next game was against the Los Angeles Sparks. I was in awe stepping into the Forum for practice, thinking about the magic made in this building with Magic,

Kareem, James Worthy and Michael Cooper, who was now an assistant coach with the Sparks.

Shalonda Enis, our starting center, got the flu when we returned to Washington and I took her place. We beat the Orlando Miracle 72-68. I was in the starting lineup for the next game in Gund Arena against the Cleveland Rockers. We beat them by one point, 63-62. The next three home games, with me in the starting lineup, we beat Cleveland, New York and Los Angeles, with an 80-45 blowout against the Rockers.

After the New York game and our fifth straight win with me in the starting lineup, an article in The Washington Times stated: "Valerie Still must be the Washington Mystics' good-luck charm. The Mystics remained undefeated last night with Still in the starting lineup and kept their slim playoff hopes alive with their fifth straight win."

Our next game against the LA Sparks was nearly sold out, 19,974. LA came in with a 17-11 record and we beat them by two, holding them to only 53 points. After the game, secret service agents filled the hallways to the locker room as Al and Tipper Gore came in to congratulate us on the win.

We were on a six-game winning streak heading to Orlando, but were beaten 81-54, knocking us out of the playoff race. We finished the season 12-20, narrowly missing the playoffs.

After the season I was offered another contract but declined. I would have to accept the fact that my knee was not the same as before the injury. Refusing the contract was difficult for me but I had played in pain the entire season. I had had one of the most adventurous and spell-binding summers playing in the most historic basketball facilities, staying at luxury hotels and meeting basketball legends while living the life of a professional athlete on a less-than-minimum-wage salary. It was tempting to return but I wanted to be able to coach and play with Aaron once he was old enough. The injury inhibited my activity level. I had always been an active person; exercising and staying in shape helped my mental health; now I was prematurely forced to a restrictive lifestyle.

I was selected for the WNBA Player's Advisory Council. The Council included Coquese Washington, Rebecca Lobo, Jennifer

Azzi, Tamecka Dixon, Sonja Henning and me as players' representatives; Pam Wheeler and Hal Biagas represented the Women's National Basketball Players Association; Val Ackerman, Renee Brown, Don Rutledge, Connie Hurlbut, Peter Smul and Jamin Dershowitz represented the league. We met in the National Basketball Players Association offices in New York. The Council addressed a number of issues, including officiating, team travel, living arrangements, expansion and the 2000 Draft. I wasn't sure what my role was but before the meeting the NBPA asked if I would address the issue of misrepresentation of WNBA players, specifically the misrepresentation of gay players. I thought it was odd that they wanted me to address this issue when players like Jennifer Azzi, who was gay, was on the Council.

The meeting was cankerous and seemed to be a formality to cover the 2-year Collective Bargaining Agreement (CBA) requirement for a player's Council. The CBA was signed early in 1999. Rebecca Lobo continued to refer to the CBA in a negative way. The issues brought up at the meeting were moot points because the CBA couldn't be changed for two years.

Once I was back in Columbus, the Valerie Still Foundation began a pilot program for middle-school girls in a public school, Still Kids Improvement Program (SKIP), which began at the end of November. I loved working with girls and put all my energy into VSF. This was the same program I had been working on with Dotti Berry when she told me about the ABL.

Aaron was growing nicely and Rob was working on his new business, Waldo Wrights Flying Service. I helped him design the logo and get a business account set up. Tammy and I began studying the Bible together and I still spoke to Mom at least once a day. Rob now seemed less stressed.

Aaron began piano lessons after his fourth birthday. I had started when I was seven and I hoped that he would gain a love for music. Mom was thrilled.

In March 2000, I started an advice blog for girls on the WNBA website called "Where's my Girls At?" Girls from across the country submitted problems and questions they had and my expert panel (Mickie, Tiff, Gabby and Elizabeth) and I gave our advice. I was thankful the WNBA allowed me to have this opportunity. The girls I worked with and became friends with were the daughters I never had.

In May, Rob's parents arrived. While they were at our house I took a home pregnancy test in our master bathroom while Rob and his parents talked in the kitchen. The test was positive. I was pregnant.

It was interesting that at the beginning of the year I had hired a nutritionist and a personal trainer and had someone treating my knee without knowing that I was going to get pregnant. Rob and I were moving in the right direction as well in our relationship. I called him back to the bedroom, not wanting his parents to know I was pregnant. When I told him, he dropped his head and looked dejected. "Oh no..." he said, lowering his eyes. "I can't afford this right now and I don't have the time. We're just getting my business started."

Although we hadn't planned this pregnancy, I thought we had time now that I wasn't playing anymore. I wanted more children and I was nearly forty years old. A couple days later, Rob left with his dad for New Hampshire. When they returned they began doing airshows together with the newly formed Waldo Wrights Flying Service.

Aaron and I headed to Lexington for an appointment with Reva. We watched the sonogram with excitement and heard the heartbeat of his sibling. I wrote in my journal that night that I had taken the home pregnancy test May 11, the same day I conceived Aaron. Aaron was "My Sunshine;" this baby "My Blessed One." With the new baby scheduled to arrive in January 2001, I decided to finish my undergraduate degree at UK. Once the baby arrived I wouldn't have time. While in Lexington I called Bob Bradley, Associate Athletic Director for Academics, to tell him my plans. He was thrilled I was finally coming back to finish my degree. Most athletes after nearly 20 years out of school did not return to do so.

The first day of June I had a scare when I noticed blood spotting. My heart sank as I remembered my experience from the previous miscarriage. I drove to the emergency room alone. The doctor was able to get a heartbeat of the baby and told me everything was fine but to see my regular doctor. I had already planned a trip to Italy but saw my doctor in Columbus when I returned.

The first week of July I awoke bleeding in the middle of the night. Once at the hospital, I felt a surging pain as I walked off the elevator. By the time I arrived at the emergency room, I had already prematurely delivered my baby in the elevator. I was devastated. I was released at 5:48 a.m. Rob and his parents left early for an airshow. Tammy and Ansul spent the day with me.

A couple weeks later, tests revealed that the female fetus had a chromosomal abnormality, an extra chromosome, Trisomy 18. I mourned the loss of "My Blessed One," my precious little baby girl. Rob never acknowledged the death of our daughter. He was gone flying every weekend between July and October.

Less than a week after my miscarriage, I met with Bob Bradley to enroll for my final semester at UK and went apartment hunting. Aaron and I would spend four months in Lexington while I finished my degree. Rob's parents and nephew moved in with Rob in Ohio. Mid-August, Aaron and I left for Lexington and I began classes. Tension had built between Rob and me with his lack of empathy and disconnection with Aaron and me.

While in Lexington, Adriano and I began communicating again. I was struggling and lonely. We began writing and calling each other. My life had changed so drastically since Adriano and I had been together but we still cared for each other.

Alone at night in the apartment, I wondered how I had become so miserable in my marriage. I wanted it to work but nothing I did made my situation better. I longed to be married and loved, having a family, but with each day a piece of me was melting away. I felt like a failure and that was unacceptable. My parents had stayed together through all their dysfunction. I would do whatever necessary to make my marriage work and keep my family together.

It was a challenge managing Aaron, school and everyday life but Mom was always ready to listen and give advice and encouragement. I enjoyed my last semester at UK. I had all production classes, which I wasn't able to schedule while playing at UK: Horse Science, Dairy Cattle Science, Beef Cattle Science and Meat Science. My Meat Science class made me become a vegetarian again. Learning how to slaughter animals and visiting slaughtering plants was the most unpleasant and difficult aspect of my studies. I had dropped this course and become a vegetarian back in the 1980s. In December I finished my last class, and the semester, on the Dean's List.

Once back in Ohio I began volunteering at the OSU large-animal clinic and registered to take a few classes in the Spring Quarter to prepare for entering the Veterinary Medicine program. I also volunteered as an assistant coach for a private Christian high school's girls' basketball team. I loved working with the young players and they were thrilled to have a former professional basketball player as a coach. We threw Aaron a surprise birthday party at my house and in March we made it to the Final Four of the State Tournament.

Shortly after, I began classes at OSU and received a call from Melissa McFerrin. She was no longer an assistant coach but now General Manager of the Mystics. They had hired Tom Maher, the Australian National Team's coach, as head coach and Marianne Stanley as an assistant but needed another assistant coach. She thought I would be perfect for the position. They would work around my schedule and allow me to start after I was done with classes at the end of May and the season would be over before Aaron's first day of school. I accepted the coaching position.

Aaron, MJ, Ingrid, Tammy, Ansul, Bonnie Hutton, and her family joined me in Memorial Coliseum on May 6, 2001 as I received my diploma from the University of Kentucky. Of all the records I set in Memorial Coliseum, receiving my diploma was the most meaningful. I finished classes at OSU and Mickie, Aaron and I headed to Washington for the summer. Mickie would help with Aaron. Mom and Francina were on the East Coast and would help when needed.

We spent the summer in executive luxury housing a few blocks from the MCI center. Michael Jordan was still president of Basketball Operations but began training in anticipation of his return to pro basketball with the Wizards in the fall. Although the Mystics finished in last place, it was a great learning experience for me. Aaron and Mickie had an adventurous summer.

Back in Ohio, after being gone all summer, I picked up my mail from the Valerie Still Foundation post office box at the end of August. There were two postcards and one letter from Adriano. I had totally forgotten to check my post office box the entire summer. The last letter I had received from him was in May before I left. I was excited that he had written me.

I quickly read the postcards written in Italian:

"I'll be in the hospital for August but I'm getting better!"

Hospital? Getting better? I wondered what was wrong as I read the second postcard:

"Everyone remembers you here and sends their greetings (Carmelo, Dario, ect.) ...From the 9th of August until the end, I return to the hospital for the definitive treatment."

Definitive treatment? Both of the postcards were from Trentino where Adriano had a house in the mountains. He was staying at a hotel there where we knew the owner. I rushed home with Aaron in the car so I could get to my office and read the letter dated July 21 in private:

Hello Beautiful,

I have not been able to write before because I have been in the hospital for 40 days. The last days of the Giro, I was not feeling well so the following day, at the conclusion of the Giro I went and had tests done. The results leukemia. Fortunately, discovered at the early stage. Now I have already done one round of chemotherapy. I must do the second, and last one, starting from August 9. For now, everything is good. I am already on the road to healing. Write me because you will not get me by phone. A big kiss. Don't worry. Now everything is O.K. Adriano.

My hands shook and my heart dropped as I read Adriano's letter. Leukemia? Chemotherapy? I sensed something terrible even though he said everything was okay. I called Adriano's house in Milano. No response. I called the hotel number from the postcard, hoping to speak to Adriano. I spoke with Carmelo, the owner. Adriano had recently left the hotel for Milano and would return the following week after his second round of treatments. He was doing better. I cried and told him to have Adriano call me. I didn't know what else I could do. I wanted to get on the next flight to Milano. I would have to wait until Adriano was done with his treatment and out of the hospital before talking to him. It hurt me that I hadn't gotten his letter and postcards before now. I knew he wanted to see me; that was why he had sent the cards and letter. I wondered if he thought I was ignoring him when I hadn't responded.

Two days later, Francina called me. "Valerie, did you hear the news...?" She asked. "Adriano died."

I closed my office door, fell to the floor and wept. In the new world I had created in the USA, I had to deny Adriano, even though I had never stopped loving him. The love Adriano and I shared was a complex one. The fact I had to hide that love was also hiding who I was. I was married to Rob and I loved Rob and wanted us to have a great relationship but I also loved Adriano. Our love was neither possessive nor unforgiving. He had moved on and I had moved on in this lifetime but we knew our love was one that endured time and space. I wept.

Adriano's funeral was the day before Aaron's first day of school. I would not be able to attend the funeral but I would make plans to visit soon. We celebrated Aaron's big day as I mourned the loss of Adriano. It was a special occasion as I kissed Aaron and he stepped onto the big yellow school bus that pulled in front of our house. I waved to him with tears streaming down my face; my baby boy was taking his next big independent step in life and I too was taking a step of independence without Adriano.

Davide called me.

I walked around in a fog. Aaron was going through some firsts, which we enjoyed together but my heart ached. Rob carried on as usual without empathy or sympathy. I was angry at him. I was angry at myself. I had allowed Rob to interfere with my relationship with Adriano. Rob didn't care that he and I were miserable together and he had neglected Aaron. Adriano posed no threat to Rob while loving me and encouraging me. We were thousands of miles apart. Now Rob and his parents were planning to move to Florida without telling me.

I felt all this personal loss, and then on September 11, after getting Aaron off to school, I took Rob to the airport. He was flying to Florida to close the agreement to work there all winter. While at the gym, my workout was interrupted by a continual flow of Breaking News. Two planes had crashed into the World Trade Center in New York. The Pentagon was hit by a plane, and another plane crashed somewhere in rural Pennsylvania. Then I watched in horror as the World Trade Center crumbled. The US was under attack. I thought about Aaron and then Rob.

I called Rob's cell. He didn't respond. I left a message pleading for him to call and let me know he was okay. I then called Mom and Francina. The phone lines were down. I couldn't help but wonder if the plane crash in Pennsylvania was near them. My heart raced harder than any time on the court. I finally got through to Francina. Thankfully, they were safe in New Jersey. Rob eventually called me back and said he couldn't talk because he was having a meeting. The only reason he called me back was because the man he was meeting with needed to call his wife so she wouldn't worry. After knowing he was safe, I watched the TV coverage of the terrorists' attacks. I cried. I had never seen something so devastating as those airplanes flying into the two massive buildings and watching them crumble as people scrambled to escape.

My plans to pay my respects to Adriano and visit Davide would have to wait until the end of the month when it was safe to fly in and out of New York.

*****

At the end of September I flew into Venice. Not many people were flying from New York; the flight was nearly empty. Erica and Zio Maurizio picked me up from the airport. I would stay with them at Hotel Noris for a night.

Adriano's driver, Joe, picked me up the following day to drive me to Milano. During our two-hour ride, I cried as Joe talked about Adriano's life since we had split up, and about his last days. He told me that although Adriano had been in a relationship he had never gotten over me and he would have dropped everything if I had decided to return. Finally arriving in Milano, I cried as we drove past places where Adriano and I had made memories.

We finally parked the car on a small street near the Duomo in the center of Milano. A handsome man with a peppered goatee and gray hair ran toward me. It was Davide. We hugged and held each other tightly. The last time I saw Davide we were just kids. He hadn't changed much besides his gray hair. He looked more like Adriano now that his hair was gray. He grabbed my bags; we said goodbye to Joe and headed up to Davide's house.

Davide told me about Adriano's cancer, and we looked over newspaper articles about his death. We cried together. Finally, here was someone I could share my grief with and someone who understood and loved Adriano as I did.

The evening was beautiful so we hopped on his vintage Harley-Davidson to go to dinner. We pulled up to one of Milano's chic contemporary restaurants. There were lots of well-dressed beautiful people enjoying good music, food and wine. Davide ordered a bottle of wine as we shared our feelings. He had always been sensitive and fun to be with. Now I could see and feel his hurt. I had hidden my hurt for so long; tears streamed down my face uncontrollably.

"I know what you are feeling," Davide said as he gently reached over and cupped my face with his hand, wiping my tears.

By the end of the dinner, Davide joked that most people in the restaurant probably thought he was a jerk for making me cry all evening. We got on his bike under the beautiful Milano sky with me holding onto him tightly and my head resting on his shoulder. We ate gelato near the castle and headed back to his place. We stayed up until 3 in the morning.

Later that morning we visited the cemetery where Adriano was laid to rest. As we arrived it began to rain lightly. I quietly sobbed as I ran my finger over Adriano's tomb plate. Davide changed the flowers and left me to have some time by myself. I missed Adriano and wished I had had a chance to see him after we had split up and before he died. The rain increased and Davide returned. He stood behind me and put his arms around my waist holding me tight.

We rode to the Duomo and lit candles. The Duomo was magnificent, majestic and mystical as usual. Sunday mass was in progress and a choir of men sang as I lit a candle for Adriano, my sister Bonnie, and Dad.

Afterward I took the Metro to Sesto San Giovanni to see La Famiglia. Davide had to meet up with his girlfriend. Being with La Famiglia was like old times. We ate, had good wine and talked about Adriano. The time flew and I needed to return to Milano.

Davide and I went to a jazz club where his friend was performing. After the performance we returned home, lit some candles, opened a bottle of wine and listened to our favorite music while cuddling on the couch. With Davide cradling my head in his lap and tears flowing, he softly kissed my tears. Davide promised he would always be my support and love me. If I needed him he would always be here for me. We fell asleep in each other's arms on the couch, listening to Giorgia . . . *Vorrei illuminarti l'anima. Nel blu dei giorni tuoi più fragili. Io ci sarò. Come una musica. Come domenica. Di sole e d'azzurro...*

*****

Rob returned to Florida when I returned home in early October and was upset I had gone to Italy. While he was in Florida, Davide had called to check on me almost every day. It felt good knowing someone cared about me and my feelings. The four days I spent with Davide were magical. I hadn't felt that alive for a long while.

When Rob returned to Ohio at the end of October, we barely spoke and he spent little time with Aaron. I accepted that Rob was moving forward with his new life in Florida but ignoring his son was unacceptable. I was willing to pretend I was happy for Aaron's sake. It wasn't Aaron's fault we couldn't make our marriage work.

I had made friends with two neighbors who had boys Aaron's age. I didn't want Aaron noticing Rob's absence. Sue Rogers lived across the street with Ben, who was a year older than Aaron, and Greg was born two days after Aaron. They became best friends with Aaron once they started riding the school bus together.

On a return visit home, Rob confronted me about emails between Davide and me that he had hacked on my personal email account. He was upset because he thought I had had sex with Davide. He had breached my trust by getting into my private emails. Of all the time Rob spent away I never questioned him or spied on his computer. After this incident, I bought a cell phone and put a lock on my office door. Rob was jealous and insecure about Davide, like he was with Adriano. I didn't want to be with Davide; I just needed someone who loved me. It had been so long since I had felt loved.

It was lonesome raising Aaron by myself in Ohio while Rob lived with his parents in Florida, and I resented that he had chosen his parents over Aaron and me. I wanted our marriage to work but that seemed unrealistic. I loved Rob but was dying inside. To compensate, I put all my time and energy into making sure Aaron's life was perfect. I kept him busy with friends, activities and school.

Rob returned in February for Aaron's birthday and stayed a few weeks. He spent lots of time on the computer in his office. I thought he was playing card games; instead I discovered he was visiting porn sites on the internet. One of his favorite websites was "Exploited Teens." When I confronted him about the site, he justified himself by claiming the girls on the website were eighteen and over. We had dealt with his pornography problem earlier but I was appalled that he was now visiting sites with teen girls when I had teen girls at my house often. I stopped allowing girls at the house. I had just had the entire girls' basketball team over for a surprise birthday party for Aaron. Rob thought I was making too much of the situation and returned to Florida.

Breaking up our family was the last thing I wanted to happen but nothing seemed to be working for us. I didn't want Aaron to have a broken family. For Spring break he and I flew to Florida to visit Rob in an attempt to try to keep things together or at least feed the illusion. After a few difficult days with him, his parents and his new friends, I took Aaron to stay with Bonnie, my best friend from college and her family, who lived in Orlando.

The Orlando Miracle had just hired Dee Brown, a former Boston Celtic player, as head coach. Bonnie suggested I inquire about an assistant coach position. Dee interviewed me and hired me. The season would start when Aaron finished school and would end before he started back in the fall. I called Mom first and then Tammy after I was hired, to give them the good news.

Tiffany came with me to Orlando for the summer to help with Aaron once school was done. Two weeks after I was hired, Dee and I flew to Chicago for the pre-draft camp at Moody Bible Institute the first weekend in April. While scouting players, Pat Head Summit came and sat next to Dee and me. We discussed players and coaching. She gave me advice on coaching and talked about how she organized for her son while she was travelling. I appreciated her advice and sharing her experience as a working mom. It helped me knowing Aaron would be okay with my travelling so much and coaching. She also wanted us to trade Pee Wee to the Mystics, for which she was still a consultant. Dee and I laughed about that once she left; Pee Wee was the best point guard in the league. I flew back to Columbus to pick up Aaron and Tiff.

Once back in Orlando for the season, I bought a car and rented an apartment. The coaching position with the Miracle was my start to regaining independence. Vonn Read, who was a video scout for the Orlando Magic, was the other assistant coach.

I reconnected with Reggie Williams from Wide World of Disney. It was good having someone I knew in the area. Pat Williams was senior Vice President of the Magic. When I was in high school he was the General Manager of the 76ers. Those were the years Dr. J played for Philadelphia. Julius Erving was now also a Vice President of the Magic. I got to know both Pat and Dr. J. This was truly magic, and with all the bad things happening in my private life, it felt like a miracle. Aaron and I were living in Orlando, of all places, for the summer, and I was climbing my way back up the mountain.

The Miracle didn't make the playoffs so Aaron and I were back in Columbus in Mid-August. We quickly got back into our normal routine — piano lessons, soccer, martial arts, and preparing for the start of first grade while running VSF. Rob returned home in September and surprised us with a family vacation to Atlantis in the Bahamas for a long weekend. We had a good relaxing time together. I hoped this was a sign that we could work things out. A month later Rob told me that he was in financial trouble with the airplane business. I offered to give the company a loan with the stipulation that I have ownership in it. Rob agreed I would own 51% of the company.

I became CEO and managed the company and Rob did what he loved doing, flying. I sent introductory letters to all of Rob's clients and his parents informing them that the company was under new management.

Although this was not in my plans, if it could help save our marriage and family, I was willing to try. Quitting was not an option. I still didn't know who I was and was willing to hold onto what I thought was stability. The more Rob and his parents rejected me, the more I wanted to prove my worth. After I became majority owner of Waldo Wrights Flying Service, RDV Sports, the managing company of the Orlando Magic, no longer wanted a WNBA team. The team relocated to Connecticut and became the Connecticut Suns. I returned to Columbus and didn't pursue renewing my coaching contract.

Chapter 18

Black and Blue

During the time I played and coached in the ABL and WNBA, the University of Kentucky's women's basketball program had been on a steady decline. The team had one winning season and never had a winning record in the SEC. It was sad to see the program that we had built in the 1980s deteriorate to a season with only six wins. I wrote the new athletic director, Mitch Barnhart, a letter welcoming him to UK and expressed my support and interest in being a part of the revitalization of the program.

On January 12, 2003 my jersey was retired in Memorial Coliseum. I was the first and only female player to have her jersey retired. At center court stood President Todd, former First Lady Gloria Singletary, Mitch Barnhart, Rob and Aaron. The Mayor of Lexington, Teresa Isaac, presented me with the key to the city. UK's hero had returned home after a long journey. The feeling was much different than when I was a young Lady Kat with oversized dreams and passion. No longer was Ottie and the Rowdy Bunch in the crowd to give me a standing ovation. Bonnie would not be waiting on me to go to celebrate at the Library together after the game. No one knew the turmoil that Rob and I shared as he and Aaron stood at half court with me. As the lights dimmed and a tribute video played, the tears I shed were for the bright-eyed girl I had lost in the 20 years since I had left UK.

It was fun reuniting with my former teammates and coaches. Debbie Yow wiped tears from my face after our seeing each other for the first time since she had left UK. She was now the Athletic Director at the University of Maryland and one of the most powerful figures in collegiate sports. I loved her. She had given a young girl an opportunity to fulfill her dreams.

Aaron, running in the hallways, met Tubby Smith, UK's first Black head coach. We had a fun-filled weekend, but once home, life returned to normal. We prepared for Aaron's first piano recital and Rob joined in the activities with us. Since we had made changes with the airplane business, the company was running smoother and Rob could spend more time with Aaron and me. Every Friday, I had lunch and recess with Aaron at school.

At the end of UK's basketball season, Bernadette Mattox resigned. I reached out to former UK teammates who had coaching experience and to Vonn Read. After preparing a rebuilding plan for the Lady Kats I contacted UK. I met with Mitch Barnhart and UK's assistant athletic director in New Orleans where the men's SEC tournament was being held. I left all my materials with them, believing I had the job.

Within a few weeks (or days) Mitch hired Mickie DeMoss, Tennessee's assistant coach. I was hurt. Mickie hired Vonn Read as an assistant. The key to the city wouldn't unlock any door if it couldn't unlock the door to UK. It seemed the jersey retirement ceremony was only to promote the school. They were unwilling to give me the opportunity to further my career in a position of leadership.

I was an exceptional athlete who had only represented the school in a positive way and was qualified for the job. In the money-making, big-time collegiate sports of basketball and football the majority of athletes were Black, while coaches, trainers, and athletic administrators were White. In women's basketball where a high percentage of players were Black, very few Black females were coaches. UK's athletic department had one of the worst records for hiring Blacks as head coaches. Maybe that key to the city I was given would unlock some back door but for sure I wasn't coming in through UK's front door now.

After UK's rejection, I plowed forward, keeping busy so I wouldn't have to deal with my real issue of low self-worth and self-hatred. I began working on a multipurpose facility for young athletes with programs that would assist players academically, athletically and spiritually, The GiG! I met with the Mayor of Columbus and a few former Ohio State players. Clark Kellogg, Jim Cleamons, Granville Waiters, Stephanie Hightower and Katie Smith all agreed to support the project. I was directed to Pastor Aaron Wheeler. He was the Chairman of Ohio Civil Rights Commission but also pastor of Mountaintop Missionary Baptist Church, which met in a small store area in a shopping mall. The church had fewer than 100 members and Aaron and I began to attend. Each member was active in church services and activities. I began playing drums and keyboards for the choir. Later I became its youth director.

With Rob gone every week, Aaron and I took a trip to Italy. Davide was excited about seeing me and meeting Aaron. We flew to Venice and stayed at Hotel Noris with Zio Maurizo. We visited Venice before Davide picked us up and spent a few days in Milano visiting the city, La Famiglia, and a former teammate. Aaron and I enjoyed Milano, Como and Switzerland while Davide worked during the day. He made arrangements for us to visit Roma and Sardegna. We stayed at the beautiful Richmond Hotel in Roma. From the terrace, where we ate breakfast, we enjoyed a spectacular view of the Coliseum and Forum. Aaron loved walking the ancient ruins of Roma, which he had studied in school.

In Stintino at night, after putting Aaron to bed, Davide and I laid out a blanket in the garden area that overlooked the Mediterranean Sea. We lay under the star-filled sky, enjoying a bottle of fine Italian wine, and talked about our lives. There was a strong attraction between us. We had always shared a platonic love but now it had become a romantic attraction. Davide shared with me that he had actually seen me the first day I arrived in Italy. He was one of the Carabinieri who were standing at customs. Throughout the years our love had grown as we became best friends and shared Adriano. Now we were destined to remain close friends and nothing more. I respected my marriage vows.

I missed Davide as soon as I boarded the flight back to the USA.

We had known each other for twenty years; he was easy to talk to and our love was strong. My trip to Italy helped me slow down but back in the States I picked up where I left off.

The GiG! Summer basketball camp for girls went extremely well. I invited Paula McGee to be a guest at the camp. Paula was now a minister and motivational speaker. I played with her on the USA national team and against her in the Italian professional league. She was a strikingly beautiful woman, standing 6'2" with short-cropped hair and a bold personality to compliment her physical attributes.

*****

With the start of school, my neighbor Sue and I met every morning in front of our house and engaged the kids in fun activities until the bus arrived. One morning Sue arrived with a bandage on her nose. Skin cancer. They removed it from the tip of her nose, but she needed chemotherapy. We began walking and monitoring our eating habits. I couldn't imagine what Sue was feeling – a cancer diagnosis with three small children.

We enrolled our boys in the same activities and attended school events together. Ben attended church with Aaron and me even though they were Catholic. A mother's worst fear is not being around for her children. Sue and I shared that fear. Our walks became therapeutic.

*****

In 2003, I was aware that UK was neither my place of opportunity nor my final destination and that my marriage would likely not last a lifetime. The more I fought to hold on to my dysfunctional relationships the more bizarre my situation became. I was holding onto the American dream of an ideal family but my reality was a nightmare. My fairy tale of the perfect family living happily ever after was being dismantled and I would have to accept that fact.

Aaron continued with his normal activities, making sure I didn't miss a single one. He excelled in martial arts, moving towards his black belt; performed in piano recitals and competitions, and kept busy in school activities. I even joined the Indian Guides, a father/

son group where we met the Schultz family who became good friends for us. Rob, living with his parents in Florida, returned periodically. Aaron learned that his father's sporadic involvement in his life was normal. I read all I could about being a single mom. I would have to efficiently navigate being a single mom, but I felt guilty.

Aaron's first official basketball team consisted of dads with their sons. The dad that coached the team knew my basketball background but the other dads who hung out during practices, shouting instructions to their sons, were clueless about who I was. I just wanted to support Aaron. I didn't miss one practice or game.

In June, after visiting Mom, Aaron and I returned to Italy. After a few days in Milano, Davide, Aaron and I, in Davide's Porsche convertible, drove to Genoa to board an overnight cruise to Sardegna. In Stintino Aaron saw old friends, made new ones and learned to windsurf. Davide and I enjoyed the beach and each other. He was in a relationship and my marriage was failing.

Chapter 19

Pathway to Freedom

On August 23, 2004 Aaron and I were invited, as descendants of William Still, to the opening of the National Underground Railroad Freedom Center in Cincinnati, Ohio. During a part of the opening ceremony, before the keynote address of First Lady Laura Bush, the descendants of prominent abolitionists were asked to participate in a dirt-laying symbolic observance. Aaron and I walked in front of the large crowd and sprinkled dirt. As a member of William Still's family, we got a private tour of the $110 million building. I didn't know much about William Still and was astonished at all the displays in the museum about him. I was so proud to be a Still. The Freedom Center was one of a new group of "museums of conscience," which challenged people to reflect on the concept of freedom and the abolition movement. After the weekend, I returned home with a passion to find out more about my ancestors and my history.

I recalled Dad's old brown book, his great grandfather's autobiography. I bought a copy and read it. I wanted to learn more about William Still so I read his classic, *Underground Railroad.* The more I read about my ancestors the more I was surprised I didn't know my history. Finally, I read *The Kidnapped and the Ransomed: The Narrative of Peter and Vina Still after Forty Years of Slavery* published in 1856 by white abolitionist Kate E.R. Pickard. It was the story of my great-great granduncle, Peter. After all the years that I had struggled with knowing who I was, in the pages of these books I discovered my identity. The more I read, the more I needed to know. I spent hours at the Ohio Historical Society and Columbus Public Library and enrolled in undergraduate African American courses at The Ohio State University in hope of getting into their Africa and African American Studies graduate program.

Rob couldn't believe I was thinking about going back to college. The Monday before Thanksgiving, we got into a heated discussion.

"Considering where you're from, you should be more than satisfied with what you have and where you are!" He concluded.

I was speechless and hurt. Our discussion was over. He packed his car and left for Florida to live with his parents. I continued to put on the facade that we were doing fine.

Rob stopped helping with bills or Aaron's needs. I met with a divorce attorney even though I didn't want to think that my marriage was coming to an end. He suggested a few books and maybe seeing a marriage therapist with Rob before making a final decision. Most days I was frightened and uncertain about life and what would happen to Aaron and me.

Rob returned for Christmas. A woman he had developed a relationship with after meeting at an airshow came to visit us. I found affectionate letters and cards she had written him. In one she told Rob that he didn't deserve to be treated the way I was treating him.

The year was ending and I was quite sure my marriage was ending as well.

*****

I had spent years in my interracial marriage with a person whose family thought people of color where inferior, but never let their painful attitudes invade my thoughts of myself as a woman, mother, or basketball player, but I had finally become conscious that my skin color could influence how certain people treated and perceived me. For years I didn't understand the level of racism in the USA because I had always fought against being identified by race, gender, sexuality, class and religion. As a child I didn't fit neatly into any box. While attending UK, with all my accomplishments, I held a privileged status that transcended race and gender and sheltered me from overt racism and sexism. As an elite athlete, with a mentality of dominance, I identified with the dominant group. Once in Europe, my world became limitless with possibilities because those restrictive labels did not hold the same power as they did in the USA. I hadn't really experienced the devastation of discrimination based on race and gender in America, or I was too naive to understand it. When I was a child I was too naive to recognize racism, and as a young adult I didn't realize its damage. But as a grown woman I finally knew and felt its pain.

Most couples experience the marital issues Rob and I experienced. We both contributed to the unraveling of our relationship as we navigated new cultures, new social statuses, and new roles, but with the support of family, our differences could have been resolved and repaired. I loved Rob but with all the past hurts it was difficult to have hope for the future and we were unable to embrace the moment.

In the pages of the books written by and about my ancestors I found solace, self-awareness and strength. Unknowingly, their spirits had guided me throughout my earth-journey but as I travelled through the darkness of my journey their manifestation made self-awareness and self-acceptance mandatory. They had traveled through the darkness of racism, during the darkest period of racism in America, but found the Divine in the darkness and their guidance for navigating through the uncertainty. They embraced and accepted any environment, knowing who they were and the power they possessed, regardless of circumstances. The secret to life wasn't about what was externally happening but discovering one's authentic self. I had begun a passage on my journey, an obscure and uncertain one that could destroy me if I remained unconscious, or enlighten me to a state of awareness if I lived consciously.

Finally as I accepted that my marriage was broken, the pieces of Aaron and me were placed neatly into the Still family tapestry. Mom always said puzzles were like life. It was impossible to see a complete composition in the thousands of individual pieces, but with patience, each piece fitted perfectly into another piece and eventually when put together correctly, they became a beautiful masterpiece.

*****

Returning to college as a 44-year old single mom was exciting but scary. Every minute of the day was scheduled and taped on our refrigerator: wake up time, breakfast time, school activities and events, sporting events, study time, playtime, reading time, bath time and bedtime. At night after winding down, I spent quiet time reading and meditating. I lay in bed many nights scared of the future for Aaron and me.

Without Rob's financial support, my savings dwindled down on mortgage payments, bills, Aaron's activities, medical and dental expenses and everyday living expenses. I was too embarrassed to share that with anyone.

For Black History Month, Aaron's teacher asked me to come and share my family's history of the Underground Railroad with Aaron's class. In his suburban school, less than 2% of the student population was of color. Most of the students knew me because I spent lunchtime with them on Fridays, but others knew I was a former professional player with the Columbus Quest; no one knew about my African American history. As I spoke to the students about Aaron's great-great-great granduncle William, who worked with Harriet Tubman and Frederick Douglass, their eyes lit up. I showed them the book William had written and read a few stories of escape including Henry "Box" Brown, who had himself shipped in a box from the South to William's office in the North so he could be free. I knew there was a need for more material for young students about the African American experience. I began writing a children's series on my family's history.

In the fall I volunteered to coach Aaron's basketball team. There were no other moms coaching boys' basketball. I enjoyed working with the young boys. For my group, having a female coach would be normal. The addition of practices and games into my crazy schedule wasn't easy, but I made it work. After the basketball season I signed Aaron up for baseball.

At the end of the school year I met with the divorce attorney again. I reached out to Dennis feeling nervous and in need of support. Dennis and I began talking regularly. He had retired from playing and was now living in Kansas with his wife and three daughters. He would be a father figure in Aaron's life.

For the summer, Aaron and I took a three-family trip to Yellowstone National Park with the Rogers and Schultzs. The Yellowstone trip was symbolic of the scary and unknown period Aaron and I were traveling. Although we would encounter frightful and unexpected things, we would always have support and love. Our three families developed a strong bond during this trip.

Aaron and I visited Mom before starting school. She was proud of me and loved Aaron.

******

The University of Kentucky had its inaugural Hall of Fame Induction Weekend in September. I was excited and proud to be the only female player in the first class of athletes. I was the only female player who had a jersey retired at UK. Tammy and Aaron came to the ceremony with me. Maryanne attended also. The elite from UK's athletic teams throughout the years attended the event. No one knew the struggles I was having personally, as I put on my public invincible persona and smiled brightly.

Chapter 20

Comfortable with Uncertainty

The African American classes in my master's program at The Ohio State University provided self-discovery for me. As an athlete I hadn't been socially conscious, and after living in Europe for so long I really didn't understand American culture. I was finally adjusting to the American way of life. I still loved Europe and dreamed of returning to live in Italy, but the more I learned in classes, the more I discovered who I was. For so long I thought I was only capable of being an athlete but now I excelled in academics.

I finished the first volume of my children's series based on my family's history and started sending it to publishing companies, including the University Press of Kentucky. Before Thanksgiving I received their letter of decline to publish the manuscript. It was my first letter of rejection, but I felt my ancestors guiding me to publish the book.

For Thanksgiving 2005 break Aaron and I visited Mom. While we were there, I had a strong urge to visit my great-great grandfather's property in Medford, New Jersey. I took Aaron with me. Dr. James Still was one of the most successful doctors in South Jersey in the 19th century and the third largest landowner when he died. Although his huge house had been torn down in the 1930s, his small 19th century office stood with a "For Sale" sign in front. My heart sang. He had written about purchasing the land and building in his autobiography. It was his pride and joy. Aaron and I walked around the property and house. Later I called about the property.

The good news was that the building was for sale; the bad news was it would cost nearly a million dollars to buy the building and land. A commercial company had bought it and was planning to tear down the office to make the area a parking lot for a large shopping complex.

I called the office of Environmental Protection of New Jersey, the Historic Preservation of New Jersey and any other state office I thought could help me. I sent out emails and solicited citizens to help me stop the destruction of the house. I contacted Charles L. Blockson. He was the leading scholar of the Underground Railroad and had the largest collection of African and African American artifacts, documents and books at Temple University.

The Blockson and Still families had old connections. William Still had assisted Dr. Blockson's ancestor Jacob in his escape to Canada. Like Jacob and William in the 19th century fighting for freedom, Charles and I were reconnected in the 21st century continuing the legacy of our ancestors together.

I returned to Columbus, sad that my great-great grandfather's property would soon be destroyed, but I continued the fight to save it.

*****

I never imagined my life as a single mom, without a job, going to school and struggling. As a child, I had huge dreams. I would have never thought Rob would take off and disregard all his responsibilities and would abandon his only son.

In the middle of the despair one of my professors gave me a book, *Comfortable with Uncertainty*. My life was filled with uncertainty and I wasn't comfortable with it. It was difficult totally embracing this principle when everything was falling apart. I tried to become comfortable with my uncertainty.

Incredibly, at the end of February 2006, the State of New Jersey purchased my great-great grandfather's property, making it the first and only African American historic site owned by the state of New Jersey. Symbolically it represented me being saved on the verge of destruction. My ancestors were protecting me and guiding me. I needed to guide and protect Aaron.

Bills became overwhelming, so I took cash advances from a credit card account that Rob and I shared, to cover expenses. My focus was on keeping Aaron as stable as possible as I was drowning. On Mother's Day I turned 45. Physically, I had begun having tremendous hot flashes that coincided with the internal heat I was feeling from all the stress in my life and my imminent divorce.

On July 17, 2006, reluctantly I signed papers to file for divorce. My signature confirmed I was a failure.

Rob challenged the terms of the divorce. I wanted full custody of Aaron and my percentage of our businesses; we could split everything else. He didn't want me to have any part of our two airplane companies. Each time we failed to agree on the terms of the divorce, it meant I would be paying additional costs. I was already financially strained; now I was coming to the brink of losing everything. Even though I owned over half of the companies, my main objective was to have full custody of Aaron. Rob didn't want custody of Aaron but he would use that as leverage to keep the companies.

Aaron and I spent Christmas with Mom in New Jersey. I needed her more than ever going into 2007. The one certainty I had was Mom. She was always ready to uplift me, encourage me, give me a positive word and be my number-one supporter. If all else failed, she never would.

PART THREE: Still Restoration

"But they that wait upon the Lord shall renew their strength; they shall mount up with wings as eagles; they shall run, and not be weary; and they shall walk, and not faint."
Isaiah 40:31

Chapter 21

"But they that wait..."

Rob and I finally agreed on the divorce terms; he would take the businesses and I would have full custody of Aaron. I would also keep the house, unaware that Rob had taken out home equity loans on it and it had a sizable mortgage. I was tired of the conflict and needed to start fresh. Financially, I was in ruins but I could recuperate once the house was sold and I finished my Master's degree.

I put the house up for sale in January 2007 as the USA began one of its worst economic depressions since the 1930s. A few days after Aaron's birthday in February we headed to New Jersey for my induction into the South Jersey Hall of Fame. Mom, Aaron, and my first grade teacher, Mrs. Arthur, attended the event in Cherry Hill. The first big snowstorm of the year stranded us in New Jersey for a few days, leaving us little to do other than spend time with Mom. I was a little concerned about her; she seemed to be slowing down. She had always been so strong and vibrant, and I had difficulty accepting the aging process.

Once back in Columbus, I couldn't stop thinking about Mom and I called her every day to check on her. Regardless of the significance of the topic she was always a light force. Near the end of March, I called Mom early one Monday morning after a restless night of worrying. She was confused; her speech was slurred and I couldn't understand anything she was saying. This wasn't aging.

"Mom, put Wendell on the phone," I said, agitated and concerned.

I sensed something was wrong as I heard people in the background talking. I didn't know who was at her house.

"Val, she's been vomiting for a few days. It might be the flu." Wendell tried to calm me.

The next day I called again and couldn't understand anything she was saying.

"Just take her to the emergency room!" I screamed at Wendell.

He did and she was admitted. I called Uncle Kenny to go check on her and then booked a flight to New Jersey.

I arrived at the hospital the next morning. Mom was unconscious and her mouth was distorted. Tubes and IVs entered and exited all areas of her body. I couldn't believe she was so sick. She looked like she had aged decades in just a few weeks..

Dennis and Sparky drove from Kansas. I stayed by Mom's side, never leaving the hospital. Although she was unconscious, I talked to her, combed her hair, bathed her and prayed with her, like she had done for me when I was sick, when they didn't know what was wrong with me.

After three days she regained consciousness. Once Mom was back home, she told Dennis and me that while she was unconscious she was in the most incredibly beautiful peaceful place. She didn't understand why she was back. Was she saying she wanted to die? That upset us. Why would she say that?

"You two have families now. You don't have to always be fighting battles. Learn to accept life. I'm ready for whatever happens."

Accept life? My life was spiraling out of control but I couldn't tell Mom. I returned home to face the fact that my house was not selling and I didn't know how I would be able to pay bills. In April I returned to check on Mom. I became her power-of-attorney, making sure her bills were paid, coordinating her medical appointments and handling all her business.

While I was trying to help Mom and get my own life in order, I heard Mickie DeMoss resigned from UK. In four years, she had taken the program from its worst and re-built its respectability. She was one of the best recruiters in the country and UK was ascending when she surprisingly left Lexington. Coaching at UK remained my dream and I needed a job but Mitch Barnhart hired Matthew Mitchell, who had been a graduate assistant for Pat Head at Tennessee and an assistant coach with DeMoss at UK for a couple of years.

In May, I was set to graduate but had to make corrections and add supporting documentation to my Master's thesis. One of my professors, Dr. Shaw, spent ten days helping me finish it so I could graduate on time. I was stressed to the maximum, but I thought about the tough times my mother faced. Both Aaron and I graduated in June. As I walked into the famous Horseshoe at OSU I didn't know how I was surviving. Listening to Bill Clinton, who was the commencement speaker, I reflected on how much had changed since the Quest team was invited to the White House to present him a Columbus Quest jersey. So much had happened to me in ten years; I wondered what the next ten years would hold for me.

A couple weeks after graduation while Aaron went to visit Rob, who was living with his girlfriend, I was accepted into The OSU Sports Humanities doctorate program. I was offered a graduate teaching assistant position that would pay for tuition. I was excited to tell Aaron, but when he returned home from his father's, he was withdrawn. His therapist helped him work through this transition during the summer. Rob seemed to be moving on happily while I was under a raincloud.

It began to pour. The day after Aaron began middle school I had to have our dog euthanized. Gladys was like a daughter to me; she was older than Aaron. Returning home I began feeling sick. When Aaron got home I couldn't get out of bed. After a few days of feeling terrible I went to the OSU student health center. An ultrasound revealed polyps on my uterus that would have to be removed. I was scared but the polyps turned out to be benign. The polyps were symbolic of my life. There were things that needed to be removed before I could move forward. Going into the next year I decided my mantra would be "2008 is going to be great!"

Unfortunately, I couldn't get anyone to buy my house. I struggled financially but continued to excel in the doctorate program. Three other doctoral students and I formed a panel to present at my first academic conference in Cincinnati. My research was about Title IX.

While I prepared for the conference, my neighbor and friend, Sue got much sicker. She was placed in hospice care.

Every day after I finished classes I sat with her, washed her, cared for her, massaged her feet and tried to comfort her. Sue and I had always talked during our walks, mainly about kids and family, but now we had esoteric conversations about life and death. As a mother, it was painful knowing that she did not want to leave her children and would miss seeing them grow up. Her oldest son Ben stayed with Aaron and me most of the time. We tried to shield her children from the reality that she was dying and planned a 50th birthday celebration but she began bleeding internally the day before. I received an emergency call from Dave, as I was heading to her house from classes, telling me Sue had died. An hour later, Sue's children and Aaron got off the school bus in front of her house. Although we had known that Sue was dying, there was no way to prepare for the death of a mother of three young children. Telling her children she had died was heartbreaking. Ben came over to play with Aaron later.

I gave Sue's eulogy at her funeral.

*****

I was invited to a basketball camp in Cagliari during the summer. Before we left I received a foreclosure letter. I needed a break and I thanked God for providing me the opportunity to get away from my problems for a while. This would be a good distraction for Aaron as well. I didn't tell him, Mom or anyone else about the foreclosure. I was just excited to be going to Italy. I hoped to see Davide. I needed to feel love and protected.

In Cagliari, we stayed at Pietro's house near the beach. Aaron made friends right away as I tried to relax and forget my problems. When Davide found out I was in Sardegna he flew to Cagliari. As soon as he saw me he put his arms around me and hugged me tightly. He made reservations for us to stay at Hotel Calamosca, a secluded, intimate hotel on the Mediterranean Sea. The three of us relaxed and enjoyed sunny Sardegna.

Once Aaron was in bed, we enjoyed a good bottle of wine or Mirto and talked until late in the night. I missed Davide so much.

"Valerie, I'm always here for you," he whispered one night as he walked me to my room.

He pressed me up against the door and gathered me in his strong arms, bringing his lips close to mine. The angst of the past few years seemed to release as I closed my eyes and soaked in the intimacy. It had been so long since I was in someone's arms.

"I've always wanted you Valerie," he said in between kisses. "Let me love you."

Davide led me to his room. He opened the window, exposing a full moon and star-filled sky and the sound of the gentle motion of the sea, and then he gently disrobed me. The passion we had concealed for so many years was unleashed and an electrifying energy exuberated between us. Usually I would worry about what the future would hold for us but I was totally captured in the moment, carefree and euphoric. I was in need of love and Davide fulfilled that need. I forgot about all my troubles and escaped into a state of ecstasy. It had been so long since I had trusted someone with my heart and was uninhibited. Davide's passionate lovemaking consumed me. I didn't know where this would lead us but the future didn't matter, for now my desire for Davide and my need for his affection trumped any thought of long-term consequences of our passion. Our relationship was enduring. Regardless of what happened, we would always love each other.

"Amore, ho bisogno di te ma devo andare," I whispered in Davide's ear after he had fallen asleep with me snuggled close to him.

Without waking him I gently kissed him with tears streaming, slipped out of bed, got dressed and returned to my room before Aaron awoke. A burnt-orange sun was just peeking up on the horizon of the tranquil Mediterranean Sea as I sat on my bed facing the window contemplating my situation with the sound of Aaron's breathing. Italy had always held my treasure. It offered the freshness of a morning sunrise, hope as vast as a calming sea, and unfettered love.

*****

Life returned to normal once I was back in the States. I enjoyed teaching. Aaron and I followed the 2008 presidential elections. I knew it would be an historically significant election with Hilary Clinton and Barack Obama running in the Democratic primary, so I took Aaron with me to cast our vote.

Obama won the elections and Aaron was selected for his 7th grade basketball team. Part of my life felt good, but in 2009, my house was scheduled for a sheriff's sale. Two days before Aaron and I would become homeless, Chuck Bluestone, a real estate attorney in Columbus whom I had met earlier in the year, petitioned the court and mortgage company for an extension. They agreed and reduced my mortgage payments while allowing me to continue my efforts to sell the house. My doctorate program would be completed in 2010. I began looking for an apartment, hoping the house would sell. Although my life continued to fall apart, I believed that eventually things would get better. My mantra was "I'm more successful than I ever dreamed possible!" Regardless of the situation, no matter how bad things got, Mom was always ready to encourage me. The times I didn't think I would make it, a quick phone call to her gave me the motivation to move forward. I couldn't pay for Chuck's services so I gave him my baby grand piano.

By the end of 2009, I had scheduled my doctorate exams and looked forward to finally closing out this dark period in my life. I began looking for teaching positions.

It had been an uphill battle since my divorce in 2007, but Aaron and I had fought through divorce, death, foreclosure, and failures in the last three years and were ready for a fresh start. No one except Mom knew of our struggles. After handing in my doctorate exams in March 2010, I could see the light.

*****

The week I was scheduled to defend my doctorate exams began normally with an early morning phone call to Mom during my commute to OSU. Those habitual conversations happened before 7 a.m. as I drove to either teach or to finish my last class as a doctorate student. It was my lifeline. She always knew what to say to motivate me to push through any obstacle. I was only ten days away from the big day.

I called her but was shocked to hear her voice weak and confused. I could barely understand what she was saying. I told her I would call her back once classes were done. I called her on my way home from OSU but my concerns were heightened with our afternoon conversation. Again, I could barely understand what she was saying.

Early the following morning I called, and again I found her in the same state. Before I pushed the end button on my phone, tears began to stream down my face as I tried to concentrate on rush-hour traffic instead of the fact that maybe Mom was beginning to show signs of Alzheimer's. I knew she was growing older but I always thought she would be one of the elderly who "stayed young."

My afternoon phone call to Mom was extremely disturbing.

"Mom, what is going on? What are you doing?" I asked. " You don't sound good."

"I'm just sitting here reading. No one comes to visit and I'm just pretty much sitting around by myself. I'm tired and just getting close to God. I'm not sure what's happening but I'm prepared for anything. I'm just so tired," she said.

I sent Wendell a text message instead of calling him. A few minutes later my phone rang.

My conversation with Wendell did not settle my concerns. I hardly slept that night. I called Mom before leaving the house the next morning. She sounded terrible. I called Dennis and then Uncle Kenny to ask him to check on Mom.

Later that evening I got news from Uncle Kenny that Mom was admitted to the Intensive Care Unit.

How could this be happening? Just a few days ago Mom was encouraging me and lifting me up, and now she was in ICU. The following day she had a seizure and was put on life support. Dennis and I made plans to get to New Jersey.

We ended up connecting on the same flight to Philadelphia from Chicago and arrived in Philadelphia at midnight. Uncle Kenny's son Mike picked us up and drove us to the hospital where Uncle Kenny and his wife Ingrid were with Mom.

The moment I finally stepped into the small room, I was taken aback by the huge formidable noise-making ventilator forcing her chest to rise and fall. The extremely intense white lights. IV machines pumped fluids and drugs into her veins. Lying in the bed was a woman I barely recognized. A once beautiful, strong, brave, invincible, unbreakable fortress, stretched out on the hospital bed draped in white sheets with plastic tubes running from all parts of her body; time stood still. An image that will forever be engraved in memory. Who is this fragile, aged person in need of help? The clear plastic bag dangling from her bed with dark brown urine. A medicinal smell permeating the room. I forced myself to move and as I stepped around the bed and lowered my head to get closer to her face, I recognized the small gold earrings with small diamonds I had brought Mom from Italy. Why hadn't they taken her earrings out? My trembling lips kissed her slightly chilled forehead as I combed my fingers through her ruffled graying and thinning hair.

"It's okay mom, Dennis and I are here," I whispered in her ear, fighting back tears and longing to hear or see a response. Dennis stayed his distance from the bed in his state of total helplessness.

I grabbed her hand. The hand that had provided nourishment, the hand that had dished out discipline, the hand that had bathed me, the hand that was always ready for a pat on the back, the hand that always reached out to help and love was lifeless.

As Uncle Kenny and Ingrid disappeared down the ICU hallway I reluctantly turned back into Mom's ICU room filled with anxiety, fear and pain. Mom's eyes had been closed since we arrived but I knew if she knew I was there she would not remain asleep. I remembered the times Aaron and I would arrive late at night and she was always up to greet us, no matter how late.

The nightshift nurse who had answered some of my initial questions when I arrived came back in for the routine check of all the machines, medical equipment and Mom.

"She can still hear you," she said to Dennis and me as she stepped out of the room and walked back to the main station in the middle of the unit.

"She's just sleeping," I softly said to Dennis, in denial, as I pulled a chair close to the right side of the bed, next to the IV stand, and cupped Mom's left hand in both of mine. I knew that would be my spot until she awakened and we could talk. Dennis paced back and forth in front of the door like an anxious caged tiger.

"How did this happen?" he murmured to himself. "I knew we should have come earlier. This isn't right. I can't believe this." Nothing was said between Dennis and me for the next hour. As kids we were usually fearless as mommy's little protectors, but now, as grown adults we were totally helpless.

"It's going to be all right mom…It's going to be all right mom… I love you," I whispered in her ear as I lay my head on her chest, which rose with each hiss of the ventilator.

Please God . . . the battle's not mine but yours . . .

In the morning, I called all my siblings to inform them that we needed to make a decision whether or not to take Mom off of life support. We would leave her on life support until each one could visit her. She had a living will that she kept in her Bible. I called Wendell to bring her Bible to the hospital. As we flipped through it looking for her will, a sheet of paper fell from it. It was notes she had written in the last few days, her last thoughts filled with encouragement and wisdom. We cried reading them. The emotionally charged environment sparked an argument between Dennis and Wendell. Wendell left.

My siblings in the Midwest opted not to return to New Jersey. Dennis and I decided that at noon we would disconnect the life support machines, despite a lack of understanding why she spiraled downhill so fast. We still didn't understand what had happened to her.

Mom's nurse entered the room at noon.

"I'm not sure how long your mom will continue breathing without the machine," she explained. "But you've made the right decision. You'll have to leave the room so I can remove the ventilator."

When we returned to the room Mom lay breathing laboriously. Dennis and I sat in anguish with her. Francine came up to sit for a while and then left. Sparky and Barry called to find out if there was anything else we could have done. I needed release from the situation for awhile; it was overwhelming for me. Dennis sat with her while I returned to her house. When I returned Dennis took a break.

I sat with Mom and prayed in the dimly lit room with her breathing becoming more irregular.

Please God, if it's her time to go don't let her linger on. She's been your faithful servant.

I never thought Mom would end up dying in a hospital without all of her children surrounding her. Her life had been all about God and her children. Now she was taking her last breaths without her children. After all the sacrifices she had made for her children, after always being available to each one of us, after always supporting us and loving us unconditionally, now she lay silently alone.

Dennis had stepped out of the room for a break as I sat next to her bed with my head buried in my hands and prayed and spoke quietly to her. "I love you Mom and will miss you but it's okay for you to move forward." Monitors buzzed. Stunned, I headed to the hallway to notify someone as Mom's nurse was already charging into the room. I called Dennis on his cell. He was sitting outside the hospital.

"Mom's gone."

I had never felt such throbbing, severe, immobilizing, breathtaking pain in my whole life. My life source was extinguished.

I waited for the funeral home attendant to arrive for her body. Watching them unload her from the body bag in an area in the back of the funeral home will always be engrained in my mind. I sobbed uncontrollably while driving back the few blocks to her house.

Uncle Kenny and Ingrid met me at Mom's house.

"I have nothing to live for," I cried to Uncle Kenny in Mom's kitchen on my knees. "Absolutely nothing!"

"Don't say that Valerie," Uncle Kenny grabbed me and held me. "You have Aaron. You gotta be strong for him. And your mom would want you to move on with your life. That's what she would want."

That night I lay on Mom's bed at home but couldn't sleep. The following morning I called Aaron to check on him and to tell him I loved him. He told me Rob had called. He warned Aaron that he could have him put in foster care because I had left him alone at home. Aaron was frightened but I assured him everything would be okay. All the pain I had inside erupted. I called Rob immediately and exploded. It woke Dennis, who was sleeping in Mom's living room. I explained to him what had happened. He called Rob and cussed him out. We cried together and then laughed about my boisterous phone call that had awoken him.

We buried Mom next to Dad in the white casket she had ordered, with a few people in attendance at the gravesite. I thought that when Mom died all her children would be around her; instead only four of us were at her burial. Later that evening I flew back to Columbus totally perplexed, still not understanding what had happened. The death certificate gave the cause of her immediate death as "seizure" which was caused by "hypoxia" and "aspiration pneumonia." I felt I had failed Mom.

As I returned to Ohio, I couldn't help but feel I had failed Mom. Those thoughts haunted me even as two days later I successfully completed the oral defense of my doctorate exams. I was numb. It really didn't matter. Nothing mattered. Dennis tried to convince me to finish and stay on track with my dissertation but I really had no life left in me. Of all the things that had happened to me in the last several years, I wanted a reason to surrender. Mom's death put me in full surrender. Through all my trials and tribulations, I had finally begun to embrace uncertainty and realized that security was an illusion of happiness.

I thought I knew Mom but I had so many questions that I wanted and needed to ask her. My journey of self-discovery, self-love and self-awareness was accelerated with Mom's death. I was in an out-of-control free fall.

Chapter 22

Through the Fire

As I still processed Mom's death while visiting Dennis, he suggested I move to Kansas so he could help with Aaron and be a support for me. I was in pain and in shock. He had opened a training facility, Ol' School Sports Academy (OSSA) and introduced me to Karen, the owner of an international trucking company whose daughter trained with Dennis and attended Louisburg High School. He wanted me to meet the principal. Louisburg High, with fewer than 500 students in rural Kansas, was about 30 minutes from OSSA in affluent Johnson County. The school was a beautiful, state-of-the arts facility and the pride and joy of the small rural town. After a meeting with the principal and girls' basketball coach we toured the school. Dennis hinted again about the possibility of Aaron and me moving to Kansas.

A month later that long shot became a reality. I didn't know Kansas and really didn't want to leave Ohio, but after I was offered the head coaching job for the girls' basketball team, I thought a fresh start for Aaron and me would be good. I accepted. Aaron and I packed up our car and headed out west for the 12-hour trip.

Aaron and I loved the setting of the town and where we lived. The view from my bedroom window was a big open field and a large farm with cattle. At night as the sun was setting in the big western sky, the silhouette of the cows grazing and walking across the plain was serene. On hot days, the smell of livestock filled the air.

The school informed me that the freshman coach, who wanted the head coaching position before I applied, would be on my coaching staff. I didn't know he was the principal's good friend. During the first week of our summer basketball camp, I experienced the first trouble.

I had Dennis do all the physical assessments and conditioning. After a few days, Dennis and the freshman coach got into an altercation. He accused Dennis of assaulting him and told the principal he feared for his life. The principal banned Dennis from the high school.

I was excited about getting back into coaching and the players were responding to the new system I put into place, but this incident and the personal attack on Dennis hurt. Dennis insisted I didn't give in to the bullying tactics of the freshman coach. I was still grieving Mom's death and Dennis was my anchor.

Even though I had some conflict with the freshmen coach, I accomplished the summer goals of establishing my system, getting to know the team members, getting them to know me better, developing team chemistry, and setting the tone for the start of the season in the fall. Players and parents were thrilled with the camp and looking forward to the start of the season.

One of the things I hadn't accomplished was uniting the parents. There were parents who hated each other and although I thought we could resolve those issues, I was an outsider coming in and they were definitely not going to allow me to control their territory.

Nuggets of racism crept back into my life again, making it more and more difficult to deny its existence now that I was on the receiving end in Kansas. At times it was blatant and easy to detect but most times it was an underlying force that remained under the surface.

*****

By the start of the school year, I had discovered that the girls' team was treated as inferior to the boys' teams. I requested the same treatment for the girls' team that the boys' team received. Louisburg had never had a Black coach or teacher and I would be the first black female coach in the Frontier League.

As I prepared for the season I requested videotapes, information and stats from the previous season but was told there were none; the boys' basketball team was getting new uniforms and even though I was able to raise money to get the girls new uniforms, I was informed that the girls' rotation for new uniforms was not this season. I had received letters from parents who accused the freshman coach of inappropriate behavior with players but these were dismissed when I presented them to the principal and was told this coach would be on my staff.

The football team was considered the elite of Louisburg sports. They had just finished a 14-0 season and won the state title for the first time in the school's history. I wanted the girls to be treated with the same respect and dignity. From the first day I met the team, I wanted them to know they were athletes and could reach any dream they set if they were willing to work.

Although the principal had forced me to keep the freshman coach on staff, I confronted the coach about the allegations I received of inappropriate relationships with players. The safety of players was important. He was infuriated that I would confront him and quit a week before the season began and began instigating problems among the parents once he was no longer on the coaching staff.

I moved forward. We won our first game 76-34 at home and were undefeated going into the Christmas break. Our defensive system was an aggressive pressure man-to-man that was not commonly used by girls in the league. We were breaking down traditional gender stereotypes.

Unfortunately, the former freshman coach continued his tactics of creating problems from afar, calling players and parents to create tension.

Aaron had made a smooth transition. He joined the band and choir and was selected for the 9th grade basketball team. I was glad he had adjusted quickly. The band was the most popular group in the school.

As Christmas break approached, I couldn't ignore a few suspicious things. I was accused of being inadequate to substitute teach because I did not follow lesson plans for a teacher who was a friend of the former coach. I was also accused by a hostile parent of trying to profit off the players because I suggested they work out with Dennis over Thanksgiving break. The same parent offered me information about other players' dysfunctional domestic situations and sexual behaviors. Although Aaron was the tallest player on the freshman team, he was not playing and when I checked in on practices he was not participating. The girls' locker room was vandalized after we fixed it up like the football locker room, with couches. I became suspicious when our beloved cat Zippy was poisoned. Now I was deeply concerned. I had never been in such a hostile environment but at the same time I enjoyed coaching and the development of the young players and I thought it would all blow over.

Karen, the owner of the trucking company, was excited I was coaching her daughter and helped me in any way she could. It was strange that although she had grown up in an environment of racism, she wasn't racist. We were sisters. As the year went on, she was embarrassed by what was happening to me.

After the Christmas break things got out of hand quickly. During our first away game after the break, at Baldwin, the officiating was lopsided in favor of Baldwin. This was the team we had beaten earlier in the season. After a few questionable calls, I approached the referee who told me instead of complaining I should teach my players how to play defense and sit down. I told him he should learn how to officiate, which resulted in my getting a technical foul. He was offended I had responded to him.

We lost four games in a row after that game. I was accused of being disrespectful during the playing of the national anthem and not patriotic. And accused of putting players in danger during an away game and of lacking integrity. The break had left its mark on the players and regaining their focus through all the distractions was difficult.

Our last regular season game was at home against our archrival, Paola. We had already beaten them and wanted to finish the season strong heading into tournament play. We beat Paola 50-46 to end our regular season and headed into the sub-state tournament optimistic. We had a great chance to go to the state tournament, which Louisburg girls' basketball team had never done.

In the semi-finals of sub-state, we faced archrival Paola again, who we had beaten twice during the regular season. The semi-finals would be played at Paola. We started the game well, jumping out to a 16-8 lead, but ended the half down by three, 25-28. We took the lead back in the third quarter, but we ended up losing the game 54-60.

The loss wasn't the most remarkable thing about the game. In all my playing years, coaching experiences or being a spectator of basketball, this was the first time that a team didn't shoot one foul shot. Paola shot 34 foul shots and we never shot one. We had four of our five starters foul out and Paola was called for only eight fouls total, most of those called near the end of the game, once it was out of reach. We outscored Paola from 2- and 3-point fields goals. I cried with my players in the locker room. They had been penalized because of me.

I received a text from the athletic director two days after the game. He and the principal wanted to meet with me.

"We're moving in a different direction," the principal said to me, barely giving me eye contact as I sat down.

"Does this mean I'm not coach anymore?" I asked, totally caught off guard.

"Yes, we're moving in a different direction," the Principal replied.

"Well can you give me some reasons for your decision?" I rebutted.

"I don't think I want to at this time," he said arrogantly.

There would be no next season for me at Louisburg High School.

My friend Cathy Schulz suggested Aaron and I get away from the town for a while. For spring break her family was heading to the Grand Canyon; they would stop and pick us up so we could spend it together. The night they arrived in Louisburg, a policeman stopped them in our driveway. When they told him they were just visiting he left.

"Val, that was really odd. That cop just followed us to your house."

"Oh, that's normal for us Cathy, we've been followed before..."

Once back from spring break, I regrouped and filed a complaint with the Equal Employment Opportunity Commission and Kansas Human Rights. I decided to fight back. It played out in the town with the local media. Aaron and I became outcasts. This was the first time that someone had stood up to these types of discriminatory tactics. At a certain point, whenever we returned to our house, a police car followed us once we reached the center of town. People from my church supported me but it was stressful in the small town with Aaron attending school there while I pursued the lawsuit against the school district. Initially, the school stopped offering me substituting assignments but when they knew of the lawsuit they began offering assignments again.

In the spring, struggling in the middle of my battle with the Louisburg school district, I received a call from a man from Kentucky. It was around the anniversary of Mom's death. He had gotten my number from the owner of a Kentucky winery for whom I had done a television commercial.

"I hope I'm not bothering you; my name is Bob Todd," he said in a strong Kentucky drawl. "I've written a novel I'd like you to read and endorse."

Bob had been an English tutor for the University of Kentucky's basketball program during the mid-to-late 1960s. He had tutored a few members of Adolph Rupp's basketball teams, including ones from the infamous 1966 team, which was defeated in the NCAA championship game against Texas Western.

Read a book about a complicated love story? Now with everything that was happening to me? I was not interested in anything but trying to figure out what other bad thing could happen to me. In July I received a huge packet with a manuscript of over 400 pages. One sleepless Saturday night I pulled out the manuscript and read the title, *In Their Tombs Unknowing*. It caught my attention right away. I thought about Mom. She was in her grave and no one knew anything about the extraordinary person she was. I called Bob the following morning.

"Good Morning Bob, sorry about calling so early on Sunday," I said apologetically; it was after all early Sunday morning and he really didn't know me.

"Oh, no, what a pleasant surprise, I'm glad you called."

I didn't know who this man was but I opened up to him after reading over half of the manuscript. I cried and cried and he listened.

My world was falling apart. I wondered why I had not had more dreams about Mom and why her life had ended the way it had. I was like a frightened little girl who had lost the grip of her mother's hand in a large crowd and was now wandering aimlessly, trying to hear her mother's voice through the confusion. I built a wall around myself so that no one could come in and hurt me again but the experience in Louisburg had shattered the wall, wounded me, and left me exposed.

"I understand, Valerie; you have gone through a period of depression and that is okay," he assured me.

Depression? Why would he make such a statement? Like my mother, I was a strong, proud woman. I was not depressed.

It was the oddest thing, after the vile racism I experienced in Louisburg; Bob's words weren't offensive; instead, they were comforting. Although I struggled for over a year, I never would have admitted to being depressed. I missed my mother and I had not moved on. My marriage ended, and I lost my job. I had been walled in for so long, I had allowed "myself," my ego, and my thoughts to dominate. Yes, I was depressed. Now the wall was being dismantled, and although it was terrifying, I could finally breathe. Exhale. I could now live.

"Valerie, have I told you about the concept of time?" Bob once asked in his nonchalant way.

"Your problem is time," Bob continued, "it's as if you are carrying a big bag of worthless rocks across your back. It's weighing you down. Instead of treating them like rocks you must treat them like pieces of gold. Instead of carrying the bag across your back, you must treat it as valuable treasure. You must embrace it in your arms in front of you, cling to it and then it won't be a burden but a blessing."

Like Plato's Allegory of the Cave, Bob's parable enlightened me. Time had become a burden for me. There was so much for me to do but seemingly so little time. With my fiftieth birthday, I had begrudgingly thrown this bag over my shoulder and as I had done so many other times in my life, "sucked it in" and carried the heavy, cumbersome load. At this point in my life, success was not as important as significance. For many, I had lived an incredibly successful life, but with my family history, I was feeling the pressure of upholding a legacy. With my mother's death, the sack had increased in weight at least a hundredfold. What significance would I leave behind? My ancestors and my mother had set the bar extremely high. If not for their sacrifices, determination and excellence, I would not be who I am. With my mother's death, I had fallen to my knees with the sack overtaking me and was being crushed by its weight. It was time to get back on my feet, pick up the sack and embrace each golden nugget in it.

Our conversations were therapeutic for me. They were just the lifeline I needed.

The situation in Louisburg reached a peak at the end of July when Aaron received threatening text messages. I periodically checked his text messages and discovered he was having an exchange with someone I didn't know. The last message left me shaking and stole my breath. I filed a police report, packed our things and left Louisburg immediately. The most terrorizing part of the numerous texts was this last phrase:

. . . i will make sure u never see earth or your relatives again because i will break your fuckin neck u fuckin nigger.

Retaliation against me was one thing I could handle but once I saw this hate-filled, racist text it was clear that Louisburg was an unsafe place for people of color. This was the worst racism I had ever encountered. I had never been called "nigger" or had my life threatened; having it happen to Aaron was frightening. It was time for us to move ahead on our journey. I had learned what I needed to learn in Louisburg. Two years later the white male freshman coach, who quit the team and was accused of inappropriate behavior with players and harassed me the entire time I was in Louisburg, was hired as the girls' basketball head coach.

I enrolled Aaron in one of the best private schools in Kansas. The boys' basketball head coach knew Dennis and we thought it would be a good school for Aaron both academically and for basketball development. The school would hire me as a basketball coach as well.

It was in Lawrence, Kansas. We were living in JayHawk basketball country. Aaron and I would get to experience the excitement and tradition of the University of Kansas. We met Bill Self and Danny Manning and experienced the "Phog" in Allen Fieldhouse at a KU basketball game.

During the school year, a young black teenager in Florida, Trayvon Martin, was shot and killed by a racist, George Zimmerman. The national case exposed modern racism in America. Trayvon was the same age as Aaron and it was sad to think that a young boy could be walking home from a store and be shot and killed by a person who had misconstrued perceptions of a person based solely on skin color. What was even more concerning was that Zimmerman was not found guilty of any crime. I realize it's impossible to understand racism when you have never faced discrimination based on race. Throughout our experience at Louisburg, I never talked to Aaron about racism in America but this killing and our experience in Kansas called for Aaron and me to have a serious discussion about race in America. I had raised him with a color-blinded, genderless perspective, hoping he would grow up untainted by intolerance and bigotry. We hadn't defined people by the color of their skin or put restrictions on individuals because of their gender, but residuals of racism, sexism, intolerance and homophobia made up part of the fabric of American society.

After the nightmare of Louisburg, I was able to pick up the pieces once in Lawrence. Bob and I started STILL Publications. Our first publication was the first volume of my children's series, *Still Alive on the Underground Railroad: Recollections of an American Family.* I loved writing and was thrilled when the University Press of Kentucky agreed to publish my memoir after I sent them a proposal and a few chapters. Their senior scholar's review "enthusiastically" supported the proposal and stated the book was "sure to garner a diverse audience and be a pioneer publication that addressed race, gender and sports in American society and the world during the 20th century." I believed that having the University Press of Kentucky publish my memoir was the perfect partnership. Apart from my love for and association with Kentucky, it was an academic press and I hoped to use the manuscript for my dissertation before having it published. The director sent a letter of recommendation to my dissertation committee. I gained a new interest in completing my Ph.D.; finishing the dissertation would be the last requirement.

During the school year, I was an assistant coach at Aaron's school and managed operations at Dennis' training facility. I also became a host on a new sports talk show on Time Warner Cable television. "Our Season" was an all-female sports talk show hosted by four women in the nation; it addressed women's issues in sports. We finished our first successful season when I realized I would have to change Aaron's school. Dennis trained Aaron and developed a good relationship with Aaron, who had grown to be 6'9," but Kansas never felt like home.

In May 2012, I contacted Valley Forge Military Academy in Pennsylvania. My cousin Mike attended VFMA for high school, and I believed it would help Aaron develop academically, athletically, and gain his independence. We had grown so close, inseparable, since it had been just him and me for so long. Although I had always believed I could raise Aaron to be a strong confident man, by instilling well-balanced and conscientious ethics, I began to question myself. Now that he was sixteen years old, maybe he needed a male-dominant environment to teach him how to be successful in a male-dominant society. Aaron was my world and making this decision was heartbreaking. It was a boarding school, so he would live on campus. How could I live without Aaron? I still wanted to be close to him; now would be the right time to move back to the East Coast.

My two years in Kansas provided me with valuable lessons about myself. Kansas had exposed racism in a way that I couldn't deny it and gave me a better understanding of racism in America; of why some people chose to be racist and why it was so difficult to not be racist in the USA. Sadly, in 2012 racism still prevailed in the USA. More importantly, I learned that although I may be attacked based on race or gender, to reciprocate that hatred was not the solution. My self (my ego) was offended by racism but I (authentic self) knew such hatred had little to do with who I am. My experiences in Kansas had set a metaphoric fire to my self, my ego. My ego would have to burn so I could become new. It was part of the refinement, the purification process of getting to the core of knowing who I am.

The mythical phoenix was said to arise from its own ashes, a new creature. I would arise from my ashes, reborn.

Chapter 23

Be Still

Reluctantly, I returned to New Jersey to check on Mom's house. It was surreal stepping inside. The renters who had lived in the house for the last two years had trashed it. I sat crying on the couch when Mike arrived. Emotionally I was in pieces. Financially, I couldn't afford to repair the house.

"Cuz, don't worry. I'll help you fix the house," Mike said. "And you and Aaron have family here."

While I contemplated what I should do, I received a surprise phone call from Nikki McCray. She was being inducted into the Women's Basketball Hall of Fame and asked me to attend the event. In June I attended the Women's Basketball Hall of Fame induction. Along with Nikki, I knew all the other inductees except one. I had played against Dawn Staley, Pamela McGee and Inge Nissen, and I knew Robin Roberts from our exchanges when I played in the ABL. After years of not seeing Pam, we bumped into each other and started talking about our sons. It was good to see that she and her son, JaVale, had done well. She had gotten pregnant while playing in Italy. Now JaVale was playing in the NBA. We talked about being single moms and the challenges of raising sons. We exchanged numbers and stayed in touch with each other.

After visiting VFMA with Aaron and John Schultz in July, I decided to enroll him, not knowing where I would get the funding for tuition. The summer was one of many trips back and forth to Kansas and New Jersey moving our stuff. We lived with Dennis for a month when the lease in Lawrence expired and while Mom's house was still being repaired.

In the fall, I drove Aaron to VFMA with a heavy heart. After his fresh clean-shaved haircut and processing, I left my plebe and drove to Mom's house with tears streaming down my face. For the first seven weeks of the plebe system I would have no contact with my son. Stepping into the nearly empty house was the final stage to my self-awareness. I was back where I had begun my journey. I sensed a presence. A stillness. A peace. A sense of welcome. I was home.

The first week in Mom's house was excruciating. I had never been totally isolated, totally alone. I missed Aaron badly. I was meditating daily when I began having vivid experiences and dreams of Mom. One night as I was sleeping the bed began to violently shake. Normally, I would have been scared but in my loneliness, I felt comfort. In the stillness, I could feel Mom. She was telling me she was in the wonderful place. She loved me and she was still with me. It was time to let go of the pain I had associated with her death. She had never left me but being in so much pain and busyness, I had had difficulty recognizing her presence. Now in her home, I could finally become conscious. It was time I knew Mom better. The tears that now flowed were not tears of sorrow or pain but of peace.

I visited her high school, Palmyra High School and met the principal, who gave me a tour of the old gym where she had classes and walked the hallways. I looked at her yearbook pictures and saw myself in her young eyes. At home, I finally sorted out things of hers I had saved. I looked through her important papers and old pictures. I read her old worn Bible with highlights and heavy outlining and heard her voice in her favorite passages. *Be still and know that I am God.*

Years ago I dreaded being alone but now in Mom's house I felt the presence of my ancestors. Then it was unsettling. I always drowned out their voices. Now in the stillness of Mom's house, they embraced me and comforted me.

I organized a small group and contacted the State of New Jersey so we could begin the restoration of my great-great grandfather's property. I began researching my family again, using information my sister Bonita had collected when she was alive. She had done extensive research but had died young at 36 years old while she was in the middle of her most important discoveries. I felt her presence as I visited the places where my ancestors had lived. I did all my traveling in the16-year-old Nissan Altima I had given Mom from the 1997 ABL championship.

"Okay, Mom and Bonnie...time to visit some relatives," I'd say, entering Mom's car before an excursion.

I visited Guineatown, which was now Bellmawr, New Jersey, where the Guinea Prince, my African ancestor, had established a community. Bonnie had documented that the Guinea Prince had arrived in the South Jersey area on a Dutch slave ship that had travelled up the Delaware River in 1630. I found information that suggested it was probably later, around 1670. I would need to do more research to pinpoint that Dutch slave ship.

The trip to the Eastern Shore of Maryland where my great-great-great grandparents were enslaved proved to be emotional. I met with the directors of the Caroline County Office of Tourism and Caroline County Economic Development; they had a historian who had done extensive research on Levin and Charity. The county directors reserved a hotel for me so I could stay in the area even though it was less than a 2-hour drive. We toured the area where Charity and Levin had lived. A slave quarters still stood. The county was in the process of restoring the structure. Next was a visit to their owner's house where Charity had spent three months isolated after her first escape. I couldn't contain my emotions as I walked up the tiny stairway to a small attic-like room. Charity's owner thought he had cured her of running away; instead the 90 days she spent isolated away from her children and family made her more resolute to gain her freedom. She planned her next escape looking out the only source of light, a tiny window with the view of a vibrant, flowing, narrow river.

I travelled to Springtown, New Jersey, where Levin and Charity escaped the first time. Looking across the Delaware River from the edge of the swamped area, I imagined what Charity must have felt when she escaped and arrived at the vast body of water that separated her and her children from her husband. They lived in fear but as a free family for nearly a year until slave hunters recaptured them. I can't even imagine that scene. One day I will walk in Charity's footsteps and take her journey to freedom. She laid the path for me.

I visited Lawnside, Medford, Burlington and Shamong, New Jersey where they eventually settled and where their bodies lay beneath the hallowed earth. Lawnside, formerly Snow Hill, was their safe haven. That is where we became the Still family, protected by an established family in a resilient community of freedom fighters. Although the Still blood may not have run through our veins, the bond of our family is more solidified than any biological bond. If not for the Still family, I would not exist. In Shamong, where Levin and Charity raised their large clan, the locals had discovered their burial site. The local elementary school had had a gravestone ceremony to mark the site and kept the small area immaculate. I took my shoes off and stepped on the large graveled area that was corded off in a secluded wooded area. For me it was sacred land. The townspeople loved Levin and Charity and were proud they were their folk.

My trip to Philadelphia included visiting the block where William Still lived and the cemetery where he was buried. Charles Blockson gave me an extensive tour over a few weeks. He had overseen the placing of historic markers on African American sites. Charles and I visited some of the schools, banks and church that Caroline Still and her husband had founded. I spent hours at the Charles L. Blockson Afro-American Collection at Temple University. He helped me put the pieces of my life together. Our ancestors were with us every step of the way.

My research took me to historical societies and visits with historians. I was totally obsessed and driven with a need to knowing who I was.

I returned to Camden. It had become the most dangerous and poorest city in the USA. I drove to my childhood neighborhood. The red-bricked public row-housing unit where we lived, 813 Ferry Avenue, had been torn down and a community center built, but the basketball court, my lifeline as a child, was still on the corner of Philip St. and Ferry Avenue. I stood on the court, now the site of drive-by shootings and drug-dealings, and watched as young children played.

I knew why I was back in New Jersey. I had work to be completed.

I obtained my substitute teaching certification so I could work in Camden public schools and started the Dr. James Still Preservation Trust so I could oversee the restoration and development of my great-great-grandfather's property. Eventually, I wanted to renovate the basketball court. Pam and I were in daily contact and I told her about the projects. She visited me in New Jersey. We planned a symposium to promote the Dr. James Still Project and educate people about the Still Family legacy.

She also wanted me to be involved in a project she was working on, a reality TV show about her and JaVale. I flew out to meet her in Las Vegas. I agreed to be a cast member of the show. We filmed a few episodes while we were in Vegas and later in the year scheduled to film the rest of the first season of "Mom's Got Game" in California and Denver. I wanted to re-enact Charity's journey from the Eastern Shore to Springtown for an episode. Unlike other reality TV shows we hoped our show would empower and uplift whoever watched. I told Pam the show would be on the Oprah Winfrey Network; she thought I was crazy.

The symposium was a huge success. STILL Publications had re-printed Dr. James Still's autobiography and many people bought copies of the book.

I was the commencement speaker for Camden High School and Palmyra High School 2013 graduation ceremonies. For Palmyra High School, the Dr. James Still Preservation Trust began two annual scholarships in honor of Mom and one of her classmates and friend, Dr. Clarence B. Jones. After graduating, he became a successful attorney and Dr. Martin Luther King's lawyer and speechwriter, and who helped pen the "I Have a Dream" speech. This was a way to keep Mom's memory alive and honor her resiliency. I contacted Dr. Jones. Hearing him share stories about his relationship with my mother and Dr. Martin Luther King, Jr. was spellbinding.

The summer of 2013 was an eventful one for Aaron and me. While he was playing in an AAU tournament, Dan Earl, the associate coach for the US Naval Academy, spotted him and began recruiting him. Aaron and I had hoped that he would have a chance to play for UK but they showed no interest in him. He wasn't one of the top players in the country. It was a business that wasn't interested in relationships but needed young athletes who could generate revenue for the school. I wasn't thrilled about the possibility of Aaron joining the military, but at least he had a Division 1 school interested in him. He had always shown interest in military stuff as a child. The thought of Aaron leaving pained me but it was part of the process of letting go.

One of my final tests of letting go was selling my vintage 1978 450SL red convertible Mercedes roadster. It was the first car I bought in the USA after playing pro ball in Italy and held sentimental value for me. I bought the car in Cherry Hill after my big contract with Como and had taken it to Italy and then shipped it back to the States when I returned. I had given up everything else I had but as I struggled to pay bills and couldn't get an advance from my contract with the show, Pam offered to buy the car for much less than I wanted to sell it for. Though difficult, I sold it. Life didn't seem to get easier because my cat Pumpkin got cancer and I had to have her put to sleep. I then headed to California to film the first season of "Mom's Got Game."

When I returned from California I was shocked to discover that the local historical society in Medford had taken over the decision-making and management of my great-great grandfather's property. As the group planned outlandish events such as the Victorian Tea with Charity Still, on his property, I met with New Jersey Park Service representatives hoping to protect my family's legacy. It was outrageous and painful witnessing the misinformation being produced by a group of individuals with no educational background or experience in African American studies or culture. My great-great-great grandmother would not have been associated with anything to do with a Victorian Tea. The Victorian era was one of most repressive and oppressive in the USA for people of color and women.

This was just one of many controversial and problematic happenings at my great-great grandfather's historic site. In the end, I was pushed out. Although it was painful, I was in a better place spiritually; my ancestors were guiding me. I had saved the property and now my role would be to continue to research and write my family's history, preserving my ancestors' sacrifices.

STILL Publications published Charles Blockson's latest book. It was monumental for me because Blockson's ancestor had interacted with William Still over 200 years previously and now we were making history together again. His book would continue the legacy and honor our ancestors.

*****

"Mom's Got Game" aired on the Oprah Winfrey Network in January 2014. Most reality TV shows were filled with drama and conflict in hopes of high ratings; "Mom's Got Game" presented a positive look at single moms raising sons, moms who had formerly been professional athletes and friends.

I continued to substitute-teach in Camden; doing so helped me deal with my dysfunctional childhood. It also allowed me to connect with children in America's worst city. Initially, I wondered if I could teach in the appalling environment that I found in Camden's schools. Maintaining order in most classes was a priority and challenge for a substitute teacher. Instead of rotating schools, I taught mainly at one particular school so I could develop relationships with teachers and students. After the initial shock of misbehavior and disrespect of many of the students, I began developing loving relationships with them.

I taught at a school built in the 1960s and the building hadn't had many renovations. The school was largely made up of Hispanic students. The environment and conditions that children had to learn in was saddening. The food that was served, I wouldn't feed to an animal. There was not an area for band or gym. The cafeteria served as gym and band room but there was not enough room to perform any physical activities and the band was set up on a small stage. It was unthinkable that in 21st century America children did not have the basics for learning.

Many of the children had been exposed to drugs and crime their entire life. It was a normal aspect of their experience. Their ages ranged from as young as 3-year old pre-school to 16-year old eighth-grade students. Many basic concepts such as respect and discipline were not part of their experience. The student body was difficult to control and maintain. My favorites were the pre-school classes. But when I worked with the older students, I shared my books and history, encouraging them to write their personal stories and to love themselves. By loving, protecting, and teaching these children, I began to love and protect little Valerie who had grown up in a similar environment. This was part of my journey to self-love.

*****

Although Aaron hadn't seen his dad in over six years, I contacted Rob so he could attend Aaron's high school graduation. My heart ached in pain and swelled with joy as Aaron broke down in tears when he saw Rob at a reception for seniors at the VFMA president's house. Tears flowed down Aaron's face as he hugged Rob. Although no longer the little boy Rob had left but a young man standing eye-to-eye, Aaron sobbed in Rob's arms like he had done so many nights with me after crawling into my bed after Rob had left.

In June Aaron was accepted into the Naval Academy Preparatory School. Aaron would attend NAPS ten months in Rhode Island before heading to the US Naval Academy.

On the long drive back from taking Aaron to NAPS, I thought about what my life would be now that he was gone. Aaron and I had been through so much together and always had each other to depend on. After a few days of hurting, I became consciously aware of my suffering. I wanted to be free of the suffering but instead I sat and breathed in the experience without trying to get rid of it. With each breath, my wounded hard heart became bigger and softer; no matter how bad I felt I continued embracing the pain; I stayed open to it and gave it more space. I accepted the moment and situation in my breathing. I knew what I wanted but more importantly what I needed to do - write my story.

After total isolation, writing and feeling connected, I received a phone call from Maryanne. The assistant coaching position at UK had become available; in fact, two of UK's assistant women basketball coaches were leaving. My heart raced; maybe it was my time to finally return to UK.

I applied for the positions, posted messages on social media expressing my interest in becoming an assistant coach at UK and called the head coach and athletic director. I wanted so badly for UK to embrace me and allow me to be a part of the program again. It wasn't about feeling entitled; I believed I was qualified and could help the program. I couldn't think of one reason why UK wouldn't at least give me an interview, and I let myself think about the possibilities of returning to Kentucky, but as the days and weeks passed, I had to accept it wasn't going to happen. I didn't even receive a phone call acknowledging my application.

Later I learned they hired other people. The third assistant coach left UK and again, I applied but wasn't recognized. Three times, three positions, and I was denied three times without an explanation or even an interview. It was clear to me that I was not wanted at UK but even more importantly, because that door was forcefully shut, I realized that UK was not my destiny.

UK's rejection was painful for me, but looking back, I know that it was the best thing to happen to me. I no longer have an unhealthy relationship with UK. I wanted to be a part of what I considered family. I was like a woman in an abusive relationship, with black and blue marks all over her body, who insists on staying because she doesn't know her worth and doesn't think she can survive without her abuser.

In 1970, psychiatrist Dr. Frances Cress Welsing's controversial paper, "The Cress Theory of Color-Confrontation and Racism (White Supremacy)," theorized that systemic racism is a cause of, and affects, many social ills in people of color including mental illness. My relationship with UK could be a case study for her argument.

As I was breaking records, UK embraced me as an elite athlete. Once I was done playing, I was discarded and replaced. Each year hundreds of young athletes will be convinced that being given the opportunity to be a "Kentucky Wildcat" is an honor in itself. My older brother, Art Still and I were exceptional athletes. Kentucky didn't recruit us thinking of our long-term future. We were both vehicles to propel UK into the national rankings. Strangely, a year after the 2014 rejection, I applied for the assistant position again when it became available. After being told by UK's women's basketball head coach that I wasn't qualified for any coaching position, I realized that being a young, talented black female athlete at UK and setting playing records was one thing but my extensive playing and coaching career didn't provide me with the qualifications needed to land a third-string assistant coaching position. That nearly drove me to insanity.

It took every ounce of my being to not take those words, "you are not qualified" personally; but it did affect my self-worth. The cathartic three-year process of accepting my mother's death and finding meaning of it by writing had made me stronger mentally, emotionally and spiritually but UK's rejection left me emotionally bruised, figuratively living Black and Blue. I was not bitter but searching for answers to my fragile mental health, the cause of my malaise.

After much research and soul searching, including discovering Dr. Welsing's theory, I've shed the veil of ignorance in regard to the significance and influence racism plays on one's mental health. More specifically I've removed any unhealthy and inaccurate correlation to collegiate athletics at the University of Kentucky with my self-worth. One of Dr. Welsing's recommendations for alleviating or treatment of this mental illness is knowing the underlying cause and having a concrete understanding of who you are.

With the 2015 rejection I was done living and playing black and blue. UK's continual rejection reminded me of my years as a young girl, being dismissed for pursuing my passion and the seeming denial of my father. I was given this final test with UK and instead of personalizing it and letting it define me, I moved forward without any negative baggage. Lexington, Kentucky was not my destiny but only a small part of my journey. I turned the page and became consumed with writing. In New Jersey at Mom's house, the hero's journey was complete.

Chapter 24

And now abideth faith, hope, charity, these three;
but the greatest of these is charity.
1 Corinthians 13:13

Completing my memoir meant going through lots of materials I had saved from college, Europe, playing professionally in the states and family research. Sorting through a box of Mom's important papers, I uncovered the final piece of the puzzle to self-discovery and self-empowerment - a death certificate. Mom had kept Dad's graduation certificate from 8th grade and his military papers. She also had death certificates for Dad and her mother and father. On her father's death certificate, Louise Still was listed as his mother. My mouth dropped. Grandpa Ricketts was a Still also? Were Mom and Dad related? I needed to know more about Louise Sarah Still.

Mom's only living sibling, Uncle Kenny, and I had grown closer since I moved back to New Jersey. They had similar personalities and mannerisms. It was strange for me initially visiting with him after Mom's death. Often I caught myself staring at him intensively as we talked. He shared with me what he knew about his grandmother, Louise Still.

"Val, I remember visiting Grandma Ricketts once. A tough little woman with long black hair who didn't say much," Uncle Kenny recalled with a smile.

"She always had a tin can close, 'cause she chewed tobacco and could spit it better than anyone!"

My search for Louise Still Ricketts led me through South Jersey, Pennsylvania, and Maryland (some of the places where my ancestors had lived) where I talked to numerous historians, all of whom led me to a fascinating discovery.

I now have a better understanding of the proud history of my paternal great-great-great grandparents enslaved, on the Eastern Shore of Maryland and given the names Levin Steele and Sidney. As a young boy, Levin promised himself that he would not die a slave and eventually bought his freedom for $500. Sydney had a resilient and determined spirit. With the birth of their fourth child they escaped enslavement.

At the turn of the 19th century Levin left the plantation as a free man and arrived in Springtown, New Jersey where he built a small secluded dwelling and farmed the land. Soon after, Sidney escaped with their four young children. Eventually, Sidney and the children were captured by slave hunters and returned to their enraged owner.

After three months of punishment, Sidney escaped again but did so making a painful decision. One night she gathered up her two young daughters, left her two little sons without waking them and escaped into the night.

She reunited with Levin in New Jersey but settled farther north in a community of freed African Americans. One of the established families in the community was the Still family. The Still family's great patriarch was the "Guinea Prince" brought to America in the 1600s on a Dutch slave ship that sailed up the Delaware River. Levin Steele changed his last name to Still and Sidney chose the name Charity to further protect themselves. More importantly, "charity" denoted freedom. I believe Sidney chose the name Charity because she believed in the power of love. With love there is no fear and no fear meant freedom. She was fearless. She was love. Charity signified self-empowerment, awakening and preservation. I believe one of her favorite Bible passages was I Corinthians 13, "... And now abideth faith, hope, charity, these three; but the greatest of these is charity." She had faith and hope but love would conquer all.

Levin and Charity lived knowing that at any moment she could be recaptured and re-enslaved but their scheme was so thoroughly planned that not only did they deceive slave hunters, their owner and everyone during their lifetime; their secret was hidden until my search for Louise Still, my mother's grandmother. I uncovered the fact that Levin and Charity were not biologically related to the Stills of South Jersey.

My research of Louise Still unveiled the masterminds of Charity and Levin and finally uncovered the secret master plan that provided them their freedom, safety and empowerment, a secret that had lasted over two hundred years.

Louise Still was a descendant of the Still family that was already in New Jersey, in the Lawnside area. Some family historians and researchers thought that the family had interbred when Cubit Still, Louise's youngest brother, married Dr. James Still's granddaughter, Juanita Still, in the early 1900s. It was the first time the two families biologically intersected; however, they were not blood-related. Louise Still married David Ricketts. One of their sons, Albert Ricketts, had a daughter named Gwendolyn (my mother) who married James Still, a direct descendant of Levin and Charity. Biologically, I am related to both lineages.

In 1870, Dr. James Still invited his siblings and their families to his Medford house for a reunion. Only the Levin and Charity blood relatives attended. There was no mention of Stills from Lawnside in attendance. Today the Still Family reunion, one of the oldest and largest family reunions in the USA, commemorates Dr. James Still's family reunion. It's held in Lawnside, New Jersey and celebrated by all South Jersey Stills. As a child we didn't attend the Lawnside reunion.

"We're not related to those people!" Dad would insist when we were invited as children.

He was right; we weren't blood related but we were related because the Stills had provided Levin and Charity life by protecting their identity. The Lawnside Stills claimed Dr. James Still and continued the annual family reunion he talks about in his autobiography because no one knew the secret. Discreetly, Levin's and Charity's children probably learned the secret but not the full story. In my family, the secret was passed down with only my father's declaration that we weren't related to the Lawnside Stills. Any of the modern relatives claiming to be related to William Still, Dr. James Still and Levin and Charity are not blood-related but that doesn't diminish the importance of this grafted family.

The Still family and Levin and Charity represent resilience, ingenuity and solidarity of a people. They are an example of the embodiment of African American families during enslavement in America. Fictive kin was a powerful tool in African American culture during slavery because families were so often separated through buying and selling. Kinships did not have to be based on blood ties or marriage. Enslaved individuals formed kinships with other enslaved, referring to unrelated women as "auntie" or "sis" and unrelated men as "uncle" or "brother." My family was the perfect example of how family grafting was used for empowerment and survival. What I uncovered about Louise Still was historically groundbreaking, and it provided me a sense of empowerment, authenticity, and identification.

For Levin and Charity and the Still family, sharing the same bloodline wasn't important because they knew who they were. They were not a race, a gender, a religion, or a class. They were on a quest for authentic self. Self-preservation was key. It astounds me to think that if they had not devised this plan, the great abolitionist William Still and Dr. James Still would have been born enslaved and missed the opportunities they pursued as free Black men. Peter and Levin Jr., their eldest sons who were enslaved, demonstrate the negative and devastating impact slavery inflicted on the potential of an individual.

The fact that William Still, Dr. James Still, Peter Still and Levin and Charity are not blood-related to the South Jersey Still family is significant, I believe, because it shows that enslaved African Americans did have agency of their own destiny and played a significant role in tearing down the institution of slavery in America. Until recently, the traditional American historical narrative gave little credit to the importance of individuals like my ancestors; however they were my life line.

Fittingly and decorously, my great-great-great grandmother Charity's journey ended in love after the forty agonizing years she had been separated from her two oldest sons when Peter arrived at The Pennsylvania Anti-Slavery office of William Still unexpectedly in 1850. Peter Friedman had bought his freedom in Alabama and had travelled back to the east coast looking for his parents Levin and Sydney. He was directed to William's office in Philadelphia. William was dumbfounded and overwhelmed realizing that he was face-to-face with his long-lost older brother. Their emotional reunion with their mother in New Jersey (Levin Sr. had already died) was the triumphant coronation of her hero's journey. Her circle of life would end as it had begun, in the loving arms of family. A significant part of Peter's journey was spent enslaved in Lexington Kentucky; it was where he was sold (probably at Cheapside Slave Auction) as a small boy after Charity's decision to escape enslavement. Ironically, nearly two hundred years later, Lexington would be a significant part of my journey. Although I wasn't physically enslaved in Lexington, I now understood how it held me in bondage and it wasn't until I discovered my ancestors that my own shackles came off. The cycle was complete.

I have followed the path laid by my great-great-great grandmother Charity, 19th century cousin Caroline, my great grandmother Louise, my mother Gwendolyn, and my sister Bonita; all strong, empowered, and influential women. Typically, males are recognized for their contribution to societies and cultures, and their legacies passed on. Often credit is given to powerful and influential male figures within the Still family (William Still, Dr. James Still, Peter Still, Levin Still) but I believe my female predecessors deserve recognition. Their stories not only reveal the significant role of women in African American history, but their survival exemplifies the important role women play in society and within families. My female ancestors, like many other valiant women of the past, are women who weren't afraid to die as a conduit for life. Women are mothers of life. That isn't based on whether we bear children but on a spiritual collective consciousness that breathes and sustains life. That consciousness spans lifetimes, generations and eons. It is timeless and universal. It is who we are.

My mother's death opened a door, a pathway to a higher awareness of life. I walked through the door, stepped onto a passageway that would take me on a journey. Life is that journey. During this journey she continues to be with me. With her love and my ancestor love, I continue my journey. Their journey is complete and I carry the legacy of love . . . the greatest of these is charity.

Epilogue

Writer and mythologist Joseph Campbell noted a common pattern in certain narratives, which he termed "The Hero's Journey." Regardless of nationality, religion, gender, race or class, a protagonist leaves a familiar environment or origin, literally or figuratively, sets off on a journey into life's great unknown, and eventually discovers the authentic self; that is, reaches that state of personal enlightenment which defines the hero – who he is, his place in the great scheme of things, a direction for his life to take. He makes peace with the world by finding his place in it. He recognizes his bliss, discovers a way to follow it, and maps his path forward.

Brian Agler, my coach from the Columbus Quest once said, "A quest is a journey, a conquesting, a pursuit of a goal...that's what we're all about." My life has been a quest, a journey. Like Odysseus, I have travelled far, seen much, and returned home finally – a different person to a different home. I too have experienced the treacheries, endured the darkness, fought through the fears, survived the Sirens' song of fame, fortune and excitement, and have come home once again to my own figurative faithful dog – the reality of who I am and an appreciation for my roots.

I have come to know happiness and joy, a sense of achievement, the beauty of meeting goals and gaining recognition; on the other hand, I have looked death in the face, only to recover and look at it again. I looked upon the death of a father, a mother, a sister, a lover, wondering each time if I could overcome the recurring feeling that this, after all, may not pass.

I believe I have been introduced to most of life's excuses and explanations and shortcuts, only to learn that each comes up empty and short. But I have found a few stepping stones on which to step as I negotiate my way across the rapids without depending on some magical, outstretched hand. "Faith," for example, a term used in thousands of ways by millions of people, I have found to be a thing of believing when there really is nothing to believe in, a matter of believing only when there is nothing else left to do. And I have made, finally, one great discovery that seems to have eluded so many, and it is a time-worn simple adage: "The best place to find a helping hand is at the end of your own arm." The trick, it would seem, is not only to continually strengthen that arm, but to know at all times the location, value, and usefulness of the hand found at its end.

Another important thing I have learned is to be able to recognize a cord and to know when to cut it and when to strengthen it. Cords such as alcohol, drug abuse, spousal abuse, one-way love, low self-esteem, hopelessness, fear, greed and selfishness can hold things together that need not be bound. These are the cords I have learned to recognize and renounce. More difficult to cut are those that bind us to good things, good friends, -- good memories, good goals -- that are ultimately unreachable or no longer important. But just as cords bind, so can their cutting free us up to pursue newer good, more nearly perfect pathways, greater goals and achievements.

In 2014, I finished the rough draft of my memoir with the title, *Playing Black and Blue: The Valerie Still Story,* hoping to inflect the significance of race. It was ironic that while I was playing at the University of Kentucky, I had never recognized racism or sexism directed at me. I was valued for my athletic ability. After a long, successful playing and coaching career, it seemed logical to return to UK to become part of the women's basketball program as a coach. However, after being rejected numerous times over more than a decade of trying, I realized that like my great-great granduncles, Levin Jr. and Peter, who were enslaved and sold to John Fisher in Lexington, Kentucky at the turn of the 19th century, my value at UK was based solely on short-term physical attributions that benefited the program but provided no opportunity of advancement for me.

My life to this point has taught me to live undefined: I no longer wish to be merely a basketball player, a woman, a mother, a celebrity. No longer am I content to be no more than rich, poor, black, educated, experienced, abused, rejected, divorced, intelligent, talented or anything else that attempts to provide shallow classification of who I am or what I am. The price I pay, most willingly, is the assumption of responsibility for my life, hour-to-hour and day-to-day. My failures are mine and mine only; I must always remember this, but never can I allow myself to forget that those times will come, do come, when I can stand briefly on a pedestal of my imagination, unseen by others, and proclaim loudly, though unheard, "I did it! It happened! This is mine and mine alone!"

Loving and rearing my son Aaron, and knowing, loving and appreciating my mother have been by far the two most significant and most painful experiences of my life. Giving up Gwendolyn Still to the eternal ages and releasing Aaron Still-Lock to the journey into manhood have been the toughest challenges I have faced. The end of basketball, the walking away from celebrity, giving up the lifestyle of the affluent – these have fallen by comparison among the lesser losses. But much of life is about loss, and on any given day any one of us could get up in the morning and write half a page of negatives without pausing.

But life does not revolve around its absences -- life is about the positives. Most importantly, I must remember that though life is, in part, defined by my relationships with others, it is also about me. I find no contradiction in such a statement, and I make it with a humility tried by the sacrificial, purifying fire of the years. I have come to realize the hollow nothingness being shouted by those who proclaim their love for God. There is no such thing as love for God without love for fellow man ("For as much as you have done it unto [...] you have done it unto me.").

I have at last made my break to freedom: I know who I am and where I am. I know how, with guidance from countless people, I got here. I know now that to live, do, be, act, think with heart is the only way to live. The only direction left for me is forward, even with great experiences and great memories safely in tow. When my journey shall at last come to a conclusion, may it at least be said of me, "She didn't take life lightly, nor did she handle it thoughtlessly." I am movement. I am Light. I am Charity. I am Still. I am.

Afterword

Om Shanti. I am Peace. I am Still.

After years of high-level competition and trying to please others, I discovered, Om Shanti at the Meditation Center, a pyramid-shaped building a few miles from my home. In late spring of 2016, after unsuccessfully finding a literary agent or a publisher for my manuscript, I decided to let go of my desire to publish my memoirs and instead found a local tai-chi class, looking for some type of peace of mind. I needed to quiet the racing, untamed monkey mind that constantly produced tens of thousands of unwanted, unnecessary and negative thoughts. It was quite a surprise for the class of older retirees moving methodically, slowly and gracefully through a routine, as I walked into the small classroom at the local fitness club and filled a spot between a tall, bald-head man and a smiling, gentle woman making space for me. After a few weeks attending the bi-weekly classes, always in my position between Frank and Pat, I not only began to gain a sense of peace from the movements, but also began connecting with the members of the class. After a couple months, I became friends with a few. Frank, in his seventies, suggested I visit the Meditation Center a few blocks up the street to find peace.

I had driven past the strange looking building surrounded by a picturesque landscape with babbling creek, towering trees and colorful flowers and bushes almost every day; the place was mystical. With Frank's blessing, I ventured into the building one Thursday evening, hoping no one would bother me. Entering undisturbed, I quietly took a seat in the last row on the far right side in the nearly empty main sanctuary. I immediately felt a sense of wellbeing, in the dim lights of what would become my haven.

The stage was empty with a large mural of what looked like sunrays on an orange background, a shining point of bright white light at the center of the image. The overhead lighting on the stage produced a warm orange aura. I wasn't sure what to do, or if there would be a program, but the softly playing, soothing music quickly calmed me, and I felt my body relax along with my thoughts. I closed my eyes and melted away as a woman's voice provided guided commentary along with the music. After an hour, the lights gradually brightened and a beautiful Indian woman dressed in a white sari stepped to the front to welcome her pupils to their seven-week foundational meditation course that was starting this night. Trying to be discreet, I scanned the room quickly, observing another elderly Indian woman seated in the back, and a few younger women, all dressed in white saris, spaced throughout the room. At least 20 people had showed up for this weekly course. Anyone was welcomed to join, and there were no fees or membership requirements. I hadn't planned on starting any course, I really didn't have the time and I couldn't make a seven-week commitment, but I wanted to find out how to make the sensation that filled me as I meditated a part of my daily routine. I stayed.

Sister Kinnari, a thirtysomething, soft-spoken woman led the class.

"Who are you?" she said in barely a whisper.

Going around the room, everyone introduced themselves by name, occupation, status, or roles such as mother, caregiver, brother. We shared a little bit of who we thought we were. Each time, Sister Kinnari would reply, "But who are you?". Those were all descriptions and roles we played.

She finally gave her answer."You are a point of light. Energy."

She went on to explain that energy cannot be created nor destroyed, and so we have always existed and we will always exist.

I was totally engaged in each word she spoke. Since my mom's death, Aaron's departure for college and no longer being physically active like I was as an elite athlete, I struggled to fill the new blank spaces before my name. This woman, this stranger, put everything in perspective with a simple statement: I am a point of light.

This would be the start of my reintroduction to myself. I attended the Meditation Center every night for public meditation and on Thursdays attended the course for an hour. In November 2016, I graduated from the course and began attending any session I could. Although the hardships in my life weren't getting better, the knowledge I acquired from the Meditation Center provided me with tools that helped me be aware of what I was thinking. The first week of December, I went to Peace Village, their retreat center in upstate New York, for a weekend workshop called Inner Peace, Inner Power. When I returned to New Jersey, I made a vow to end the year in peace and to maintain it in 2017.

At the end of January, I reached out to Dr. Clarence B. Jones to update him about the status of his scholarship. We hadn't been in touch since 2014. He offered to help with the funding of the scholarship and to also get his friends to contribute. The next day, I reached out to Joe Martin, the principal at Palmyra High School, to see if it would be possible to honor Dr. Jones and bring him back to Palmyra. Joe was no longer principal, but the school district was excited about the idea of Dr. Jones coming back. They had tried to contact him a few years earlier with no luck. Getting Dr. Jones to come back was a long shot, but with the support of the school district, I asked Dr. Jones if he would be willing to return to Palmyra High School.

"Valerie, you plan it, and I'll do whatever you decide," Dr. Jones told me.

My heart raced, my mind raced, my thoughts raced. I nearly exploded with the joy of hearing those words, but my experience with mediation helped me stay emotionally detached and maintain my peace. Still, it was incredible that this civil rights icon, legend, hero, a man who had walked and talked with Dr. Martin Luther King, Jr., who had helped him write one of the most iconic speeches in world history, a man who was a friend and classmate of my mother, would be coming back to Palmyra just because I asked him.

Should he be honored with an award? Should we ask him to be the 2017 commencement speaker? Or should we go for the stars on this? I decided to push a little more and requested that the school district honor Dr. Jones by naming the library after him and establishing the Dr. Clarence B. Jones Institute for Social Advocacy. The school district and Board of Education agreed to both my proposals. In all this, Dr. Jones put full trust in me. We had deep conversations about his childhood, and I realized he was returning to also tie up all the loose ends from his childhood in South Jersey. He had many questions that needed answering, and I would help him find those answers. This process led to my knowing this honorable man in a way I could have never imagined. By the end of the process of bringing Dr. Jones back to Palmyra for his much-anticipated homecoming at 86 years old, we would become godfather and goddaughter. The sisters at the Meditation Center had become my spiritual family. They taught me how to love, yet be a detached observer. They shared the knowledge of the Source of unlimited love that sees each person as a brother or sister, all in the same family from the same spiritual Mother and Father. It was amazing after mourning the loss of my mother and the death of my earthly family, now I was gaining a new, chosen tribe.

As godfather Jones shared stories of his experiences with Dr. King during our time together in June for his homecoming, one of the stories that touched me most was the story of how Dr. King was "personally afraid, but fearless." I questioned godfather Jones as to what this meant.

"I'll give you an example. Martin, myself and maybe a couple other friends could be walking down a street in a southern state when a car would backfire. The only one to immediately cower, to instantly take cover, would be Martin. We always knew it wasn't a matter of if but when, he would be assassinated yet he continued his public fight for social justice and equality for all in America. He was personally afraid but fearless."

This would be what I imbibed. What I wanted to be an embodiment of.

As I continued my activism and advocacy work in Palmyra, eventually joining the school district's administration as the communications officer, a newfound sense of purpose banished the past versions of myself that haunted me. For the first time, I could accept that the person who became the all-time leading scorer and rebounder for the University of Kentucky, an entertainer, an American Basketball League champion and one of the first WNBA players was behind me, and I began to live the way I know my mother would have wanted. But as soon as I could let go of Valerie Still: professional athlete, the Naismith Memorial and Women's Basketball Halls of Fame appeared around January 2018 to revisit those former labels.

I'm honored by the Naismith nomination and to be one of the 10 finalists selected for the Women's Basketball Hall of Fame Class of 2018, but my happiness does not hinge on my photo joining the ranks of extraordinary athletes in those halls. My life has truly come full circle — the literary quality of my biography is not lost on me, and it is this very quality that has made me a favorite with South Jersey's local news outlets. But I could never anticipate the phone call to which The Burlington County Times' coverage of my nominations and work in Palmyra's schools would lead.

When I returned home from Taiwan in 1980 after playing with the USA National Team and a bacterial infection that should have killed me, according to the doctors, there was one person whose determination to save me matched my own will to survive. Dr. Louis Baxter, a young chief resident at Cooper Hospital in Camden, had a crazy theory that my blood was contaminated with Salmonella Enteritidis, a hypothesis his colleagues strongly doubted. It is Dr. Baxter's tenacity and out-of-the-box approach to my case that now I credit with having saved my life, and so when I heard his voice on the other end of the line nearly 40 years after I left the hospital, I couldn't help but be overcome with gratitude and emotion.

I had no idea Dr. Baxter was involved in my case until he called to tell me he read the article in the Times profiling the athletic excellence, research and advocacy work I went on to contribute to the world thanks to his fearlessness in diagnosing me. After all this time, he said, my case stuck with him because he could sense God had a plan for me, and be it through divine intervention or not, Dr. Baxter put his reputation on the line to save me from certain death.

As I reflect on Dr. Baxter's role in my life, my family history dating back to my ancestors' arrival via the slave trade in Lexington, and their subsequent involvement in the Underground Railroad, I can't help but recognize the magnitude of Dr. Jones' description of Dr. Martin Luther King Jr.: "personally afraid, but fearless." All women, all people of color, all God's creatures who find themselves subject to oppression must suffer a constant and pervasive sense of fear as they struggle for equal footing and self-esteem.

Yet, regardless of the categories we are placed in — so often dictated by our gender, religion, race, social class, age and sexuality — what unites us and empowers us, gives our lives meaning is knowing that though we may be personally afraid, our true selves are peaceful, loving, powerful, blissful, pure and, of course, fearless.

Acknowledgements

I thank all the radiant stars, beings of light, sparkling brightly, generating unlimited energy that helped make this book possible. One of the most fulfilling, meaningful and challenging experiences in my life has been writing my memoirs. I began officially writing in the spring of 2011 and through many ups and downs, my dream of honoring and carrying on the legacy of my ancestors by writing and publishing our story has become a reality. Throughout the process, I've felt my ancestors guiding me.

I was motivated by my great-great-grandfather James who wrote and published his autobiography in 1877 and also by my great-great-granduncle William who wrote and published the classic Underground Railroad in 1872. My great-great grandfather defied all odds by becoming one of the most respected physicians in South Jersey with only three months of education and then wrote his story. By the time of his death he was the third largest landowner in South Jersey. William risked his freedom and life for individuals who were disenfranchised, dehumanized and marginalized in the United States of America. Today, many express disgust and contempt and label certain types of social protest "unpatriotic" and "disrespectful" such as football players' kneeling during the national anthem or protest movements such as Black Lives Matter but William Still's form of protest during the antebellum period was illegal and the most radical form of civil disobedience and breaking civic laws.

William unselfishly risked everything knowing that he was on the right side of history. And with time, all those brave individuals who William encounter through the Underground Railroad, individuals who didn't have the platform or importance that professional athletes, entertainers and politicians have today, have been vindicated and are credited with truly making America a great nation. Lest we forget.

Of course, my mother was and is my constant guide and energy. The times when I felt like quitting, I was reminded by her words, "someone needs to write a book on your story." The truth is someone needed to write a book about her. Hopefully, in the limited time and space of this book, her essence radiates. Like my mother, my great-great-great grandmother Charity provides me with the perfect role model; strong, brave, resilient, intelligent, curious, adventurous, loving, powerful and personally afraid but fearless.

Although I have my posse of mighty angels, I'm extremely grateful for having a brother that would go through the fire with me. Thank you Dennis. We were a fighting tag team as children but we've learned that it is better to light a candle than curse the darkness. I love you.

Words are inadequate to describe my gratitude to my inner circle, my stable undertow of support, love and strength, Charles L. Blockson, Bob Todd and Dr. Clarence B. Jones. This book definitely would not have come to fruition if not for you. Thank you, Thank you, Thank you.

A special thank you to April Ellis and Mary Ellen Cagnassola who helped me bring everything together and let me know I had a story that was worthy of sharing.

Finally, I know who I am and whose I am, thanks to the guidance of the Brahma Kumaris…all thanks and praise and worship is given to the Supreme Soul, God, Shiv Baba, my Mother, my Father, my Source, my Eternal Energy. Love, Remembrance and Namaste.

READING RESOURCES

- Early Recollections and Life of Dr. James Still (1877) by Dr. James Still

- The Kidnapped and the Ransomed (1856) by Kate E.R. Pickard

- The Underground Railroad (1872) by William Still

- New York Times Article (1999) - "A 15-Year Playing Career Is Quieted but Not Her Voice" by Valerie Still

- Still Running (2014) by Nate Northington

- The Bluegrass Conspirarcy (2001) by Sally Denton

- The ISIS Paper The Isis Papers: The Keys to the Colors (1991) by Dr. Frances Cress Welsing

- The Cress Theory of Color-Confrontation (White-Supremacy) (1970) by Dr. Frances Cress Welsing

- Jubilee by Margaret Walker (1966)

- "How I Wrote Jubilee," by Margaret Walker in How I Wrote Jubilee and Other Essays of Life and Literature (1990)

- The Yellow Wallpaper and other Stories (1892) by Charlotte Perkins Gilman

- Roots: The Saga of an American Family (1976) by Alex Hailey

- Alex Haley and the Books That Changed A Nation (2015) by Robert J. Norrell

- The President's House Revisited Behind the Scenes: The Samuel Fraunces Story (2013) by Charles L. Blockson

- Damn Rare (1998) by Charles L. Blockson

- Big Blue Nation: Kentucky Basketball's Native Sons and Daughters (2012) by Russell Rice

- Playing in a New League: The Women of the American Basketball League's First Season (1998) by Sarah Gogol

- Venus to the Hoop: A Gold Medal Year in Women's Basketball (1997) by Sarah Corbett

- Mad Seasons: The Story of the First Women's Professional Basketball League, 1978-1981(2006) by Karra Porter

- The Quiet Storm: A Celebration of Women in Sport (1997) by Powe-Allred, A. & Michelle Powe

- Sport and Identity (1972) by Patsy Neal

- A New Season: Using Title IX to Reform College Sports (2003) by Brian Porto

- Sporting Equality: Title IX Thirty Years Later (2005) by Rita J. Simon

- Beer and Circus: How Big-Tiime College Sports Is Crippling Undergraduate Education. (2000) by Murray Sperber, Murray

- A Place on the Team: The Triumph and Tragedy of Title IX (2005) by Suggs, Welch

- University of Kentucky NCATE / EPSB INSTITUTIONAL REPORT (2007)

- Understanding Race, Class, Gender and Sexuality (2010) by Lynn Weber

- Playing Nice and Losing: The Struggle for Control of Women's Intercollegiate Athletics, 1960-2000 (2004) by Ying Wushanley

- The Way of Man According to The Teaching of Hasidism (1964) by Martin Buber

- The Impersonal Life (1941) by Joseph Benner

- Comfortable with Uncertainty (2002) Pema Chödrön